Brother Gardner's
LIME-KILN CLUB

By

Charles B. Lewis

LITERATURE HOUSE / GREGG PRESS
Upper Saddle River, N. J.

Republished in 1970 by
LITERATURE HOUSE
an imprint of The Gregg Press
121 Pleasant Avenue
Upper Saddle River, N. J. 07458

Standard Book Number—8398-1159-4
Library of Congress Card—76-104513

Printed in United States of America

M. QUAD AND CHARACTERS.

BROTHER GARDNER'S

LIME-KILN CLUB:

BEING THE

Regular Proceedings of the Regular Club

FOR THE LAST THREE YEARS.

WITH SOME PHILOSOPHY, CONSIDERABLE MUSIC, A FEW LECTURES,
AND A HEAP OF ADVICE WORTH READING.

---

*NOT COMPILED IN THE INTERESTS OF CONGRESS, OR ANY
DEPARTMENT OF GOVERNMENT.*

BY

M. QUAD AND BROTHER GARDNER.

Illustrated by GEAN SMITH.

CHICAGO:
DONOHUE, HENNEBERRY & CO
407-425 DEARBORN STREET
1890

COPYRIGHT
1883.
BY BELFORD, CLARKE & CO.

DEDICATED

TO THE MEMBERS OF THE

DETROIT LIME-KILN CLUB,

AND TO

THE FRIENDS AND WELL WISHERS

OF

THE COLORED MAN IN AMERICA.

BROTHER GARDNER.

PREFACE.

It is not any ways probable that the production of this work will add anything to the general happiness of the world; and the purchaser must not hold me responsible if his crops fail or his lottery ticket hits a blank. It has become quite fashionable to write and publish books. They are handy to box the children's ears with; are good property to lend to your neighbors; and when the baby has torn the covers off, they can be worn as chest-protectors and liver-pads. The only thing I warrant about this book is that it contains no vegetable poisons, and will not explode when handled by innocent children.

Affectionately,

THE AUTHOR.

CONTENTS.

About Art	114
About Kind Words	145
About Liars	99
About Progress	128
Agriculture	40, 147
All a Sham	52
As You Find Him	152
A Champion	282
A Divorce	61
A Few Reflexhuns	60
A Generous Offer	81
A Great Gain	143
A Heathen Body	79
A Narrow Escape	91
A Painful Report	47
A Statesman's Descent	68
A Word to Cranks	242
Banks and Wood Piles	219
Beauties of the Ballot	256
Beyond the Vale	199
Bouncing Brudder Scott	25
Brudder Howker	295
Can't See Why	36
Champion Poets	133
Cussin' De Times	289
Cum Down	65
De Circus	179
De Comet	74
De Comin' Power	98
De Good Ole Days	120

Contents.

De Good Man	126
De Goneness	112
De Sun Do Move	251
Death's Grip	56
Dread Scott Decision	142
Endin' Up	162
First Annual Election	17
Guess Not	83
Having Fun	66
He Had a Pucker	29
How Uncle Pete Died	122
Human Nature	103
It Doan' Pay	150
It Must Be Crushed	49
It Pays To Be Good	291
Judge Cadaver	89
Junius Henri Bates	192
Killwilliam Smith	84
Let 'Em Divorce	233
Mary Jane's Petishun	203
More Baseness	108
Missing	187
Nine Horses and a Dog	209
No Lunatics Present	267
No Sore Heel Relief	213
None o' Your Business	129
Not a Congreshunal Body	22
On Terms	154
On the Fence	174
On De Wait	34
Only Sons, a Protest	139
Prof. Artichoke Huggins	286
Sartin People	157
Serene Toots	107
Silent Sorrows	95
Sign "X"	229
Some New Proverbs	24
Some Observations	134
Some Valuable Relics	158
Something Was Up	234

Contents.

Striking' De Average	35
The Amende Honorable	147
The Airy Perkins	118
The Case of Smith	166
The Honest Man	30
The Hon. Solo Bomby	46
The Hon. Standoff	44
The Influence of Music	278
The Lawyers	273
The Only Reliable	224
The Revised	105
Thanks and Modesty	206
That Strange Nigger	75
Their Dander Riz	39
To Patriots	261
Trapping a Hyena	271
Valuable Time	169
Washington's Camp Chair	212
Whistled Fur His Dog	53

ILLUSTRATIONS.

FRONTISPIECE, WITH PORTRAIT OF M. QUAD..................

GIVEADAM JONES SETTLES PATENT OFFICE SMITH............ 18

BROTHER GARDNER, PRESIDENT OF THE LIME-KILN CLUB.... 44

HON. WILLIAM JOHNSON ON THE COMET..................... 74

WHAT MIGHT HAVE BEEN..................................... 92

SERENE TOOTS AS A ROMAN BRIGAND......................... 108

BROTHER GARDNER IN THE BOSOM OF HIS FAMILY............ 120

THE DEFEAT OF KYFUSTUS................................... 149

WAYDOWN BEBEE.. 156

DISTINGUISHED MEMBERS OF THE CLUB....................... 178

BROTHER GARDNER AND REV. PENSTOCK...................... 194

BROTHER GARDNER'S
LIME-KILN CLUB.

FIRST ANNUAL ELECTION.

DELEGATES to the first annual election of the Lime-Kiln Club began to arrive on Thursday, and when the club was called to order in Paradise Hall, at 7 o'clock Saturday evening, 378 honorary members, representing every State in the Union, were on hand to participate in the exercises. The largest delegation was sent by Alabama, consisting of eighteen members.

Among the honoraries were sixteen ex-judges, twenty-four colonels, seven generals, twenty-two elders, eight deacons, thirteen reverends, ten majors, twelve captains, six trustees, five "squars" and thirty-eight "hons."

A Reception Committee of six active members was constantly at the landings and depots, and as fast as visitors arrived they were escorted to Paradise Hall, and tendered a half interest in a water melon and a pound of crackers.

ON THE ISLAND.

AT 11 o'clock, A. M., the crowd embarked on a steamer for Fighting Island. Such had been the vigilance of the Committee on Agriculture, that nothing was lacking to make the ride enjoyable. Ice-water, warm water, buttermilk, lemonade, root beer and ginger ale were furnished in abundance; and six bushels of peanuts, and ninety-eight water melons contributed to the general harmony.

While no special provision had been made for amusements, six dog fights occurred at convenient intervals. There was also a wrestling match between Canterbury Jones of Wisconsin, and Judge Holdback Johnson, of Vermont, in which the Canterbury's heels flew around with such vigor that two dogs and a delegate from Rhode Island were knocked overboard.

A set of boxing gloves furnished opportunity for Giveadam Jones and Patent Office Smith to limber up a little, and during this performance Mr. Smith was knocked into the middle of next week, and did not recover consciousness until nearly a gallon of first-class lemonade had been wasted in bathing his head. Jumping and wrestling matches were held on the boat, and after her landing at Belle Isle there was a running race, a sack race, and various other sports.

The following prizes were distributed to the successful champions:

Judge Holdback Johnson, champion wrestler by a large majority—A water melon once owned by Henry Clay.

Giveadam Jones, champion boxer—A photograph album, worth forty cents.

Regulation Jones, champion jumper—A linen duster which can also be used for a bootjack.

Snowball Piper, champion climber—A hand-painted, silk embroidered, double-action wheelbarrow, can also be used for a hammock.

GIVEADAM JONES SETTLES PATENT OFFICE SMITH.

Quite Right Hastings, champion runner—A pair of No. 14 Arctic overshoes, can also be used for spare beds in case of a rush of company.

Evidently Smith, champion gymnast—A hand-sled with "Remember Thy Creator" painted on the seat.

DINNER.

At 2 o'clock the multitude sat down to the several long tables loaded down with the following luxuries, nearly all of which were contributed by the liberal-hearted citizens of Detroit:

Beef,	Mutton,	Potatoes,
Cabbage,	Onions,	Turnips,
Mustard,	Pickles,	Vinegar,
Green Corn,	Mustard,	Pickles,
Mustard,	More Mustard,	
Bread,	Crackers,	Pickles,	Mustard,
Coffee,	Mustard,	Pickles.
Mustard,	Pickles,	Mustard.

AFTER DINNER.

After the banquet was disposed of, the games were renewed and the festivities maintained until nearly sundown, when the crowd re-embarked for home. On the way up the Rev. Smith lost a mouth organ which had been in his family for twenty-one years, and Judge Calkins fell overboard. The mouth organ would not float, but the Judge did, and he was pulled in by the hair, and rolled on a barrel until he recovered his usual spirits.

OPENING SPEECH.

At the hour of 7:30, Paradise Hall was thrown open, and the meeting called to order. The following eminent gentlemen had seats on the platform:

Gibraltar White, of Arkansas; Sozo Smith of Georgia; Liberty Brown, of Virginia; Remembrance Tracey, of Alabama; Kinderhook Taylor, of New York; Industry Keets, of Massachusetts, and Vandyke Peters of Canada.

"You am crowded togeder on dis occashun to hold our first anyual 'leckshun," said Brother Gardner, as he arose. "A little ober fo' y'ars ago, seben men an' a dog met at de Central Market, aroun' de co'ner, an' organized dis Lime-Kiln Club. At de nex' meetin' we had eight men an' fo' dogs, an' it has kep' gwine on dat way till now we hab a membership of 3,256 pussons, sayin' nuffin' 'tall 'bout dogs. In de las' y'ar we hav' absorbed twenty-two different societies, collected ober $2,000 in cash, los' five members by death, expelled three fur unbehavior, paid out $103 fur de relief of de sick, increased our library one-half, added much to de interes' of de museum, an' am now runnin' as smoothly an' happy as any branch of de gov'ment. We am on good terms wid ebery department of de guv'ment 'cept de Interior; we jine hands wid de Concord Skule of Philosophy: we am all O. K. wid leadin' 'stronomers; we has de friendship of all societies, an' our prosperity am all dat could be looked fur. We has met dis evenin' to 'lect officers fur de ensooin' y'ar, an' to transact odder bizness, an' we will now purceed to de work in hand."

THE PRESIDENCY.

An informal ballot was taken for President, with the following result:

Brother Gardner, - . . . . . - 370
Rev. Penstock, - 1

Pickles Smith,	1
Judge Congo,	1
Scattering,	5

On motion of Elder Smasher, the election of Brother Gardner was made unanimous, and the old man took the honor in a well-chosen speech twenty-two feet long.

The following is a list of the other officers elected:

Vice-President—Judge Congo, of Tennessee.
Treasurer—Waydown Bebee, of Detroit.
Secretary—Trustee Pullback, of Detroit.
Grand Legal Adviser—Magnesia Jefferson, of Virginia.
Honorary Poet—Lazarus Bunkers, of New York.
Grand Chaplain—Rev. Penstock, of Detroit.
Keeper of the Bear Trap—Avaricious Johnson, of Detroit.
Librarian—Hon. Goneback Fisher, of Canada.

Committees were also appointed on Judiciary, Agriculture, Fisheries, Lighthouses, Astronomy, Finance, Harmony, Pomology, Botany and Encouragement of Vice.

MUSIC AND POETRY.

Judge Congo made a speech of ten minute's length, in which he stated his belief that music had done more to keep the colored race happy and peaceful than any other influence. He believed in music and song, and the Lime-Kiln Club, as the representative of 3,000,000 colored people, should hold out encouragement. He would move that a premium of $20 be given each year for the best song and chorus sent in by the composer, and he would favor any move to put music in the hands of the masses.

FISHING.

Liberty Brown favored fishing as well as music. The art of fishing was yet in its infancy. He had known colored men to fish all day long and not get a nibble. What is wanted is a new kind of hook—one which will bait itself and pitch right into hard work while its owner finds a shady spot and goes to sleep.

Speeches were made on various other subjects, several songs sung by the Glee Club, and it was on the stroke of midnight when the meeting broke up and adjourned to a barn to attack a barrel of lemonade and 112 watermelons.

NOT A CONGRESHUNAL BODY.

"It may be well to menshun a leetle sarcumstance right heah an' now," said Brother Gardner, as the next meeting opened, "I want it distinctly understood dat de rules of Congress doan' govern de purcedins of dis club only to a sartin figger. Fur instance, if Calculation King and Romance Floyd should make use of dis floo' to call each odder liars an' blackguards, an' to make a display of muscle, an apology nex' day would have no effect on dis club. Kase why? Kase de two members wouldn't be heah to apologize! Dat's de remark I war gwine to set fo'th, an' we will now go on wid de reg'lar bizness."

COMMUNICATIONS.

A letter from David Field, of Lynn, Mass., made inquiries of the club as to whether the rain-fall in

Michigan during the past twelve months was above or below the average.

The Rev. Penstock, who has been very qniet and humble-minded since his jump from the back window, got upon his feet and replied: "I 'spose dat queshun 'peals to me personally, kase I 'spose I'm de only member of dis club who watches sech things. It am my opinyun dat de rain-fall for de last ya'r am far below the averidge."

"Brudder Penstock," said the President, "you am a valuable member of dis club, an' de club would be mighty lonesome to lose you, but still what you doan' know about de rainfall would lay de foundashun fur a heap o' dry weather. My old woman keeps a bar'l under de spout to ketch rain-water, an' I is confident dat de quantity of rain-water in dat bar'l fur de last y'ar has been moah dan for eny y'ar in ten y'ars. De secretary will reply accordingly.

NO NEPOTISM.

At this point Jamestown Smith arose to a question of privilege, and said rumors were afloat to the effect that the janitor was employing his son to help him around the hall, and paying him out of the club funds. Mr. Smith moved for an investigation.

"De janitor will please step to de front," said the President, "dis club investigates on de spot."

"Gem'len," began the janitor, as he limped out, "I has heard de charges an' am ready fer trial. I has been charged wid workin' my son into a fat job. Whar's de fatness? Whar's de son? Way back in de y'ar forty nine, when me an' de ole woman was livin' on de Rapidan, we had a son bo'n to us, but arter he growed up big 'nuff to let de hot stove-poker alone, he died. Dat's de only son I eber had. If Ize got anoder aroun' heah I'd be mighty glad to shuk hands wid him."

A brief investigation disclosed the fact that Mr. Smith was the victim of a put-up job, and he was fined one dollar for the benefit of the library fund.

SOME NEW PROVERBS.

"I wouldn't gin a cent fur de man who quotes old proverbs an' adopts second-han' mottoes," began the old man, as the crunching of harvest apples suddenly ceased. "Dis am an aige fur ebery man to hold his own plow, an' who am content to let some one else hold it must be satisfied wid cobs in place of co'n. Ef I was so poo' an' low-down dat I had to pick rags, I would have my own maxims an' mottoes. Instead of sayin' 'Doan' put off till to-morrow what kin be dun to-day,' I would have it: 'Now, ole man, you git right up 'n dust, an' sling mo' rags dis week dan any odder chap kin in a month.' De odder day I met Comeback Jones. You know he am about sixty y'ars old, on' about as hard up as a woodchuck in a b'ar's grip. I axed de ole man how he was keepin' up wid de pursheshun, an' he replied: 'Wall, ize mighty hard up, but dey say it am a long lane dat has no turn.' Just fink of an ole man wid one No. 13 in de grave waitin' fur a turn in de lane to bring him heaps to eat an' lots to w'ar? All frew life he has carried dat second-han' sayin' wid him, an' am yet a believer in it. Why didn't he hab one of his own? If he had said, forty years ago, 'Doan foller any lane, but cut cross lots', de wolf wouldn't be arter him to-day. A man who hes de will to make a motto hes de pluck to make it a success. 'Buckle down to bizness' am a better motto dan any book kin give ye. Let me, in closin', quote some of de mottoes an' maxims belonging to members of dis club:

"Sir Isaac Walpole—'Doan drap fifty cents reachin' fur a dollar.'

"Waydown Bebee—'When you can't dig fru a wall climb ober it.'

"Giveadam Jones—'Git dar' if it takes a leg.'

"Pickles Smith—'Ye can't swim a ribber by sittin' on a bank.'

"Samuel Shin—'Sot yeralarm clock fur six in de mornin.'

"Trustee Pullback—'If de road am up hill, stiffen yer backbone a little mo'.'

"Kyan Johnson—'De man who w'ars his hat on his ear, shows de empty side of his head.'

"Brutus Johnson—'Hoe co'n wid yer hans an' arms 'stead of yer mouf.'

"Elder Toots—' Take a job at fust sight, but doan' trade hosses till yer fink it ober.'"

BOUNCING BRUDDER SCOTT.

"AM Brudder Abraham Scott in de hall dis evenin'?" inquired the President, as he looked down the aisles.

"Yes, sah," answered a voice from the northwest corner.

"Den please step dis way."

Brother Scott scuffed forward, head down, and his countenance betraying about seventeen different emotions, and when he reached the mark the President continued:

"Brudder Scott, in gwine ober to de ole man Johnson's las' nite, to borry a hunk o' butter fur breakfast, I diskivered some one lyin' on de sidewalk. My fust thought was to yell murder. My nex' thought was to smell of his breaf. Dat settled de case to once. It wasn't a murder, but a case of dead drunk. I turned de subjeck ober to git a look at his face, an' who d'ye 'spose it was?"

Brother Scott gazed straight at a bust of Venus and had nothing to say.

"It was Brudder Scott!" whispered the President. "Although two of his children am bar'fut, his wife needs cloze, an' he hasn't a dozen taters in de house, he had taken good money from his pocket an' paid it out fur bad whisky. He wasn't a man when I foun' him. He was a hog—a great big hog. I could smell his breaf six feet away, an' it would have made a dog sick. He had lost his hat, rolled in de slush, an' den fallen into a stuporish sleep. I got help an' toted him home, an' to-night he comes to dis meetin' to have a wote among men who work hard, respect demselves an' lib sober lives."

"Ize sorry, sah."

"No doubt of it; but dat am no defense. A fool excites pity, kase God made him dat way. A lunatic draws sympathy, kase he has met wid misfortune. A drunkard arouses nuffin' but contempt. He deliberately goes at it to make a brute of hisself. You have heard me speak of dis matter on seberal prevus occashuns, an' you know how de majority of dis club feels on de subjeck. In de las' two months you have bin drunk fo' times."

"Yes, sah; but I'll quit."

"I hope you will, but I doubt it. You had ebery thing to lose by gettin' drunk de fust time. You have lost character, respect, money an' standin', an' dar's leetle hope dat you will see any reason to quit. We kin guard agin thieves by lockin' up our money. We kin put de murderer in prison an' hab him outer de way. We kin expose de liar an' kiver him wid confusion. But de drunkard—de hog—de beest, who kin trust him? Who kin believe in him? Who wants his society? Who am not degraded by walkin' beside him? Brudder Scott, you am a bounced man! Your name will be crossed from our rolls, you will be refused admission heah, an' we shall furgit dat you war eber numbered wid us. Let us now attack de reg'lar order o' bizness."

PREPARING FOR A PANIC.

Waydown Bebee desired to call the attention of the President to the fact that the only means of egress from Paradise Hall was a single door which opened into the room. In case of fire, and a rush, a calamity might occur which would fill hundreds of Detroit houses with wails and lamentations.

"De President has had dat ar' fack in mind fur de las' six months," replied Brother Gardner; "an' now dat de queshun has bin called up, I deem it my dooty to arrange a programme to prevent accident. In case de janiter puts a stick in de stove dat has bin loaded wid powder, or some of dese lamps explode, our fust dooty will be to try an' distinguish de flames. In case of failure, I will walk out of de hall fust, followed by Sir Isaac Walpole, Waydown Bebee, an' Giveadam Jones, at reg'lar intervals. De rest of you kin foller on in single file, an' I figger dat not a coat-tail will eben be singed. My reasons fur gwine out fust am dat I may see de fire engines when dey arrive, an' tell de men whar to frow water to keep our safe from heatin' its contents."

FALL RATES.

The Committee on Modern Philosophy reported the following amended scale of prices for the fall season, being an increase of fifteen per cent. over summer rates:

For whitewashing an ordinary kitchen ceiling and carrying away a cat to be drowned, fifty cents. Where there is no cat the price will still be the same, as the whitewasher is not to blame if the family has not provided itself with a feline.

For blacking an office stove which has been spit on for the last four months, twenty-five cents. Where the stove has escaped no abatement will be made, as it could have been spit on as well as not.

For blacking stove-pipe which has been piled up in the yard all summer, seven cents a joint, with an extra charge of three cents for wrinkled elbows.

For whitewashing a board fence eleven feet high between two loving neighbors, the charge will be thirteen cents a yard. If they are not loving neighbors an extra twenty-five cents will be collected on the job.

For whitewashing trees, a charge of ten cents each, irrespective of size.

Where gold-leaf is worked in, or work is done to imitate the old masters, the price will be $2 per day, with the privilege of attending any dog fight occurring not over four blocks away.

These prices are to be strictly adhered to by all members of the club, and any cut will subject the delinquent to a fine of $300.

SONG.

The hour for closing having arrived, the Glee Club tuned up as follows:

> De gentle spring am almost here,
>   De sun am gettin' high;
> De snow am gently slidin' out,
>   De ice begins to fly.
>
> In thirty days, or dar' abouts,
>   De grass will take its green;
> An' all of us kin slosh aroun'
>   In April mud an' rain.
>
> De robin will begin to rob,
>   De blue-bird will feel blue;
> De crow will crow-bar on his way,
>   De buzzards buz anew.
>
> Now let us all feel proper glad,
>   An' lose no time, indeed;
> In castin' roun' among our friends
>   To borry onion seed.

HE HAD A PUCKER.

JUST before the hour arrived for opening the meeting Pickles Smith went to the water pail to quench his thirst. Judge Cahoots was there and had possession of the dipper. Owing to the fact that he is in the habit of drinking out of a jug, he consumed so much time that Brother Smith said something about a hog. Then the judge said something about a baboon, and from words they proceeded to kicks and blows. The judge was knocked over a bench, and Pickles was landed with his head under the stove, and for a moment a general row seemed imminent.

Elder Toots peeled off his coat and uttered a warwhoop; Samuel Shin danced around, and even the placid Cadaver Blossom, who is considered the soul of good nature, threw down his hat and jumped over three red stools and a bench.

But in two minutes all was over. The judge held out his hand, and explained that the peculiar pucker of his mouth obliged him to drink like a horse with a bit in his mouth, and Pickles took the proffered hand, and said that he had just left a home where the old woman was sick with the mumps, and three children were whooping around with the measles.

Both were deeply grieved and heartily ashamed, and by the time Brother Gardner reached the head of the stairs, harmony prevailed by a vote of 169 to nothing.

THE HONEST MAN.

"IF I should find a perfeckly honest man—honest in his expressions, honest in his dealings, sincere in his statements—I shouldn't like him!" said Brother Gardner, as the meeting was called to order. "He would be a lonesome object in dis aige. He would seek in vain fur companionship. While I believe dat honesty am de bes' policy, I doan' look to see it practiced beyond a certain limit. When I trade mules wid a man, I kinder like to doubt his word.

I want to feel dat he am keeping still 'bout de ring-bones an' spavins, an' dat de beast he says am jist turnin' fo'teen y'ars, will nebber see his twenty-first birthday no moar. It am monotonous to deal wid a man who am perfeckly honest. If I lend a man money I want him to be honest 'nuff to return it, but if he kin trade me a watch worth $3 for a gun worth seben, I shall think none the less of him.

"If men were so sincere dat we felt obleeged to believe whateber dey asserted, we should hab no use fur theories an' argyments. When I gib my note I expect to pay it. When I ax a man how he would like to trade his wheelbarrow fur my dog, I'm not gwine to inform him dat Cæsar am all bark an' no bite, an' he am not gwine to tell me dat he borrowed dat wheelbarrow in de night, an forgot to return it. If a grocer leaves me in charge of his sto' Ize gwine to sot fur half an hour beside a box of herrings an' keep my hands in my pockets all de time. Yet, if dat same man sells me a pound of tea he expects me to try an' pass off on him a half-dollar wid a hole in it.

"Continer, my frens, to believe dat honesty am de bes' policy, but doan' expect too much of so-called honest men. You kin trust men wid your wallet who would borrow a pitchfork an' nebber return it. You kin lend your hoss to a man who would cheat you blind in tradin' obercoats. You kin send home a pa'r o' dead ducks at noon-day by a man who would steal your live chickens at midnight.

"When I lend my naybur Mocha coffee I like to wonder if he won't pay it back in Rio. When de ole woman buys kaliker on a guarantee she rather hopes it will fade in de washin'.

"I solemnly believe dat de world am honest 'nuff, jist as it am. When you gin your word stick to it if it busts de bank. When you do a job of work do it well; when you make a debt pay it. Any man who am mo' honest dan dat will want you to cut a penny in two to make out his shilling; he will ring you up at midnight to return your mouse-trap; he will take one shingle from your bunch an' offer you de one-hundredth part of what de bunch cost; he will borrow your boot-jack an' insist dat you borrow his wash-board to offset it. We will now proceed to bizness."

PLEASE ARREST HIM.

The secretary announced a letter from the Hon. Occupation Buckworthy, of Portsmouth, Va., stating that a colored man calling himself Judge John Waterman, and claiming to be an active local member of the Lime-Kiln Club, was in that city disposing of photographs supposed to represent Brother Gardner. He sold the photographs at twenty cents each, and claimed that the funds were to be sent to Liberia, to establish a mouth-organ factory. The photographs represented a colored person with a broken nose, a squint eye, front teeth gone, and ears large enough to throw a shadow over a wall eighteen feet high. Was it all right, or was the man an imposter?

Brother Gardner was jumping two feet high before the secretary had finished, and it took him only four minutes to write and send out a telegram asking the Portsmouth man to arrest the imposter if it cost $200.

In this connection it may be well to state:

. The Lime-Kiln Club employs no traveling agent.

2. It offers no chromos.

3. None of its members are allowed to attach their names to medical inventions.

4. It favors no scheme to build observatories in Liberia, or orphan asylums in the Sandwich Islands.

5. It publishes no dime novels, sends out no hair dyes and has no Presidential candidate for 1884.

UNPLEDGED AND UNCERTAIN.

The secretary announced a letter from the State Department of New Jersey, inquiring if Brother Gardner favored the annexation of Canada to the United States, and the old man carefully felt of his left ear and replied:

"Dat's a subjeck which has troubled me a great deal, an' up to de present time I am onsartin and unpledged. De same toof-brush which am sold for twenty cents on dis side, kin be bought fur fifteen ober dar. If we annex Canada, we kin hab cheap tooth brushes. On de odder han', de same rat-trap dat we sell fur twenty-five cents on dis side, can't be had ober dar fur less dan thirty. If Canada annexes us she am suah of cheap rat-traps. Dar it am, you see, an' whether we should annex Canada or Canada annex us am a queshun which I cannot decide to my own satisfaxun."

THE MUSEUM.

The keeper of the bear-traps and director of the museum reported that he had received during the week:

1. A bust of Andrew Jackson with both ears missing.

2. Plans of a smoke-house, drawn by old Cato.

3. An ink-bottle supposed to have been used by Mary, Queen of Scots.

4. A paper collar inscribed: "From Diogenes, to his dear friend Smith."

The secretary was requested to return thanks to the various donors, and amidst sweetest harmony the triangle sounded and the procession moved.

ON DE WAIT.

"Patriots of de nineteenth century," began the President, as Waydown Bebee finished breaking out a pane of glass with his elbow, "It hez pained me to obsarve on various occashions dat de cull'd populashun of dis kentry am on de wait. Dey am given to sittin' down in de house or on de fence an' waitin' fur de good time comin'. I war ober to see ole man Penny las' night. He ar' on de wait. He's bin waitin' fur de las' fifty y'ars, an' de good time hain't got 'long yit. I foun' him wid the raggest sort o' cloze on ye eber seed, pockets empty, wood gone an' flour out, an' de way he looked up at me as I walked in was 'nuff to bring on a chill. All de odder folks roun' him had work an' plenty to eat, but de ole man was waitin' fur somebody to come 'long an' take him out to hunt a job in a keeridge, an' pay him fo' dollars a day. He ain't de only man 'round heah who am waitin', stead o' gwine out an' lookin' fur work; I tell you dis big world doan' car' a copper wedder such men starve to death or not. De world owes nobody nuffin. De man 'spects to git 'long an' hev sunthin to eat an' a place to live hez got to bounce aroun' an' let de world understan' dat he's on de *git!* If any well man, no matter what de culler, walks dis town wid an en pty stomach, it am his own fault, an' I hain't gwine to fill it fur him. Now let de purceedings purceed.'

STRIKIN DE AVERAGE.

"What I was gwine to remark," said Brother Gardner, as the back end of Paradise Hall grew quiet, "was to say to you dat the pusson who expects to injoy dis life mus' make up his mind to strike de world on de gineral average. He who neglects to do so will meet wid daily sorrows and dispintments.

"Doan' expect dat de man who happens to agree wid you on the weather am sartin to agree wid you on politicks. It doan' foller dat de man who agrees wid you on politicks will feel bound to accept your kind of religion. De fack dat you lend a naybur your shovel doan' bind him to lend you his wheelbarrer. He who looks for honesty whar' he finds gray ha'rs will be as sadly disappointed as he who argues dat an old coat am de sign of a thief or a beggar. Put faith in human natur' an yet be eber ready to doubt.

"I expect to meet about so many mean men in de course of a y'ar.

"I expect de summer will be hot an' de winter cold

"I expect to have chilblains in December, an' shakes of de ager in April.

"I expect dat a sartin per cent. of dis world's populashun will lie to me, steal my cabbages, frow stones at my dog, and hit me wid a brickbat as I go home from de lodge.

"On de odder hand, when I come to strike de average, I kin put my hand on men who will lend me money, go on my bond, speak well of me, an' sot up all night to protec' me.

"No man am perfec'. He may strike you at first sight as werry good or werry bad, but doan' decide until you average him. He may beat a street kyar company, an' yit be honest wid a butcher. He may crawl under de canvas to see a circus, an' yit pay his pew rent in advance. He may lie to you as to how he woted, an yit tell de truf about a spavined hoss. He may cuss on de street, an' yit be a tender father at home. He may incourage a dog-fight, an' yit walk a mile to restore a los' chile to its parents.

"Accept no man fur his fine talk—reject no man for his old clothes; stand him out in de sunlight an' average him. You will be certain to fin' sunthin' bad about him, but you will also be sartin to fin' sunthin' good.

CAN'T SEE WHY.

A communication from Winchester, Tenn., stated that sixty-three colored residents of that town had been converted and baptized within the last three months, and yet poultry continued to disappear with the same regularity and dispatch as before the revival began.

"I doan' see nuffin' strange 'bout dat case," replied Brother Gardner as he scanned the letter. "Gittin' religun an' being baptized doan' ginerally affect de appetite. If a pusson has a taste fur chickens, its gwine to take an awful shakin' up to make him prefer salt pork or corned-beef."

AGRICULTURAL.

The committee on agricultural reported:

1. That the spring tramp had come forth and was in condition to make a summer tour of 1,0 0 miles.
2. Farmers are recommended to plant a larger area of melons, and to locate the patch at least half a mile from the house.
3. Seed corn which has been kept in Saratoga trunks behind the cook stove all winter has escaped the frost and promises well.
4. Any farmer who hangs a bell on a harvest apple tree, or sets a bear trap around his smoke-house, or places a spring gun to guard his hen-roost is a silent enemy of American liberty.

RESOLVED.

Prof. Tranquility Hanover then offered the following resolution:

"*Resolved*, Dat in case a circus comes 'long, an' a member of de Lime-Kiln Club in good standin' can't raise de necessary wealth to buy a ticket, it am not derogotary to his character to crawl under de canvas."

Giveadam Jones objected to the resolution. He always began saving up right away after New Years, and by the middle of May he could lay his hand on a half dollar to go to the stupendous combination of world-renowned celebrities,

Pickles Smith hoped that no such resolution would pass. He had crawled under the canvas without being seen, and he had crawled under and had his neck broken with a tent-pin, and in both cases he had a feeling that he had derogatoried his character. The best way was to carry water to the elephant and get a free ticket.

Several others spoke in the same vein, and upon a vote being taken, 128 voted against and only three for.

THE JANITOR.

This individual submitted a bill for extras amounting to sixty-four cents, and attempted to make a speech defending the Peruvian policy, but his bill was cut down to seventeen cents, his speech sat down on, and he fell over three dogs on his way out.

THE MUSEUM.

The Keeper of the Sacred Relics reported that he had received from Dalton, Ga., a pair of cow-hide boots left in the neighborhood by De Soto when he was looking for the Mississippi river. Also, from Chattanooga, a relic of the Aztecs in the shape of a pipe. He recommended a new lock for the door, asked to be reimbursed for a bottle of ink he had purchased with private funds, and was given leave of absence for three days to bury his uncle.

THE CLOSE.

There being no other business which would sour before the next meeting, Pickles Smith was given leave to take home the ice left in the water pail, and the meeting adjourned, with a sweet smile illuminating every countenance.

THEIR DANDER RIZ.

A COMMUNICATION from M. B. Smith, of Cincinnati, conveyed the intelligence that he was a member of the Bar of Ohio, in good standing, and that he would be glad to do the legal business of the club by the year for a reasonable compensation. His rates for defending members of the club were given as follows:

For defending a murderer, $25; a burglar, $20; an incendiary, $18; a bigamist, $15; a horse-thief, $15; an embezzler, $12. For defending four common thieves in a heap, and proving an alibi in each case, $50; half in advance and the remainder in thirty days.

The reading of the letter was not interrupted by even a cough, but bushels and bushels of short hair could be seen trying to stand up straight in indignation. Brother Gardner had a dangerous roll to his eye as he got up and began:

"Misser Secretary, you write to dat man wid de biggest kin' of a pen, an' in de plainest language, dat if he ever strikes dis town he'd better keep cl'ar of Paradise Hall."

REPORTS.

The Committee on the Fisheries reported that little or nothing had yet been done towards introducing whales and sharks into inland waters, and that their communications to Secretary Evarts in regard to this matter had met with no answers. They were perfectly satisfied that both whales and sharks would thrive and do well in Erie and other lakes, and that their introduction would greatly enhance the fun of taking a dive off a lumber pile or going out for a sail in an old boat. The Secretary was instructed to write Mr. Evarts to the effect that he was only a servant of the public, and that Mr. Hayes would not be the next president.

NATURAL HISTORY.

This committee was instructed last fall to investigate and report on the statement that native game and fowl were gradually dying out. They reported at this meeting that only part of the statement had any foundation. They had found quite a scarcity of elegible wild cats, deer and bear, but other game was on the increase. They estimated the following increase in round numbers of the animals named in one year:

Rabbits,	24,000,000
Woodchucks,	6,000,000
Possums,	3,000,000
Chipmonks,	75,000,000

As to fowls, the increase in hens alone is estimated by the committee to be at least 55,000,000 per year, not counting the spring chickens which mysteriously disappear every dark night in the fall. Great pains have been taken to verify those figures, and the commissioners of agriculture, stock-brokers and candidates for the Presidency can depend upon them in making up their semi-yearly reports.

AGRICULTURE.

The committee on the internal resources of the country reported that they had been unable to secure any reliable statistics as to what crops flourished best on side-hills. Some writers had seemed to favor buckwheat, aud others had partly declared for long-necked squashes, and the committee had about concluded to settle on onions.

"Onions!" added the chairman, "kinder fill in whar odder crops hez got to spread out. De onion am all solid. You doan' have to loose anyfing in de peelin. Ye kin bile, fry, roast or bake it, an' de sensashun am right dar all de time. De onion had radder grow wid de top up, but am perfectly willin' to go long any odder fashion. De rain doan' hurt it, de sun doan affeck it, an' de frosts can't kill it. Darfore, dis committee am inclined to go heavy on de onion, an' let de tulip an' rose take car' of demselves.

POLITICAL.

Brother Gardner said he had a remark or two to say in regard to the coming election, and he said:

"Go to the polls airly; git right away from dar jist as soon as you hev put in your wote.

"Doan' wote but once, kase de second wote won't count fur unffin'.

"Doan' stan' aroun' de polls talkin 'bout de hard winter or de late spring, kase 'lection hezn't nuffin' to do wid de weather.

"Doan' blow aroun' 'bout de candydates. Let de candydates do dar own blowin'.

"Doan' mix up in enny fouts, kase fouts am none o' yer bizness, an' folks may git dar ribs broken.

"Doan' try to make enybody believe dat de salvashun of dis kentry depends on de success of your ticket, fur it don't. Dis kentry would go right along to glory if dar wasn't a ticket put up from now till Halifax.

"Dat's all. Let de meetin' be abided fur one week."

PETITIONS.

Some fifteen or sixteen petitions were received during the week, but the bundle was accidentally knocked off the secretary's table, and probably burned up by the janitor when he built the fire. The janitor offered to make affidavit that his kindlings consisted of two old ink-bottles and a railroad map of Texas; but he is a man who often labors under fits of absent-mindedness.

NOT ANY FOR THEM.

When the bean-box had been laid away, Waydown Bebee secured the floor and said that the time was not far away when all men annually decided to "swear off" from all bad habits, take a vow to save money, and keep a diary for the next year. He would like to know if the club had thought of taking up any action as a club.

James K. Polk thereupon introduced the following:

Resolved, That this Lime-Kiln Club does not sw'ar off from anything, nor save an extra cent, nor keep no diary, an' dat de fust member who resolves to be any gooder in 1880 dan he was in 1879, be fined fifty dollars, an de cost of a new wood box fur dis hall.

"Question" was called, and the resolution was adopted, and ordered spread on the minutes of the meeting.

THE SEASONS.

A communication from Harvard College requested the President of the club to explain what caused the four seasons of the year, and after some hesitation Brother Gardner arose to reply.

"What we call de fo' sezuns of de y'ar am caused by varus causes," he began. "De sun hez consid'rable to do about it, an' de moon helps along all she kin. I doan' s'pose dat sickness in de fam'ly hez anyfin' to do wid de changes of sezun. I s'pose dey'd come 'long 'bout de same anyhow. De sekretary can answer to de effeck dat sickness hez nuffin to do wid it, an' dat de winter sezun am no doubt caused by so much cold wedder comin' down all of a sudden."

GUESS NOT.

Axletree Jones said he arose to defend the American nation from the aspersions of the Canadian press. He had lately read in a Canadian paper that this nation was living too fast, and that it must soon become bankrupt. Such unwarranted attacks on his native country thrilled him with indignation clear down to his last bunion, and if the press of this country would not resent them he would.

"Livin' too fast!" As he repeated he drew himself up. "I hez worn dis same paper collah free weeks. Am dat livin' too fast? Heah am a west ober ten y'ars ole by the almanax! Am dat dressin' to kill? Look at de red woolen patches on de knees of dese black pants, an' tole me if it looks as if this nashun was death on sto' cloze? Livin' too fast! Why de werry ideah am imposturous! Am 'taters biled wid de hides on an' pieced out wid bacon an' co'n bread livin' too fast? On behalf of de American people I protest! On behalf of dis nashun I warn de Stait of Kennedy dat we can't be sassed beyond a certain pint. When dat pint hez bin passed dar will come a demand for gore an' revenge."

The speech was received with great applause, and Satisfaction Rice next took the floor and said:

"Civil war an' its horrors am to be deplored an' shunned—but if she mus' come—if we mus' resort to de force of arms to preserve our honor, den let us resort! Let us gird on de armor of right, an' march forward wid brave hearts. He who sasses dis nashun sasses de Lime-Kiln Club."

It was then resolved that this nation was not living too fast, and that Canada had best beware, and the meeting adjourned.

THE HON. STANDOFF.

"GEM'LEN, a curus anecdote happened at de cabin of the Hon. Licurgus Standoff las' nite," said Brother Gardner, as the janitor lighted a fresh lamp.

"De brudder am not heah, owin' to resuns to be menshuned a little furder on, an' de case am one to which de attenshun of de club has bin called by seberal white men, an' an investigashun demanded. De facks in de anecdote seem to unwind as follows: De Hon. Standoff was about to retire fur de nite. De ole woman had already sought de downy couch of sweet repose; de chill'n were dreamin' of apple-blossoms an' angels, an' de cat an' dog had dropped down behin' de stove in blissful harmony. Dar was a hot fiah in de stove. De Hon. Standoff lingered

BROTHER GARDNER, PRESIDENT OF THE LIME-KILN CLUB.

behin' to injoy de refreshment, an' he had just leaned ober to spit under de front doahs when sunthin' happened. De top of dat stove riz up. So did de ole tea-kettle, a hot brick, an' moah or less fiah. De Hon. Standoff also riz up, an' got out doahs an' yelled 'murder! at de top of his voice. It was a riz up time aroun dat house, an' folks say dat fam'ly was de wildest-lookin' lot o' niggers eber seen in Detroit. Now, den, what caused dat 'sploshun? It wasn't gas. It wasn't low water in de biler. White men say dat it was caused by powder in a stick of wood, an' dat de wood didn't belong to de Hon. Standoff, who now lies in bed wid blisters all ober him. Was it powder? Was dat powder in a stick of wood? Did de brudder incorporate dat wood from some surroundin' naybur? Let de members speak."

Samuel Shin was first to break the silence. Rising to his feet with a blush of philosophy covering his face, he said:

"Bekase dar was a 'sploshun in de stove, it doan' foller dat dar was powder in de wood. 'Spose one of de chil'en had dropped a bottle of hoss-medicine in de fiah befo' goin' to bed. I've knowed dat wery thing to happen in my own house, an' whar's de man who says I stole wood?"

"If I war to be axed for my opinion on dis subject," remarked Waydown Beebe, as he took the floor, "I should say dat dar mought have bin powder in de wood. What of it? If de Hon. Standoff had a mind to, couldn't he put powder in his own wood? Dar's no law to prewent him. De white folks ain't de only folks who kin put on style an' plug deir stove-wood wid powder."

"I fink I see how all dis hapened," said Blackberry Williams, as Bebee sat down. "Fur instance. De Hon. Standoff owns wood. He sees dat woodpile growin' smaller—meltin' away like he had six stoves goin' 'stead o' one. He plugs a stick wid powder. He furgits which is de stick. It finds its way into his own stove, an' where am dat stove to-day?"

None of the other members seemed inclined to tackle the subject, and Brother Gardener said:

"De Hon. Standoff am hereby acquitted of de charge of takin' fiahwood belongin' to somebody else, but de Cha'r feels it his dooty to warn de brudder to be a little more keerful in de future."

THE HON. SOLO BOMBY.

THE above-named gentleman, who was on a short trip from his home in Arkansas, to try the effect of the northern climate on a stiff knee, having appeared at Paradise Hall, was invited to lecture; and, after being escorted to the platform, he placed his hand on his breast and began:

"My fren's, I did not arrove heah to-night to make a speech. I simply wanted to gaze on your hall, congratulate ebery member, an' go home wid Brudder Gardner to save hotel bill. [Cheers.] I should have jined dis club fo' y'ars ago, only dat I was led to believe dat a man wid a glass eye would not be taken in. I hev diskivered my error to-night, and my application hes been filed. [Cheers.]

"I am astonished wid the Norf. I neber saw so much land to de acre in all my life. White folks seem to hev plenty of money, an' ebery cull'd fam'ly owns from one to six dogs. I am also highly surprised an' greatly delighted at de progress which you'uns hev made in intelligence an' eddecashun. Yesterday I asked a cull'd boy not ober ten y'ars old who diskivered America, an' he answered Abram Linkum quicker'n a wink. [Applause.] Cull'd men know when de train goes out jist as well as white folks. Dey keep track o' eclipses, comets, freshets, an' odder excitin' news, an' dey om a long ways ahead of de Souf on dictionary words. [Cheers.]

'I'm glad to see all dis. No thought of jealousy rankles in my breast. On de contrary. May de emblem continer her indivisibility until the unrewarded requisition contests de apparent reliability of de gondolier. In fact, let me say wid Jefferson: '*Ignis fatuus hos de combat, faux pas ex abrupto est modus in rebus,*' and don't you forget it!"

For a minute the hall was as silent as a graveyard. Then Samuel Shin rose up and whooped, and cheer upon cheer rolled up and down and could not be suppressed until someone outside threw a turnip through the window and missed the Rev. Penstock's head by the millionth part of an inch.

A PAINFUL REPORT.

CANESTOGA JOHNSON, of the Committee on Hereditary Privileges, arose with business in his eyes and announced that he was ready with his monthly report. Two weeks since his committee had been informed of a dastardly attempt to wrest one of the most cherished hereditary privileges from the hands of the colored race, and he had sent to Memphis to secure all particulars. He was now ready to report that a white man in that city had invented and brought out a machine known as "The Dead Give-Away." It was an explosive torpedo made up to resemble a spring chicken, and its position on the roost at night was so natural that a person who had eaten 10,000 hens would be deceived. It had been brought out on the quiet, and before the colored population of Memphis knew what was up the place was full of shattered constitutions. Large orders had poured in on the inventor, and one firm in Detroit had telegraphed for 3,000. In six months every nen-roost in America would have its torpedo chicken, and the 6,500,000 colored people might as well prepare for a change of diet, unless something could be done. He would urge prompt and speedy action. Every day of delay put fifty additional torpedo chickens on the market.

"I hab neber said dat de cull'd people war' eben de wictims of suspishun when a hen-roost was robbed," replied the President; "but yet it seems to me dat dis torpedo bizness orter be squelched. Dey may accidentally go off an' kill all de hens; dey may blow up leetle chill'en who go out arter eggs; dey may 'splode while we am whitewashin' de fence; dey may git mixed in wid de poultry at de markets, an' be de means of seperatin' fond husbands an' lovin' wives. De Committee on Emergencies will darfor' meet wid de Committee on Hereditary Privileges to take such axshun as am deemed best."

IT MUST BE CRUSHED.

THE person or persons who, sometime during Friday night, climed upon the roof of Paradise Hall and filled the chimney with old hats, straw, boots, etc., are hereby warned that it was the practice of such deviltry as this that brought Capt. Kidd to the gallows. When the janitor started the fire the hall soon filled with smoke, and the opening of the meeting was delayed twenty minutes by the joke.

The roll had scarcely been called when Pickles Smith offered the following:

"*Resolved*, Dat we do hereby express our deep indignashun at dis exhibishun of human depravity; and

"*Resolved*, Dat we ax ourselves wid alarm whar' dis infringement of de rights of freemen will end; and

"*Resolved*, Dat we denounce de perpetrators of dis appallin' outrage as outlaws, imbeciles and orators of the deepest dye."

The resolutions were adopted and filed, and Brother Gardner quietly observed that this fresh outrage was another evidence to him of the drift of the times toward barbarism. If the chimney on Paradise Hall could be choked up with old hats, what was to prevent the City Hall from being blown up by the same gang? It was a spirit which must be suppressed and crushed at any cost, and he would authorize the Secretary to offer a reward of $500 to any person who would capture, convict and send the perpetrators of this fiendish crime to State Prison for fifty years.

CANCELLED.

The President announced that he had cancelled the following certificates of membership for **reasons** given:

No. 3084, being the certificate of the Hon. Gonawanda Hooker, of North Carolina. Evidence was furnished the President that Hooker had three wives and yet ran away with the fourth.
No. 5,163, being the certificate of Col. Hunter, of Wisconsin. Evidence was furnished to prove that he was the biggest colored liar in that State.
No. 6,062, being the certificate of Elder Rackabout, of Kentucky. The Elder was convicted of stealing two bags of flaxseed, giving up a mule to settle the case, and then hiring a man to steal the mule.

AGRICULTURAL.

The Committee on Agriculture, to whom had been intrusted the query from Indiana: "Are we advancing in agriculture?" reported that they had spent seven weeks in investigating the matter, and were quite ready to answer in the affirmative. Among other instances of progress in agriculture might be mentioned that of hoeing corn. A dozen years ago the plan was to lean the hoe against a stump in the field and go off fishing. It is now done by giving a chattel mortgage on three steers and hiring a neighbor to do the work. Ten years ago turnips were heaped up in the barn or cellar and supposed to be fit food for only cows and calves. To-day they are carefully wrapped in tissue paper, laid in bureau drawers, and are considered a fit diet for even a Senator. When wiped off with a dishcloth, and scraped with a butcher knife, they furnish a very bracing and enervating diet. Progress had been made in plowing, dragging, reaping, and many other particulars, and the committee felt safe in saying that the time was not far distant when a farmer could sit in an arm chair in a lager beer saloon and raise sixty bushels of wheat to the acre

WHERE DUTY ENDS.

"I am in receipt of a query from Pittsburgh," said the President as he displayed a letter, "axin' me whar' our dooty to our naybur begins an' ends up. To be nayburly wid a naybur am one of de highest and greatest principles on airth. Our dooty begins when we let his chickens scratch up our garden, his chill'en ride our gate, an' his dog chase our cat widout complaint. Our dooty ends when we have lent him our hoe, shovel, spade, ice-tongs, ax, sugar, tea, coffee, milk an' butter, and he has forgotten dat he owes us anythin' beyan' a request dat we will come ober an' turn grindstun fur him to sharpen a crow-bar."

INTERNAL HARMONY.

Giveadam Jones, Chairman of the Committee on Internal Harmony, reported a sad state of affairs existing between Pickles Smith and Kyan Jones, starting originally with a dispute over the ownership of twelve feet of clothes line. The members had not only used violent language towards each other, in the presence of a grocer who sells two boxes of sardines for a quarter, but had clinched and rolled in the mud, and solemnly vowed each other's destruction. The two members being called to the desk, it was discovered that the piece of rope belonged to neither, and Brother Gardener said:

"Gem'len, I doan' ax yer to fall on each odder's neck an' shed tears, but I want you to understan' dat if dis gulf ain't bridged ober befo' de nex' meetin' you will h'ar sumthin' drap. As de case stands, you am bof fined $5, which money de Treasurer will place to de credit of de fund to purchase silk stockings fur de widows of deceased cull'rd poets."

The two members retired to the ante-room for a short time and returned to report that all was joy and harmony. A motion was then made to remit the fine, which was carried, and the reunited pair returned to their seats and lovingly chewed on the same bologna.

THE CLOSE.

All the public business having been disposed of the Keeper of the Bear-Trap reported everything clear in the West, with a tendency to skip dividends on railroad stock, and the meeting broke up with the Glee Club sweetly singing the plaintive melody of "Old John Brown."

ALL A SHAM.

"Feller Kentrymen," said the old man, as he laid down his stick of licorice and stood up, "I war ober to de widder Smith's the odder eavnin' to see if she could lend my ole woman her wash-board de nex' day, an' de widder she spoke up an' said: 'Misser Gardner, dis world am all a sham.' I war in de co'ner grocery de nex' day, an' de grocer he hove a sigh as big as my fist as he leaned ober de counter an' said: 'Misser Gardner, dis world am all a sham.' I was blackin' a stove fur de doctah down on de co'ner below dat same day, an' when I got frew wid de job he drapped a quarter inter my hand an' softly whispered: 'Brudder Gardner, dis world am all a sham.' Now, gem'len, all dat talk am cl'ar bosh. De world am all right. Who says de hoss am a sham? Who says dat de cow an' mule an' dog an' de cat am shams? De man who falls down finds solid bizness. De man who buys codfish doan get mutton chops. When I ax fur kaliker dey doan' gin me silk. Once in a while we may frow a boot-jack at a cat an' hit nuffin' but an ash barrel, but de world in gineral am plenty good 'nuff fur de kind of people who put in deir time heah. De man who scratches his back agin de City Hall will tell you dat de world am all a sham. De chap who's wife supports him by washin' an' sewin' feels dat de world am sham all ober. De noodle-head who sots out to captur' de public wid a little cane an' a good deal of brass is no sooner stepped on dan he cries out 'sham!' till ye can't rest. I doan' wont to hear dat 'spreshun aroun' heah, kase it won't go down wid men who work ten hours a day an' pay deir honest debts."

WHISTLED FUR HIS DOG.

IN opening the meeting, Brother Gardner stated that he would be unable to do much talking, owing to the condition of his throat. Three or four days ago he was advised to hold a brass overcoat button in his mouth to cure the earache. In whistling for his dog, he swallowed the button, and it will be some time before his throat gets over the strain.

MERE FORMALITY.

The Committee on Navigation, having been instructed to report why the term "Honorable" was used in connection with the Common Councils of cities, explained as follows:

"As nigh as dis committee could l'arn, de use of dat word am descended from de English, an' it am used in mere formality. No Common Council am honorable, an' no one expects anything honorable from sich bodies. We believe de word should be stricken out of all petishuns an' communicashuns. De time has gone by in dis kentry when you kin blind a man wid a sheet o' white paper."

The report was accepted and adopted, and the Secretary was instructed to erase the word "honorable" from his next official communication to any Common Council.

NOTHING SPECIAL NEEDED.

The Secretary further announced a letter from Indianapolis, in which the writer asked what special qualifications were necessary in this State to fit a man for the office of Justice of the Peace.

"So far as I have obsarved," replied Brother Gardner, "nuffin speshul am needed. No justice am required to know anyfin' of law. He need have no character fur sobriety or honesty. He am 'spected to decide ebery case in de favor of de plaintiff, an' he will do so ebery time onless afraid dat de defendant will appeal. De posishun of justice of de peace am one which any one kin fill, an' which few decent men hanker arter."

THE LIME-KILN CLUB. 55

THEY WILL OBSERVE.

Giveadam Jones offered the following preamble and resolution:

"*Wh'aras*, George Washington was de Father of his kentry, an' could not tell a lie; an'

"*Wh'aras*, De anniversary of his birth should be observed by all good an' patriotic citizens, wedder dey kin tell a lie or not; now, darefore,

"*Resolved*, Dat de Lime-Kiln Club sot apart de 22d as a day of feastin' an' rejoicin', an' gwine to a dance in de evenin'."

The Rev. Penstock moved to strike out the words, "Gwine to a dance in de evenin'," and substituting the words, "Take our way to prayer-meetin' in de twilight." But he was voted down with a pressure of 200 pounds to the square inch, and the resolution was adopted in its original form.

ASTRONOMICAL.

The Committee on Astronomy submitted their regular monthly report as follows:

Number of dark nights since last report, twenty-two.

Number of comets discovered, three; but too far off to cause any run on the bank.

Lime-Kiln Club estimate of the distance to the sun, about five miles; to the moon, about the same.

The committee further announced that they had changed the name of Venus to "Sarah," of Jupiter to "Charles Henry," of Mars to "Andrew Jackson," and of Saturn to "Sam Johnson." Astronomers throughout the country will please take notice and govern themselves accordingly. Further changes will be made as spring opens and the roads improve.

THEY WERE CONSIDERING.

Waydown Bebee announced that he had received a letter from Si Doodlebat, of Pittsburgh, complaining that his application for membership had been neglected. Brother Gardner called upon the Committee of Petitions to explain, and the chairman said that he had been investigating the character of the applicant. He had written to the Mayor of Pittsburgh regarding the petitioner, and the information might be summed up as follows:

1. He wears two watch chains.
2. He carries a cane, wears an ulster, and is followed by a four-ounce dog wearing a red blanket.
3. He goes to the postoffice three times per day and loudly inquires for letters—but never gets any.
4. On several occasions he has tried to pass himself off as a member of the Legislature.

The committee having discovered that he was this sort of a man, were waiting for further evidence, and the President indorsed their action and told them to go slow.

EATH'S GRIP.

THERE was sadness in every eye as the members of the club softly filed in and took their seats. Each one had seen the crape on the Hall door, and each one had been told that death had again entered Paradise Hall. The officers moved about very quietly on the platform and held whispered consultations, and the voice of the triangle when it called to order echoed and re-echoed like the notes of a sad refrain.

"Gem'len," began the President, as he rose up and looked down the Hall at the vacant seat bedecked with crape, "anoder soldier hez gone down while fightin' de battle of life—anoder member of our club hez listened to de woice of de bell rung on de furder shore of time to guide de speerits of de dead across de dark an' rapid riber dat flows 'tween life an' eternity. It am my painful dooty to inform you dat Brudder Torpedo Hunt am no moah on dis earth. He passed away las' night arter an illness of only free days. A week ago he sot in dat cheer dar' an' seconded de moshun. To-day he am ready fur de grave!"

There was a sensation in the hall. Elder Toots covered as much of his face with his hands as he could, and Pickles Smith, Trustee Pullback and Rosin Johnson looked out of the window to hide their agitation.

"Torpedo was our brudder, an' an airnest worker in de cause," continued the President, "but if I stan' heah to yulogize him, I mus' not furgit dat he had his faults. If de truf can't hurt de livin', it can't harm de dead. Torpedo was a great han' to git up airly in de mornin', an' to work hard all day, but his chill'en went bar'foot all winter jist de same. He was kind to his wife an' felt bad fur de poo', but he neber played yuker widout hevin' two extra bowers up his sleeve. He didn't git drunk, but no rail fence had any bizness widin a mile of his cabin in de winter. He didn't ingaige in rows an' riots, but his enemies got hit wid brick-bats all de same. We saw him at church on Sunday, settin' a good 'zample fur de young, but he'd turn in nex' day an' try to win de big prize in a lottery. It was about half an'-half wid him. When we say dat of any man we hev hit him pretty clus. When we hev given de dead all de praise dey sought to gain when livin', no man's mem'ry kin ask fur more. Torpedo was up to de aiverage, an' he am dead. What ackshun will de club take?"

Sir Isaac Walpole moved a committee of four to prepare resolutions of respect to be presented to the widow, and such a committee was appointed.

Waydown Bebee moved that the Club take charge of the funeral, and march in procession to the grave, and the same was adopted.

The Hon. Juneberry Killfish said that he was with the deceased in his last hours, and that Brother Torpedo asked for and ate nearly a pound of beefsteak half an hour before he died, and that he seemed worried for fear that his dog would be misused after he was gone.

Several other speeches bearing on the character of the deceased were delivered, and it was then resolved that out of respect for his memory the regular business of the Club be postponed for one meeting. This made room for further speeches, and Col. Damson Brown took the floor and said that life was short and uncertain, and it behooved every man to have his house in order. He wanted to make a confession and clear his conscience. Six years ago he poisoned a dog belonging to Esquire Smith, of Hastings street, a neighbor of his. Both were now members of the Club, and in the presence of all he would confess, ask forgiveness, and pay what the canine was worth.

There was a great clapping of hands as he sat down. Then Esquire Smith arose, his face wreathed in smiles, and he replied that he distinctly remembered the dog case, but that the Colonel didn't owe him anything. The dog hadn't been dead six hours when he killed and ate the Colonel's goat and stole half a cord of his wood, and he thought the thing was about even.

Major Spoon-holder wiped his eyes on a red napkin which he had picked up somewhere and remarked that all had to die. If any colored man thought he could escape the king of terrors by moving to Canada or Oberlin, he was greatly mistaken. He would move that the Club sing a hymn.

A DOLLAR BILL.

The Club didn't sing one all the same, and Samuel Shin got on his feet. He felt contrite and broken up, and he also had something to confess. About three months ago he found a dollar bill in the Hall. He knew it must have been lost by some member, and yet his selfishness and dishonesty whispered to him to keep it. He did so, but now the owner of the bill had only to reveal his identity and his money should be restored and his forgiveness asked.

Brother Gardner crooked his finger for that "William." Sir Isaac Walpole leaned forward and held out his hands. Waydown Bebee and twenty-nine others took the floor in chorus, and tried to say that they would receive back their lost bill and grant a free pardon. A rapid look over the hall and a count of noses showed forty-seven men who had lost a dollar and were ready to forgive Samuel Shin. He was called forward by the President, who asked:

"Did any of us gem'len drop a dollar bill on dis floo'?"

"We did!" called forty-seven voices together.

"I resign my claim," sighed Brother Gardner, as he looked up and down and realized the situation.

"Was it a greenback dat you losted?" asked Samuel.

Forty-seven voices wildly answered "yes!"

"Dis was a Kennedy bill I foun'," softly continued Samuel, and amid an awful silence he returned to his bench.

A committee of three was then appointed to draft an inscription for the tombstone of the deceased, and the meeting adjourned.

A FEW REFLEXUNS.

"DE odder night, in de Club library, I heard a member of de Club grievin' cause he wasn't a great man," said the President, as the Hall grew quiet. "It am nateral 'nuff dat we should all want to git ahead. It am not onreasonable in any man to want to be top of the heap. Preachers, poets, editors an' lecturers all incourage us to dig 'long an' strive to carve our names on de cupalow of de temple of fame. An' yit what a holler mockery fame am. Dar was Shakspeare. He had de toof-ache same as a common man. He had his blue days, same as de poorest white. De rain pored down on him same as on Samuel Shin—he fell in de mud, same as Elder Toots--his grocer wanted cash, same as mine. Dar was Byron de poet. His name am as high as de steeples, an' yet his corns ached, same as Waydown

Bebee's—butcher-carts run him down, same as Trustee Pullback—street kyar drivers rang de bell on him, same as on 'Squar Williams. Dar was Queen 'Lizabeth. She had a big palace, heaps o' waiters an' lots o' cloze, but she had big feet, got bald-headed, an' couldn't see any more of Niagery Falls for five dollars dan my ole woman did for two shillins. Greatness may bring store cloze, but it doan' allus bring happiness. Fame may bring a house purvided wid a burglar-alarm, but de higher de fame de higher de gas-bills. If greatness comes foolin' around you, cotch him by de coat tails. If he nebber comes, be content widout him. A home—wife an chill'en —plenty to eat—pew-rent paid an' a pig in de pen, am good 'nuff fur any man, an' he who seeks to climb higher am jus' as apt to bust his 'spender-buttons as to git dar. Wid dese few inflexshuns on de incontestancy of earthly greatness, we will now disband ourselves to bizness."

A DIVORCE.

Brother Gardner looked down upon the bald head of Sir Isaac Walpole for a long minute, and then began:

"Gem'len, dey say dat ebery man's house am his castle, an' I'm de las' one to bring up a brudder's domestic matters in dis Club; but de tears of a wife an' de hungry wails of de chill'en am crowdin' me to say a few words at dis meetin'. Lat' night de wife of Brudder Simcoe Davis knocked at my cabin doah. I kicked out de dog, chased out de cat, frew de boot-jack under de bed an' my boots under de table an' toled her to come in. She was weepin' like a green bay tree. My ole woman helped her to sot down on de aige of de wood-box, an' arter de fust convulshuns of grief had passed away, de woman tole us dat she an' de chill'en hadn't a bite to eat in two days, an' de cook-stove was as cold as a crowbar. Brudder Simcoe Davis was at home an' in de bes' health, an' while de chill'n were cryin' fur bread he was lyin' on de floo', perusin' de 'Life of Kit Carson' an' stoppin' to spell out all de big words. I went ober dare an' seed it wid my own eyes. I doan' say dat he has broken any of de laws an' rules of dis Club, but I do say dat a nigger who will lump down on his back to read a novel when de fiah am out an' de cupboard empty, am not fit to sot heah 'longside of hard-workin' men."

"Hear! hear!" came from all parts of the Hall, and in about two minutes Simcoe Davis was divorced from the Club by a unanimous vote.

A VISITOR.

The Janitor having made known the fact that the Hon. Robert Beeson, of Washington, had arrived at the Hall from the depot, the Secretary was dispatched to greet him and bring him in. Mr. Beeson is a gentleman of fine education and liberal views, and is now seeking to stir up his race on the subject of discovering the East and West Poles, leaving the North and South to be found by the white folks. In his brief speech to the Club he stated his belief that an open sea existed around the West Pole—a sea whose waters were as tranquil as a meadow, and tasting like gin and sugar with nutmeg grated in. The bark which entered this sea would pass over

THE LIME-KILN CLUB. 63

beds of purest coral, be surrounded by mermaids, move in an air of choice flowers, and be certain to return laden with diamonds, rubies and pearls. Mr. Beeson was soliciting aid to enable him to charter a vessel and buy provisions, and it had been his idea from the first to invite at least two members of the Lime-Kiln Club to accompany the ship. He left a subscription paper on the Secretary's desk, and in less than an hour and a half the following amounts were subscribed:

Samuel Shin, - - - - - - - 2c
Waydown Bebee, - - - - - - 1c
Elder Toots, - - - - - - - 1c

A FAILURE.

The Rev. Penstock gave notice that the efforts of the Club to secure a law to abolish brush-boys in barber shops had failed, through the treachery of the State Senator who had the matter in charge. This Senator had solemnly agreed to introduce such a bill, but he had at the last hour basely turned about and sent in a bill making it obligatory on every barber shop in the country to employ at least two brush-boys with a fixed fee of ten cents each. The Club's bill for the better protection of the woodpeckers of Michigan had also failed to pass.

COMMUNICATIONS.

A letter from the Sixteenth Assistant Secretary of State at Washington asked the co-operation of the Club in preserving to future generations the historic spots of Michigan. Brother Gardner was scratching his head and re-reading the letter, when the Rev. Penstock arose and said:

"Perhaps de worthy President of dis Club doan' 'zactly know what dem historic spots am. If so, I'll——"

"What!" interrupted the President; "I doan' know what historic spots am! Misser Penstock, do you emagine dat I was brung up in de second story of a cider mill, an' dat no books or papers war printed till arter you war bo'n?"

"I simply frowed it out as a suggestion," was the humble reply, as the brother sat down.

"Doan' frow out any moah digestions, Misser Penstock! When de time arroves dat I can't pint out all de historic spots in dis part of de kentry, I'll resign my posishun in dis Club. De Secretary will answer to de effeck dat de Club will help preserve de spots. If any member of dis Club happens to run across a new historic spot dat I doan' know of, a postal keerd will reach me at my house, or he kin drive up in a coupay."

LAID ON THE TABLE.

The Secretary announced a petition from Mary Jane Crawford, of Detroit, asking the Club to use its influence to secure the right for women in this State to cast a ballot. Opportunity was given for debate, and it was discovered that Samuel Shin was the only member present who favored the idea. The petition was therefore laid on the table.

THE PENSION BILL.

The Secretary was instructed to make out a list of colored people in Detroit entitled to increase of pension under the new law, and to include in it all ex-soldiers who sprained an ankle, fell off a fence, or were afflicted with pains and aches at any time for ten years previous to the war, and to be sure to make special mention of the case of the widow who claims to have lost three husbands in the battle of City Point.

CUM DOWN.

"My dear friends," began the President, in a voice damp with pathos, "I doan' want ter keep peggin' away in dis yere Club 'bout finances all de time, but de weekly colleckshuns am growin' mighty lean of late. De sum total in de hat las' week was jist 'nuff to patch one o' de holes in de roof, an' it wasn't a first-class patch eider. Of course we has got a few hun'ered dollars in de bank, an' of course we am tidy 'nuff in heah, but de only way am to keep fings goin'. I doan' say dat de man who puts in de moas' will hev de biggest crop o' taters next fall, but I speck his onions an' mellyuns will turn out mighty fine. Now let de hat purceed."

The hat was passed. There were sixty-one members in the hall, and the collection counted up nineteen cents, and it was certain that Sir Isaac Walpole threw in a dime.

"Gemlen, if it takes fifty-nine men to frow nine cents into a hat, how many minutes will it take me to adjourn dis meetin'?" asked the President as he looked down the Hall.

There was silence.

The soft tread of cats could be heard on the roof.

The Elder Toots arose and said that there must be some mistake. He meant to throw in a quarter at least, and he thought many others did, but when the hat passed him he was scratching his back and wondering when the next run of sleighing would come along. He hoped that the tile might come around again.

It was sent, and the sum total amounted to over nine dollars.

"I tell you, de way to cum down am to cum down," observed the President as he finished counting. "Shingle-nails an' shirt-buttons may do for de church hat, but dey doan' pay fur our kerosene an' rent."

HAVING FUN.

"Seberal letters hab come to me doorin' de pas' week, axin' me to define my posishun on dis queshun of amusements," said the old man as the lamps were turned up. "Ebery once in awhile dar am a yell fur reform, an' sartin men an' women weep an' wail ober de gineral wickedness of de world. De church pitches into de theatre, de prayer-meetin' whacks away at dancin', an' de Sunday school teacher tells de little boys dat de circus am nex' doah to perdishun. It has bin my opinyun fur de las' fifty y'ars dat dis was a wicked world. It was created fur a wicked world. De Lawd wanted it dat may, an' he made it to please Hisself. De Scriptur's states dat wickedness shall abound in ebery co'ner of de land; dat men shall murder an' rob, an' women go astray; dat chill'en shall deny deir parents and brudder turn agin brudder. All such fings am predicted an' to be 'spected, an' looked fur, an' nobody has any grounds to howl an' weep. If dis war a good world we should have no need of preachers, deacons an' Sunday school teachers. Preachers will tell you dat man am imperfect, an' dat de Lawd made him to go astray, an' yet dey will turn aroun' an' wonder dat he am not goodness biled down.

"Deed, gem'len, but de only better world dan dis am Heben itself. You have got to hunt fur wickedness to fin' it. You have got to prejudge de case if you can make wickedness out of de jokes of a circus clown or de plot of de ordinary drama. If I had to praise God by findin' fault wid de world he made an' de people he put yere, I'm afraid it would be faint praise. De preacher who can't go to de theatre widout feelin' wicked had better stay away. If he wasn't on de hunt to find wickedness he wouldn't see it any mo' dan de rest of us. Me an' de ole woman kin go out an' dance Virginy Reel fur fo' hours an' cum home wid cl'ar consciences fur family prayers. We kin sot down to keerds an' not furgit to be honest an' charitable an' forgivin'. We kin go to a circus an' come home an' fank God dat our lives have bin spar'd anoder day, an' dat we am still left to cumfort de sick an' forgive de errin'. If gwine to sich places makes a preacher feel dat Satan has got a mortgage on him, den he'd better stay home.

"No man airnest in de good cause wants to fight agin human natur'. Man am a social bein'. He likes to be pleased an' amoosed. Make a tombstone of him, an' he'll soon hate hisself. When I see a man who claims to be too good to watch a circus purceshun pass 'long the street, I neber work fur him widout de cash in advance. When I fin' a man who am down on amoosements, I doan' work fur him at all. A y'are ago, when me an' de ole woman was joggin' ober de circus, we met a man who said we war gwine straight to Texas. He said he would sooner see his son in his coffin dan in a circus, an' he scart de ole lady most to death. I kept track of dat tombstone, an' in less dan six months he left town widout payin' his gas bill, water tax, butcher or grocer, an' he am no 'ception in his class. Look out fur solum-faced men. Bewar' of de men who weep ober de wickedness of a world made so by de Lawd fur reasons of his own. Have no truck wid men who neber laff. A man widout faults am a man widout reason. A man widout wickedness am a man widout argyment."

A STATESMAN'S DESCENT.

"In case Brudder Cinnamon Carter am in de Hall to-night, I should like to have him step dis way," said the President, as Pickles Smith got through blowing his nose and Elder Toots secured an easy rest for his back.

The member inquired for, rose up at the back end of the Hall and came forward with a look of surprise cantering across his countenance.

"Brudder Carter, when did you jine dis Club?" asked the President.

"'Bout six months ago, sah."

"What was your object in becomin' a member?"

"I wanted to improve my mind."

"Do you fink it has helped your mind any?"

"I do, sah."

"Well, I doan! In de fust place, you has borrowed money from ebery member who would lend you eben a nickel. In de nex' place, I can't learn dat you has put in one honest day's work since you became one of us. You war' sayin' to Samuel Shin las' night dat de world owed you a livin'."

"Yes, sah."

"I want to undeceive you. De world owes no man only what he airns. You may reason dat you am not to blame for bein' heah. Werry good; de world kin reason dat you am to blame for stayin' in it when it costs nuffin' to jump inter de ribber. Brudder Carter, what has you done for de world dat it owes you a livin'?"

"I—Ize—Ize——"

"Just so!" observed the President. "You has walked up an' down, an' wore cloze, an' consumed food an' drink, an' made one mo' in de crowd aroun' a new buildin'. An' for dis you claim de world owes you a livin'? You has made no diskiveries, brought out no inventions, written no song an' held no offis. Not 500 people in de world know of you by name. You can't name one single man who am under obligashuns to you. You eat what odders produce. You w'ar out de cloze odder people make. An' yit you have the impudence to sot down on a bar'l of dried apples, cross yer legs an' fold yer hands, an' say dat the world owes yer a livin', an' by de great horn spoons mus' gin it to you! Brudder Carter, look at yerself a few minits!"

"Yes, sah—ahem—yes—I'ze sorry, sah," stammered the member.

"What fur? Sorry kase you've bin found out? Sorry kase you've entered dis Hall for de las' time? Brudder Carter, we doan' want sich men as you in dis Club. De world doan' owe us a cent. On de contrary, we owe de world mo' dan we kin eber pay. De man who argys dat he am entitled to any mo' dan what his brains or muscle kin airn him am a robber at heart. We shall cross your name from de rolls, show you de way down stairs, an' permit you to go your own road frew life. If you kin make de world clothe, feed an' shelter you fur de privilege of seein' you hold down a dry-goods box in front of a sto' which doan' advertise, dat will be your good luck."

Brother Carter thought the matter over and decided that the world owed him a place in Paradise Hall, but he was mistaken again. The Committee on Internal Revenue stepped forward at a nod from Brother Gardner, and the expelled member only struck the stairs twice in going from top to bottom.

DE OLE MAN LEE.

"Las' nite as I war gwine pas' McGuffy's grocery," solemnly began Brother Gardner, as Samuel Shin finally got through pounding the stove, "as I war gwine pas' McGuffy's grocery, dar sat de ole man Lee. I reckon you all know de ole man. He sat dar on a box, hat on de back of his head an' feet obstructin' de sidewalk, an' he was sayin' to de crowd dat de present greatest need of dis kentry was an increase of currency. Las' winter all he got to eat cum from de poo'master, an' all de close his family wore cum from charitable people. I doan' reckon he has dun one squar' day's work dis hull season, an' I'm quite sartin dat his wife am bar'fut an' his chill'en hungry, an' yit he sot dar spoutin' 'bout de needs of de kentry same as if he war carryin' half de States in his west pocket.

"Let me say to you all right yere dat none of you need shoulder yourselves wid any responsibility in regard to dis kentry. Jist let 'er slide. If she runs off de track, dat's none of your look out. I know a dozen cull'd men in dis city who am continually worried about de expanshun or contracshun of de currency, free trade or purtecshun, an' odder queshuns, an' ebery one of 'em am ragged an' hungry. Doan' you lose any sleep fur fear America won't git up right end fust in de mawnin'. All you have to do am to begin work at seben an' leave off at six, an' if de kentry busts her biler you'll have sunthin laid by to emigrate on. I doan' keer two cents fur de political fucher. Let 'em contract or expand, swell or shrink, nail down de kiver or leave de box open—I'm counted out. When I have dun, my day's work an' got my pay I have no furder claims on de kentry. While I pay my debts an' obey de laws she has no furder claims on me. We will now enter upon de usual reckless programme of bizness."

RESIGNATION ACCEPTED.

The Secretary announced that the resignation of Three-Ply Hastings had been handed to him for action by the Club, and Brother Gardner explained that he had accidentally overtaken Mr. Hastings one evening with a sack of flour on his shoulder. He claimed to have won it at a raffle, but a grocer claimed next day to have had such a sack taken from his door. Three-Ply could not describe the place where the raffle was held, and the fact that he emptied out the flour and burned the sack as soon he reached home still further strengthened the suspicions that instead of winning the flour at a raffle he had found it hanging to the limb of one of the maples in the park. His resignation had, therefore, been asked for, and he had been invited to make a defense. Not being present, was considered an evidence of a desire on his part to work his own corners in flour, and the resignation was accepted by a unanimous vote.

HOW TO GET EVEN.

Elder toots, after a brief but earnest conference with Giveadam Jones, arose to make a personal statement. He said he had taken two shirts to Wah Hap, a Chinese laundryman, to be washed and ironed, but that Celestial had perversely, if not indignantly, refused to do the work, presumably on account of the Elder's color. He now sternly demanded to know whether a Chinaman was better than a colored man. If so, he wanted to die of a tape-worm and be buried under a swamp-elm. If not, then old as he was, and as much as he deplored blood-shed, he would ask the Club to sustain him in going over to the laundry and putting a head on the yellow-faced barbarian from over the sea.

"Elder Toots," replied the President, as he solemnly scratched his ear, " de queshun as to wedder de African an' de Mongolian am de bes' man am bound to cum up fur discushun in de near fucher, but jist at de present time I reckon de bes' way fur you to git eben wid dat Chinaman am to refuse to whitewash his ceilins or blacken his stove. Please sot down an' go to sleep."

SOME NEW RULES.

The Secretary then announced the following new rules, which will be rigidly enforced until further orders:

1. No member shall address the meeting without having both shoes on.

2. No more than forty dogs will be allowed in the Hall at any meeting. The other fifty or sixty shall be tied up in the alley or left in the ante-room.

3. Religious or political discussions between individuals will not be allowed while the meeting is in session.

4. In rising to address the chair, members will face the chair.

5. Peanut-shucks, apple-cores, banana-rinds, orange peels and other foreign substances must not be thrown about when there is a question before the meeting, as a member who is hit on the jaw is liable to have his attention distracted.

THEY PARTED.

The hour for adjournment having arrived, the janitor reported that the stove had broken its last leg, and four new cracks had lately appeared in the bottom plate. He was instructed to confer with some scientific men to see if some solution could not be prepared to draw the cracks together, or if there was not a preparation to fill such crevices, and the procession moved down stairs to the tune of "Daddy's Coming Home."

DE COMET.

As the meeting opened, Brother Gardner announced that the Hon. William Johnson, of Port Huron, was awaiting in the ante-room for admission, and on motion of Assassination Smith the Committee on Reception were instructed to bring him in. When the duty had been performed, the President introduced the visitor, made him welcome, and Mr. Johnson led off as follows:

"What am de comet? Who is she? Which is it? What am he heah fur? How many of you kin answer dese queshuns? My frens, de study of astronomy am full of intres' an' pleasure. But fur astronomy how could we hev known dat de moon am peopled by a race of one-eyed giants, an' dat de distance to de sun am so great dat if we was to sot out an' trabble on a hoss kyar it would take us fo' weeks to git dar? Astronomy teaches us dat de atmosphere in de planet Jupiter am so cl'ar an' transparent dat you kin see a hoss-fly six miles away. In de planet Mars de air is so cool dat a dead dog kin be left in front of a first-class hotel fur nine weeks. In de planet Venus it am allus good weather fur goin' a-fishin', an' de air am so bracin' dat de women allus split deir own wood. De planet Saturn furnishes its inhabitants strawberries an' cream de hull y'ar round, an' de wery bes' kind o' lager beer kin be had fur sixty-eight cents a keg. Way back in de dark aiges nobody knew wedder de sun was ten miles or ten million miles off. De sight of a 'clipse skeered chill'en into fits an' made strong men crawl under de bed fur safety. De stars war' supposed to be pieces of tin nailed to de midnight air, an' men would no mo' believe dat de earth turned round dan

HON. WILLIAM JOHNSON OF PORT HURON.
"Whar am de Comet? Who is she?"

you now believe dat de day will soon come when men will go sailin' frew de air at de rate of two miles a minute.

"But I doan' wish to take up de waluable time of dis meetin', an' I will close by deservin' dat all occashuns seem supplementary to de general debility of de furlong. Dar am no mo' reason why all of you shouldn't agitate generosity of de sincerity dan dar am fur de elocution to operate disastrusly against de terribleness of de octavo."

Elder Toots cheered.

Pickles Smith fainted dead away, and he did not regain consciousness until Waydown Bebee ran the cold handle of the water dipper down his back.

Mr. Johnson was taken out in such a weak and exhausted condition that the janitor had to fan him with a lump of coal, and run around the corner after a whisky straight. It has been long weeks since Paradise Hall was favored with such a tremendous oratorical effort.

THAT STRANGE NIGGER.

"WHAT I was gwine to remark," began the old man, as the calcium light at the lower end of the Hall shone full on his clean shirt and garnet necktie, "am to de effeck dat you can't depend on a man till you hev gone ober a mill dam in de same boat wid him, an' eben den it am safer to keep de doahs locked. I am led to dis reflecshun by de fack dat about fo' days ago a strange nigger knocked at my humble doah. He was a meek an' humble lookin' man, an' he tole me a story of woe an' misfortun' dat almoas broke my heart. I took him in. I fed an' warmed him an' felt bad fur him. Yesterday, while I was out lookin' fur a job fur him, he dodged de ole woman an' made off wid all my summer 'skeeter-bars, an' I heven't cotched him yit. De ideah of a man stealin' 'skeeter-bars in de winter am bad 'nuff of itself, but to steal 'em from a fam'ly dat had warmed his heels, clothed his back an' filled him up wid bacon an' taters, am sunthin' that I can't get ober right soon. I shall go right on trustin' folkses, same as befo', but in de sweet bime-by dar will be a clus board fence eighteen feet high 'tween me an' sich people as can't eat two meal a day an' pay a hundred cents on de dollar. We will now enter into de reg'lar concordance of de meetin'."

THE AGRICULTURAL COMMITTEE.

The Committee on Agriculture, which had been requested to investigate the cause of the scarcity of apples the past season, reported as follows:

"Dis committee was in correspondence wid seberal pusons who know all about de fruit bizness, an' de gineral impression seems to be dat de scarcity was due to de fack dat de trees didn't b'ar many apples. Why dey didn't b'ar was owin' to de scarcity, an' dat's all we could find out, 'cept dat it am much cheaper to eat pop-corn at five cents a quart dan apples at forty cents a peck. You doan' hev to frow away any cores when you eat pop-corn, an' your committee will eber pray."

THEY BEAUTIFY.

Some time since the Committee on the Preservation of Natural Scenery were asked to investigate the subject of barber-poles, and report as to whether they beautified a street or were a source of annoyance to the artistic eye. The committee now submitted the following:

"Dis committee buckled right down to bizness, an' didn't lay off an' eat oysters on de half-shell, same as some committees dat we know of. We found dat of all de signs in a city de barber-poles am de freshest, cleanest and brightest. De eye dat am lookin' up de street fur a saloon, or down it fur a peanut stand, lights on a barber-pole an' am rested an' relieved. A barber-pole will beautify an old shanty or adorn a marble front. It looks well wherever you put it. Dey lay right ober signs of soda water, an' knock de spots off of signs of ice cream. Dey doan' show off in de night quite as well as a drug store, but dar am no smell about 'em. Dey doan' quite come up to a Fo'th of July parade, but dey contain nuffin' to blow up de public or set bildin's on fiah. Dis committee decides dat barber-poles am useful, ornamental and healthy, an' recommend dat dey be protected by de laws which governs de high seas."

RED PEPPER.

The report was no sooner ended than Pickles Smith arose and demanded to know if members of the Club could be insulted in open meeting with impunity.

"Who's been insulted?" asked Brother Gardner.

"I hez, sah; an' so hez de odder members of Committee on Astronomy! Dis report jist read speaks of a committee eatin' oysters on de half shell. **Dat was my committee, sah!**"

"Well, didn't de oysters taste good?" innocently inquired the President.

"Dey did, sah, but dis report seems to refleck on us—seems to cast a slur on our reputashun as a committee. I demand an apology, sah!"

"Pickles Smith," said Brother Gardner, "doan' neber ram de bullet down afore you git de powder in. Please sit down."

Pickles sat.

THE SICK.

The Chairman of the above committee said he was glad to report an "unusual wellness" among the active members of the Club. There was no one on the sick list except Xerxes Black, who tried to hold the handles of an electric machine until a bystander could count ten hundred. He was now laid up with tickling in the elbows and a goneness in other joints, and the committee had refused to recommend his case for relief.

"De committee am perfeckly k'rect," replied the President. "When a member of dis Club goes to foolin' 'round wid 'lectricity, he takes all de chances an' reaps all de glory. Let Brudder Black keep on ticklin'."

HE OBJECTED.

The Hon. Celluloid Johnson now arose to a point of order. He said he had been deeply grieved and pained at sight of a weekly spectacle to be seen in Paradise Hall ever since frosty weather set in, and he could stand it no longer.

"Misser President, look up an' down de isles," he added, as he waved his hand. "Here am fi'teen members wid deir boots off to scratch deir chilblains!

Am dis respectable an' polite to de Club? Am it courtesy towards Paradise Hall? I move dat each one of dem be reprimanded or fined."

"KINDER SYMPATHIZED."

"Gem'len," began Elder White, as he arose with a boot in his hand, "I can manage to sot frew a short sermon an' keep my butes on, but when it comes to puttin' in two long hours in dis Hall, I'ze either got to scratch dat heel or take chloroform! I kin stan' a head-ache, de toof-ache, a shake of de ager or a hard chill, but when it comes down to chillblains I can't stand 'em off."

The President was observed drawing his own heel across the boards and squinting up one eye as he replied:

"De chilblain queshun am a serus one. It affects de hull foot. It takes in ebery heel in America. At some fucher time we will give it de considerashun it deserves, and in de meantime members who hev to scratch will please keep deir feet down an' be as quiet as possible."

The Glee Club then sang several selections from Mozart, the janitor locked up the water-dipper and the match-box, and the meeting was carefully adjourned.

A HEATHEN BODY.

THE Hon. L. C. Briggs, of Charlotte, Mich., failed to appear last week as advertised, having been delayed by the death of his aunt. His presence was now announced by the Keeper of the Bear

Trap, and he was escorted to the platform by a committee of three. After a general introduction to the Club, he began.

"Gem'len, de objeck of my awovin' heah at de present time am to warn you all to bewar' of de present an' all future Legislachures. De pop'lar ideah am dat de body am imposed of men of high honor an' noble minds, but doan' you believe it! It was stated in de papers dat I went out to Lansin' at de front end of de present seshun to secure de place of head nigger of de cloak room. So I did. Dey haft to have one dar, an' if I can't run a hat-rack as well as a man wid a mole on his ear den I want to die befo' night. Wall, I got out dar on time. I spoke to Senators wid bald heads an' all odder kinds, an' dey was pleased to pat me on de back an' remark dat I was fo'teen rods ahead of all other candydates. Dey smiled on me; dey winked at me; dey said dat providence must have tumbled me down dar fur de special good of de Senate. I walked high an' was happy; I felt suah of de place, an' de way I made common niggers stan' back was tough on shoe leather. But am I bossin' dat cloak room? Am I hangin' up hats an' bowin' befo' de great esquires? I reckon not; but why not? Kase dose baldheads sold me out an' gin de place to a man who shows ebery toof in his head when he bites into a peanut. Dey am all on de sell, an' de truf won't stick to 'em onless nailed on an' clinched on de furder side. I warns you all to bewar of de hull crowd. I hear dat de Club am reck'nin' to go out dar on a 'scursion. Doan' you go! Dey will smile on you wid one elbow an' knock your teef down your froat wid de odder!"

A GENEROUS OFFER.

"Let a pusson do what am right an' squar, an' friends will riz up fur him on ebery han'," said the President, as he fished up another letter from his coat-tail pocket. "Heah am a letter from a bizness house in New York, sayin' dat dis Club will be furnished all de French-plate mirrors wanted by members at twenty per cent. below de usual price. Dis am a dun gone savin' of twenty dollars on a hundred, or one hundred dollars on ebery five hundred dollar purchase. We can't ax for nuthin' better, an' de seckretary am requested to return our warmest thanks."

"It strikes me," began the Rev. Penstock, as he solemnly arose, "dat not moar dan seventeen out of twenty members of dis Club will eber want to invest five hundred dollars on a looking-glass."

"Is dar a queshun befo' de house?" mildly inquired the President.

"It am my opinyun——" continued Penstock, when the President interrupted:

"Is dar an opinyun befo' de house?"

The Rev. Penstock sat down, and called up a vision of a seven-hundred dollar French mirror leaning against the white washed wall of a negro-cabin, and the liberal-minded epistle was filed on the wire in due form.

A SOLEMN WARNING.

The Committee on Claims and Accounts submitted written charges as follows:

1. That Alexander Goldsboro Swipes, an honorary member of the Club, residing in Vicksburg, had represented that the Club indorsed his new

toothache cure and corn eradicator, when the Club had done nothing of the sort.

2. That the above-mentioned person has falsely represented himself as Waydown Bebee.

3. That he has contracted debts, and had the bills sent here to the Club for payment.

His case was taken up under a suspension of rule three, and, at the finish of the debate Brother Gardner said:

"De seckretary will write to Misser Swipes, dat dis Club disanamously rumpudiates his actions, and dat just one more complaint, even if no bigger dan a free-cent piece, will obviate his name off our rolls widout onnecessary slowness. He will be held up an' shook ober de yàwnin' gulf of corrpushun as a solemn warnin' dat no crookedness am allowed in dis Club, even on a call of de eyes an' nose."

COL. CLARKE.

The distinguished visitors mentioned last week, could not remain to address the Club, as was hoped for, but Col. Clarke. of Kansas City, arrived unexpectedly, and declared his willingness to deliver a brief address on the subject of "On Time." When escorted to the platform he seemed to be as much at home as a major-general three miles in rear of a battle, and his few words on the organization and growth of the Club were well received.

Time, the speaker said, had considerable to do with the daylight of this country. If some sharp man hadn't thought of inventing clocks and watches the world would have been in a bad muss. No one could have told whether it was yesterday, to-day, or day after to-morrow. Some people would have been eating breakfast while others were splitting kindlings for night. Some men would be starting out for a day's fishing while others were going home to get ready to attend one of Bob Infidel's lectures. Luckily for the world, time had been invented, patented, and divided up to suit everybody but a man with a bank note to meet. He believed it was of the greatest importance that every man should be on time. Fortunes had been lost by people being two or three minutes late. Kingdoms had been won by men who were on time. The Colonel held that even a murderer going to the gallows should step right off and be on the drop at the right tick. His promptness might not bring a reprieve, but it could not fall of exciting the admiration of those accustomed to having dinner at 12:30.

When the Colonel concluded his remarks, Samuel Shin presented him with a spring bouquet on behalf of the Club, and a resolution was passed to escort him to the depot in a body.

GUESS NOT.

THE Secretary reported the following inquiry from the office of Secretary of State of New Jersey:

"Are the barriers of American liberty being gradually demolished?"

The question being open for discussion, Trustee Pullback said he couldn't see any signs of such calamity. When an American could open a grocery in one end of a building, a saloon in the other, and a poker room up stairs, it didn't look as if American liberty was in very great danger.

Samuel Shin said he had carefully studied the subject of the barriers of liberty for many years past, and he had of late come to the conclusion that as long as a red-faced young man could blow a brass horn all the evening next door to where a child lay dying, the barriers were all right and sound as a dollar.

Giveadam Jones observed that he had also kept his eye peeled for any signs that a central government was seeking to undermine the barriers erected by Washington and cemented with the blood of patriots. When an American could sit on dry-goods boxes all summer and make charity support him all winter, there need be no alarm for the safety of the Republic.

Several other members spoke in the same vein, and the President closed the address by saying:

"I think dis Club am purty well satisfied dat de barriers of liberty am all solid, an' on behalf of de organizashun I feel to assure de kentry at large dat all de rights and privileges granted by our fo'faders am still worf a hundred cents on de dollah. Now let de Glee Club strike up dat good ole air 'Gwine Down de Lane', an' as we rush fur he doah it will avoid complicashuns fur all to remember de fust pa'r of obershoes on de left as you go out belongs to me."

KILLWILLIAM SMITH.

"What I was gwine to remark," said Brother Gardner, as the siege opened, "was to de effeck dat Killwilliam Smith, ginerally known as de 'Demosthenes of de South,' am now waitin' in de aunty-room for an invitashun to deliver his orashun on 'De Great Men of de Past.' He has come heah from Lynchburg, Va., fur dis speshul purpose, payin' his own fa'r part of de way an' walkin' de rest on de railroad ties, an' if dar am no objecshuns we will bring him in."

"Did I understan' de cha'r to say if deir was no dejecshuns?" asked the Rev. Penstock, as he suddenly popped up.

"You did, sah."

"Dejeckshuns—ah. Didn't de cha'r mean to say if deir was no——"

"Brudder Penstock," interrupted the President, "when dis cha'r says dejeckshuns he doan' mean infleckshuns, direckshuns or defleckshuns. De las' time you interrupted de purceedins of dis meetin' you war toled dat de nex' display of capfulness on your part would dissult in a fine. Painful as it am to me, an' as much as I feel fur your wife an' chill'en, I shall repose a fine on you of $400 an' costs. De costs, as nigh as I kin figger, will be about $600. You will consider yourself impended from membership until de fine am paid."

The Rev. sank down on his chair. His eyes rolled, his breathing was labored, and he suddenly fainted away and dragged Napoleon Shrewsbury with him to the floor. During the excitement eight or ten persons received the contents of the water-pail. Melon rinds flew about in a perfect shower, and a cantelope, which struck Ten Thousand Collins between the shoulders, broke open and extinguished three lamps, and knocked down the grub-hoe with which Washington crossed the Delaware. Brother

Penstock finally revived and bound a wet towel around his head, and Colonel Hi-Hi-Smith arose to make a statement. He was intimately acquainted with the pecuniary resources of Brother Penstock. His earnings the past year were exactly $483.29. His expenditures were exactly $483.25. The balance on hand was therefore only four cents. This year the balance would be closer still, and even in the best year to come there was no hope of a great increase. Giving four cents as the average yearly balance, and it would take Brother Penstock about 250,000 years to pay his fine and secure his restoration to membership. The speaker hoped that mercy would prevail and the fine be withdrawn. After a brief consultation with Sir Isaac Walpole and Waydown Bebee, the President arose and announced that he would remit the fine and costs, and that the member's narrow escape from being killed stone dead would be a great moral warning to him throughout the rest of his days.

DEMOSTHENES.

The Committee on Reception then donned their red neckties and escorted the great orator into the Hall. He was given a general introduction from the platform, a glass of water and a lemon placed at his left hand, and after clearing his throat and adjusting his necktie, he began:
"Whar' am Cicero? In de y'ars gone by de world cheered at his name. When he recommended any maker's liver pills dem pills war' considered boss. When he acted as judge at a hoss race no man dared appeal. When he entered a street kyar everybody hitched along. When he rode out in his keer

idge butcher-carts turned pale and took a back street. De newspapers glorified him, de public applauded him, an' banks fairly ached to cash his checks. But whar' am he to-day? His sweet song am silent; his dog has quit barkin', an' eben his name am forgotten except by de few interested in faro an' de string-game. [Cheers by Elder Toots.]
"Whar' am Plato? Ask 'em at de toll-gate an' dey can't tell you. Ask 'em at de depots an' a shake of de head will tell de sad story. Gone! Gone! When he crossed de Rubicon de world thundered with applause. [Applause from Samuel Shin.] When he crossed de Alps nations trembled. [Cheers from the back end of the Hall.] When he wrote 'Paradise Lost' de world wept. [Suppressed applause from Cassowary Bottomlands.] But he am passed away. De blight an' de mildew struck him an' he faded, an' only now an' den, as you see a game of dominos, do you h'ar his memory referred to. [Prolonged cheers.]
"But I did not come yere to take up the time of dis meetin'. [Applause.] I simply desired to present you wid a few gems from my oratorical album, an' to say to you dat yereafter I kin be found at 2057 Croghan street, dis city, where I shall be ready at *all* times to cuah co'ns, bunyons, cracked heels an' so' toes, an' deliber my full lectur' at de low price of twenty-five cents a head—chill'en free. [Cheers and applause, and a fall of eleven joints of stovepipe.]

BEWARE OF HIM.

When quiet had been restored, the Secretary read a communication from Happy John Franks, of Vermillion, Marshall Co., Ks., stating that a one-eyed straw-paper colored man, giving his name as Pickles Smith, had been in that vicinity for the last two weeks collecting money for the erection of a colored church in Michigan. He had credentials, but hesitated and exhibited guilt when asked how many of the bald-headed members of the Club wore a buckskin plaster on top of the head in fly time.

The Secretary was instructed to reply that the real Pickles Smith had not been outside of Detroit for a year, and to ask the people of Kansas to receive the base imposter in the way he deserves.

VENTILATED ENOUGH.

The Committee on Sanitary matters reported that they had spent thirteen days investigating the inquiry: "Do the colored people of Detroit appreciate the benefits of proper ventilation?" The committee rather thought the colored people did. Out of 200 houses visited 180 had broken windows, cat holes in the roof, and door-panels busted out, and it was pretty plain that the inmates were having all the ventilation any one family could take care of.

There was no need of disinfectants. Dead cats and decayed vegetables were passed from yard to yard until the outskirts were reached, and the presence of dogs in the house effectually crippled the injurious effects of sewer gas.

THE CLOSE.

The Keeper of the Relics reported that the bear trap and other articles of reverence were in good order, the janitor was ordered to give the stove pipe two coats of paint during the week, and the meeting softly adjourned.

JUDGE CADAVER.

"Am Judge Cadaver in de Hall to-night?" softly queried Brother Gardner, as he looked down the aisle toward the stool on which the fat and juicy Judge was unanimously reposing.

"If de Judge am in de Hall he will please step dis way," continued the President, after a moment of deep silence.

The Judge slowly arose and meandered forward, energetically chewing a piece of slippery elm to hide his agitation.

"Brudder Cadaver, I have a few words to say to you to-night," said the President, as he looked down upon his shiny baldness. "De odder day I happened to pass a policy shop, an' I saw you gwine in. Dat same evenin' as I was gwine past a saloon I saw you standin' at de bar wid a glass of whisky in your han'. I kin also recall de fack dat I hev not seen you at work for de las' month."

"I hasn't bin feelin' strictly well," pleaded the Judge.

"You war well 'nuff to play policy."

"I—I—didn't put up but ten cents."

"An' what about de whiskey-drinkin'?"

"I was feelin' powerful weak, sah,"

"Too thin—too thin," replied the President, as he shook his head. "Now, den, I want to spoke to you. In some respects you am a good man. I doan' believe you would steal, I hev never cotched you lyin', an' I reckon you am a good man at home. Now, if somebody told you dar was a gold ring in de bottom of de ribber somewhar, would you pay ten cents a chance to fish fur it?"

"No, sah."

"Sartin, you wouldn't. Policy am a long, wide, deep ribber. De gold ring at de bottom am a $5 prize which some poo' critter fishes out after payin' ten or fifteen dollars fur de chance. You wouldn't frow money into Lake Erie an' 'spect to git it back, but you'll frow money into de pond of policy an' 'spect to git out ten times as much as you tossed in. Drap it—drap it, Brudder Cadaver, befo' you lose de title of Judge an' get dat of Fool."

"Yes sah; I'll drap it to once."

"An' you drank whisky. De man who goes into a saloon am no better dan de man who keeps it. If I should ax you to put your foot agin a hot stove you would think me crazy. An' yit, when you burn your stomach, befuddle your brain an' make a brute of yourself, an' hev to pay fur de privilege besides, what shall I think of you? God made de idiot, but it was left to whisky to make de fool."

"I'll nebber tech de stuff agin, sah—nebber."

"An' you hev big loafin' aroun'. Brudder Cadaver, all wickedness begins wid laziness. A loafer am as much despised as a drunkard. When laziness comes home, pride goes away to visit de nayburs. Whisky may break a woman's heart, but laziness will freeze her to death. When you go home to-night spit on yer hands an' ax de boys to grease yer butes. When you turn outer bed in de mawnin', freeze hold of de ax, or spade, or brush, an hunt fur a job. Dissolve partnership with laziness, cut de acquaintance of whisky, an' de next time you am tempted to play policy come ober to my cabin an' ax me to kick you all roun' de doah-yard. You kin now sot down."

A NARROW ESCAPE.

AND still another fiendish attempt to destroy human life and demolish Paradise Hall must be recorded. As the janitor was making ready for the Saturday night meeting, he opened the stove to take a chew of tobacco from a box he had been keeping there since it was decided not to build any more fires. To his horror, it was discovered that some one had placed a two-pound can of powder in the stove, and under ordinary circumstances he would have started a fire without seeing it. The result would have been appalling. Samuel Shin, who always sits nearest the stove, would have gone out of the opposite window and demolished the entire rear end of a second-hand clothing store. Giveadam Jones would have been lifted off his stool and dashed into the ante-room, knocking down the Keeper of the Pass-Word and utterly smashing a jug containing five pints of kerosene oil. Waydown Bebee would have been subjected to a pressure of 22,000 pounds to the square inch, and under this terrific strain he must have gone scooting up the Hall and plumped dead against Sir Isaac Walpole, mashing the old man to pulp in the wink of an eye. Brother Gardner would have been blown against the iron safe containing over $700, and rebounding from thence he would have struck Elder Toots, killed him stone dead, passed close to Pickle Smith's ear, and brought up against the chimney, falling to the floor a lifeless mass of dark-colored clay. Every lamp chimney would have been broken—every window demolished, and every one of the nineteen joints of stove-pipe would have struck a separate head in falling. Paradise Hall might not have been entirely demolished, but it would have taken at least $13 to cover actual damages, to say nothing of the loss of valuable lives.

THE EYE OF PROVIDENCE.

"Let dis be anoder warnin' to you dat de eye of Providence am allus watchin' out," said Brother Gardner in his opening. "De good am sartin to be protected, while de bad will sooner or later arrove at some awful end. Had we been de Common Council, a political convention, or a State Legislature dat fiah would have been built; dat powder would have gone off, an' dis Hall would have been de picture of desolashun an' death. De janitor, who now receives a salary of seventy-five cents per week, will have it increased to eighty, an' in fucher his seat will be under de bust of Andrew Jackson. We will now pass de water an' purceed to bizness."

A PETITION.

The Secretary further announced a petition from twenty-four colored men of Richmond, asking the Signal Service of the United States to give at least twenty-four hours warning of the approach of earthquakes. No arrangements have been made for reporting earthquakes at all, and the colored population had to depend on luck alone. Brother Gardner announced that the Lime-Kiln Club would indorse the petition and forward it to Congress.

DELAYED POETRY.

The Secretary announced that he had received from Prof. Bagdad Pratt, of Brownsville, N. Y., a poem to be entered for the Waydown Bebee premium. The entries had been closed and the prizes

WHAT MIGHT HAVE BEEN.

awarded, but on motion of Pickles Smith the Secretary was instructed to read the poem in a voice full of emotion. He therefore read:

ON DE NEGLECTED GRAVE.

By de co'ner ob de melon patch,
   Among de bloomin' clover,
I sot me on a grassy mound
   To look de melons ober,
De bee was buzzin' in de sun,
   A makin' ob de honey—
De skeeter borin' at my shin,
   As if he worked for money.

A stirrin' ob de melon vines—
   De win' blew from de souf;
An' powerful de melons pumped
   De water in my mouf.
An' den I think, "how soon—how soon,
   No melons I see shall—
How soon—how soon I shall not hear
   De buzzin' ob de bee."

Dis darky's fleetin' bref done gone!
   (For life am neber long),
De melon-longin' hushed—an' hushed
   De banjo an' de song.
Den lay me in de groun' right heah,
   An' let de skeeter rave!
De melon shuah will ripen on
   De poo' neglected grave.

On motion of Waydown Bebee, the Secretary was instructed to forward the thanks of the Club, together with a letter introducing the poet into the best society in the principal cities of the Union.

IT DOES NOT.

After lowering the contents of the water pail an inch and a half, and raising two windows to admit more oxygen, the Secretary announced the following inquiry:

GLENROSE, TEXAS, March 14, 1882.

DEAR BROTHER GARDNER.—There is a superstition among the negroes of the South that all lawyers go to the bad place. Does such an idea prevail among the members of the Lime-Kiln Club? By answering this question, you will oblige greatly,

Your distant friend,
COTTONSEED WHITE.

"I neber heard dat dis Club entertained any such superstishun," said Brother Gardner, in reply. "So fur as de average lawyer goes, dis Club has no particular respect fur him. De average lawyer isn't a bit better dan de average criminal he keeps out of jail. De thief breaks de law to git money. De lawyer defends the thief for de same purpose, an' it most allus happens dat de thief am dun cleaned out when de lawyer am frew wid him. But de greatest criminals an' de meanest men am generally giben time to repent. Arter de lawyer begins to grow old an' de rheumatism cotches on, an' his wife dies, an' his house burns up widout insurance, he am forced to reflect on his past life, an' dat refleckshun probably brings repentance. I doan' 'spose Heaben am crowded wid lawyers, but I reckon dat 'nuff of 'em squeeze in to keep fings pretty lively fur sich angels as disturb de peace or obstruct de sidewalks.

SILENT SORROWS.

"DAR am sartin folkses I want to keep away from," began the old man, as the voices of the Glee Club died away on the last strains of "Sarah Jane's Baby." "I mean dat class of people who groan ober de wickedness of de world, an' who have heartaches an' sorrows to peddle aroun' de kentry at de reg'lar market rates. Dar' am de ole man Turner. He comes ober to see me now an' den, but he can't sot still kase somebody stole his dog, or hit him wid a brickbat, or beat him out of seventy-five cents. He fully believes dat de world am gwine to smash at de rate of fifteen miles an hour, an' it would eanemost kill him to lose his ole wallet an' find a man honest 'nuff to return it.

" De widder Plumsell comes ober to borry some butter fur supper, an' she draps down on a cha'r an' heaves a sigh as big as a barn doah an' goes on to say dat dis am a cold an' unfeelin' world. 'Cording to her tell all men am dishonest, all women extravagant, an' all chill'en jist ready to come down wid de measles. Tears run down her cheeks as she tells how she has to work an' plan while eberybody else has money to frow inter Lake Erie, an' she wipes her nose on her apron as she asserts dat dis wicked world can't stan' mo' dan fo' weeks longer.

" Deacon Striper draps in to eat pop-corn wid me on a Friday ebenin', an' he hardly gits out from under his hat befo' he begins to tell what his first wife died of; how his second wife run away; how his third broke her leg by fallin' off a fence an' cost him $28.14 for doctor's bill, an' befo' he gits frew you couldn't make him believe but what de hull world was dead agin him. He predicts a late spring, a hot summer, poor crops, high prices, a bloody war, an' goes home feelin' dat he am stoppin' on airth only to accommodate somebedy.

"I have no sorrow of my own. I've been robbed, but dat was kase I left a winder up. I've been swindled, but dat was kase I thought fo' queens would beat fo' aces. I've bet on de wrong hoss; I've bought lottery tickets which didn't draw; I've been sick unto death, an' I've been shot in de back wid a hull brickyard, but I do not sorrow an' I do not ax fur sympathy. De world am plenty good 'nuff fur de class of people livin' in it. Honest men am not lonesome fur company, an' honest women am sartin to be appreciated. De janitor will now open fo' winders an' we will purceed to bizness."

PRIZE AWARDED.

The time for receiving poetry entered for the special prize offered last fall by Waydown Bebee having expired, that gentleman announced that he had received thirty-two different specimens, of which seven were poems, six idyls, twelve sonnets and the remainder were odes to spring, fall, winter, dead folks, rolling oceans, green meadows, spotted cows, handsome women and codfish balls. He had read and re-read, and had come to the conclusion that a poem entitled, "The Tears They Blind My Eyes," by Prof. Goneby Jackson, of Alabama, was entitled to the prize of $5 in cash and a fire shovel eleven feet long. The following is the first verse of the poem:

> I ar' lookin' down de lane whar' de chill'en used to play,
> An' de shadows of de ole persimmon tree,
> War' frown across de roof of de little cabin home,
> Whar' ole Dinah watched de hours away fur me,

THE FOURTH.

Giveadam Jones offered a resolution to the effect that the Lime-Kiln Club celebrate the coming Fourth of July in becoming style, and after some considerable discussion the resolution and the following programme were adopted:

1. National salute at sunrise of twenty-seven shot guns—provided there is a sunrise.
2. Breakfast at 7 o'clock—providing there is anything in the house to eat.
3. Assemble at Paradise Hall at 10 o'clock. Addresses by Pickles Smith, Trustee Pullback and Samuel Shin.
4. Street parade at noon.
5. Reassemble at the Hall at 2 o'clock. Patriotic songs, speeches and declamations by Waydown Bebee, Pickles Smith, Boneless Parsons and others.
6. Display of fireworks in front of Paradise Hall in the evening—front seats reserved for ladies. The display will be in charge of Condensed Johnson, R. A. M., and Prof. Clingstone Fairbanks, of the Concord School of Philosophy. The principal attractions will consist of "Washington Going up the Spout;" "ex-President Hayes Crossing the Brandywine;" "Napoleon at Waterloo;' Susan B. Anthony at Chicago," and "The Dying Sleepingcar Porter."

MORE VILLAINY.

The janitor reported that he had just unearthed another villainous plot to work harm to the Club, if not injury to life and limb. Some unhung villain had secretly entered the hall and removed the quicksilver from the thermometer and replaced it with a drop of lard oil. The janitor had used up three old barrels, two boxes and a heap of wood in trying to raise the temperature to 106 degrees, and it was only after the legs of the stove began to turn red that he cast about to discover the cause of his failure.

Giveadam Jones offered the following:

"*Resolved*, Dat any pusson who will steal de inside of a thermometer am base 'nuff to rob graves, an' dat de sum of $20 am hereby sot aside as a reward for de diskivery of de said hyena in wolf's clothin'."

The resolution was promptly seconded by Trustee Pullback, Jerusalem Smith, Kyann Johnson and others, and after being unanimously adopted, the meeting was hung up to dry for one week.

DE COMIN' POWER.

THE Committee on Scientific Research having been requested to furnish the Club with a list of the various motive powers in daily use, and suggest any new ideas on the same subject, reported as follows:

"Motive power am de power which makes fings move. Steam am a motive power, kase it makes de ingine in a distillery move, an' ward politishuns am thus furnished wid capital stock to pack caucuses an' pull wires. Water am a motive power, kase it turns de wheels of de saw-mill, an' thus purvides us wid sidewalks full of holes. Wind am a motive power, kase it lengthens de sessions of Congress an' de varus Legislachures. 'Lectricity am a motive power, but de rates am so awful high dat we didn't investigate. De bite of a dog, de sting of a hornet, de toe of a boot, an' de squint of a man's left eye am numbered among de minor motive powers. Gunpowder, when properly used, has been known to blow up hoss-barns an' kill elephants. Dis Committee feels safe in sayin' dat de nex' decade will bring forth other motive powers. De time am comin' when our butes will be pulled on an' off by machinery; when de chill'en will be put to bed wid four revolushuns of de big fly-wheel; when de sarvint gal who doan' come home in time to get supper will de snaked along at de rate of a mile a minute; when a Tom an' Jerry will be mixed an' stirred up by simply pressin' on a button let into de bar, an' when de man who comes home at midnight an' can't open de front gate, will be lifted up frew a second-story winder an' sobered off in about twenty ticks."

ABOUT LIARS.

"Who am a liar?" asked the old man, as he rose up in his usual place and glared around him.

"Pickles Smith, Trustee Pullback, Samuel Shin and Evergreen Jones started and turned pale, and there was a deathlike silence as Brother Gardner continued:

"An' what shall we do wid him—wid de liar an' de liars? De liar am wid us an' of us an' among us. He gits up wid us in de mawnin' an' lies down wid us at night. Go to de grocery, an' de grocer smiles an' nods an' lies. Go to de dry-goods man, an' he has a welcome an' a lie. De tailor promises a suit when he knows he can't finish it. De shoemaker promises a pair of butes for Saturday when he has three day's work on the nex' week. De ice man charges us wid twenty-five pounds an' delivers sixteen. Our carpets are warranted, an' yet they fade. De plumber plumbs an' lies. De painter paints an' lies. De carpenter planes an' saws an' cheats. De dressmaker not only lies but steals de cloth. We all lie like troopers fifty times a day, an' de man who won't lie doan' stan' any show.

"An' yet, my frens, whar' will we bring up in de end? When Waydown Bebee axes me fur de loan of a dollar till Saturday, he lies. He knows he can't pay it back under fo' weeks. I know he knows it, an' I lie. I tell him I jist paid out de last shillin' fur a wash-bo'd an' can't possibly raise no mo'. If I ax Judge Hostetter Johnson to sign a bank note wid me, he lies when he says he promised his dyin' gran'mother neber to do so. We lie when we wa'r better cloze dan we kin afford—when we put on airs above us—when we put on our backs what orter be fodder fur our stomachs. We has become a red-hot go-ahead dust-aroun' nashun, but we has also become a nashun of liars, cheats an' false pretenders. We adulterate our goods, cheat in weight, swindle in measure, an' put on broadcloth coats to hide de absence of dollar shirts. Our society am full of false pretenders, our religion furnishes a cloak fur hypocrites, an' our charity am but a high-soundin' name fur makin' a dollar bring back ten shillings. I doan' know what de principal wickedness of Sodom consisted of, nor wedder de folks in Gomorrow tole lies or pitched pennies, but if either one could beat an American town of the same size fur lyin an' decepshun dey mus' have got up werry airly in de mawnin', an stayed awake all night long. We lie, an' we know we lie. We play de hypocrite, we cheat an deceive, an' yit we want the world to pick us out as shinin' examples of virtue, an' we expect our tombstones to bear eulogies georgious 'nuff fur angels. Gem'len, let us kick each odder into doin' better! Let de kickin' begin jist whar' it happens, fur we can't hit anybody who doan' need it."

'ROSE TO INQUIRE.

Waydown Bebee arose to inquire if he had ever borrowed a dollar of the President and neglected to return it on the date specified.

"You has, sah!" was the prompt reply.

Waydown scratched his head, looked around for a soft spot to break his fall, and finally sat down with a look of melancholy creeping over his complexion.

ELECTION.

"Gem'len, befo' purceedin' to de bizness in han'," said Sir Isaac, as he stood up, "let me beg de privilege of admittin' dat I am a liar. I whitewash a lie. I black stoves an' lie. I beat an' put down ca'pets an' lie. I am an aged liar from de word go, an' I am ashamed of it; sorry fur it, an' I promise to quit de bizness from dis time out. I will now pass de bean-box. Please remember dat one black bean rejects a candydate, an' may bring sorrow to a hull back township."

He then began his preambulations, and the followlowing gentlemen of off-color were unanimously elected in the order named. Trustee White, Moses Adew,

Rev. Pilaster, Judge Tremaine, Elder Dodo, Nemesis Scott, Col. Peachtree Williams, and Lord Conducive Jones.

THE FOURTH.

The committee having in charge the arrangements for the glorious Fourth for the colored element throughout America, reported the following programme, which they trust will be strictly adhered to:

"Arouse yourselves at 5 o'clock A. M. Describe the battle of Bunker Hill to the children. Breakfast at 6. Describe the battle of Trenton to the old woman. Down town at 7. Lemonade—lager—cocoanuts—peanuts—bananas. Meet at some appointed place at 9 o'clock. Encourage each other to be patriotic and strive for a pension. Let some orator in the party make a speech glorifying the American Republic.

"After dinner take the children down to see the proud bird of liberty. Have the old woman hold up both hands and swear that she will never wash a shirt or scrub a kitchen for a tyrant.

"Fireworks in the evening. Lemonade grows weaker. Grand flight of sky-rockets and hurrahs for the best country under the sun. Wallop the children and jaw the old woman when you get home. Nothing like it. Hip—hurrah!"

The programme was discussed at length but on the motion to adopt, there was not a negative vote.

KILLED IN THE BUD.

Trustee Pullback then offered the following resolution:

"*Resolved*, Dat usurpashun am de death blow of liberty."

"Brudder Pullback," said the President, as he looked at the member over the top of his spectacles, "do you know what usurpashun means?"

"I—I—'spect I does, sah."

"What is it?"

Brother Pullback hesitated, scratched his ear, rubbed his elbow, and was evidently fast-aground on a sand bar.

"You had better take dat resolushun an' place it softly on top de stove," resumed the President. "Dar am too much chin-music in dis kentry 'bout usurpashun, monopoly, centralizashun, loss o' liberty, an' so on. If anybody wants to usurp let him go ahead. As fur loss o' liberty, we has got such dead loads of it dat we kin afford to lose a sheer. Sot down, Brudder Pullback—sot down, an' remember dat shootin' off big words doan' pay fur meat an' 'taters."

HUMAN NATURE.

The blowing of noses in the northwest corner of Paradise Hall finally came to an end, and when Trustee Pullback had flung his whole soul into one grand effort to cough his head off, and failed, Brother Gardner arose and said:

"My kentrymen, when you meet a man who knows jist whar' he kin borry a dollar—who has friends in boaf political parties—who gits invitations to all church festivals—who am ginerally spoken of as a good feller, you have foun' a man who makes a study of human natur'. De student of anatomy carves up a cadaver to diskiver how de bones am put togedder—whar' de muscles lie—how de vital organs am nailed on. De good feller studies de livin' 'stead of de dead—de mind 'stead of de body. De human mind am full of co'ns. Tread on one of 'em, an' dar' am a back-ackshun to once. If I should want a five dollah bill airly Monday mornin' I should slip ober an' ax Deakun Jackson fur it. His big co'n am de belief dat no one kin be saved onless he am baptized in de riber, an' I have been keerful to walk all aroun' dat co'n. I go ober to his house wid a jug o' cider in one hand an' baptismal argyments in de odder, an' sometimes he feels so good dat he'd like to douse me in de rain bar'l.

"If I wanted some onion seed I'd go ober to Elder Tiffs'. De Elder's co'n am de belief dat he was bo'n fur a great preacher. I've walked all ober him a hundred times, but I'ze neber stubed my toe agin dat co'n. I've sot down wid him an' praised de build of his head, an' de shape of his mouth, an' his pose an' gesture, an' I've stuck to de cha'r while he talked an' cavooted fur a straight hour. If I wanted onions, he'd fall down cellar to git 'em fur me.

"If you come across a man who imagines dat he am an orator, doan' gibe his booms; it won't hurt anybody to let him keep right on finkin' so, but it will make him your deadly enemy to try to conwince him dat he was cut out fur a blacksmif. Dar' am people who write stuff an' call it poetry. Ize got a naybur who writ fourty-four varses of sich stuff las' fall an' read it to me, an' axed my candid opinyun. Did I tell her it was bosh? Did I jump frew de winder when she reached de second verse? Not much! I listened wid de utmos' diligence, an' when she finished de las' line I advised her to publish a book o' poems. De nex' week I fell sick, an' dat poetess was de fust on de groun' wid chicken-brof an' currant jell.

"When I meet a man who has made up his mind dat our city guv'ment will go to smash if he don't git office, I incourage him. I incourage de young to become Washingtons. I incourage de ole to hang on till de world has to recognize deir greatness. A word at de right time means de loan of a dollah—means thirty off when you want a new whitewash brush—means a bushel o' lime free gratis —means a recommend if you want to jine de purleece fo'ce. Tech my co'ns an' I'll want to kick ye. All men am de same. Call 'em co'ns or call 'em hobbies, but he who goes slashin' aroun' widout carin' whar' he puts his feet, will make twenty enemies whar' he gains one friend. Study your man. Take him apart—put him togedder—fin' out whar' his co'ns lay, an' den step high an' softly. Let us now irregulate to bizness."

THE REVISED.

"I TAKE pleasure an' satisfaction," said the President, as he held up a parcel, "in informin' you a worthy citizen of Detroit, who does not car to hab his name menshun'd, has presented dis revised edishun of de Bible to de Lime-Kiln Club. We do not open our meetins wid prayer, nor do we close by singin' de Doxology, but, neberdeless I am suah dis gift will be highly appreshiated by all. Dar has bin considuble talk in dis Club about dis revised edishun.

Some of you hab got de ideah dat purgatory has all been wiped out, an' heben enlarged twice ober, an' I have heard odders assert dat it didn't forbid lyin', stealin', an' passin' off bad money. My frens, you am sadly mistaken. Hell is jist as hot as eber, an' Heben has'nt got any mo' room. In lookin, ober some of de changes, las' night, I selected out a few paragraphs which have a gineral b'arin. Fur instance, it am jist as wicked to steal water mellyons as it was las y'ar or de y'ar befo', an' de skeercer de crap, de bigger de wickedness.

"No change has bin made in regard to loafin' aroun' de streets. De loafer am considered jist as mean an' low as eber he was, an' I want to add my belief dat he will grow meaner in public estimashun all de time.

"De ten commandments am all down heah widout change. Stealin', an' lyin', an' covetin', an' runnin' out nights am considered jist as bad as eber.

"I can't 'find any paragraph in which men am excused for payin' deir honest debts, an' supportin' deir fam'lies.

"I can't fin' whar a poo' man or a poo' man's wife —white or black—am 'spected to sling on any pertickler style.

"Dog fights, chicken liftin', polyticks, playin' keerds fur money, an' hangin' aroun' fur drinks, an' all sich low bizness am considered meaner dan eber. Fact is, I can't fin' any change whateber which lets up on a man from bein plumb up an' down squar', an' honest wid de world. Dey have changed de word 'Hell' to 'Hades,' but at de same time added to de strength of de brimstun an' de size of de pit, an' we want to keep right on in de straight path if we would avoid it. Doan' let any white man make you believe dat we's lost any Gospel by dis revision, or dat Peter, or Paul, or Moses hab undergone any change of speerit regardin' de ways of libin' respectably an' dyin' honorably."

SERENE TOOTS.

ELDER TOOTS has been alluded to in the proceedings of this Club as an individual of serenest countenance and sweetest repose. Having to go to market for a bottle of horse-raddish and a quart of beans, he decided not to return home previous to putting in an appearance at the Lodge. As a consequence, he was on hand half an hour ahead of the usual time, and was left in charge of the Hall while the janitor prospected up the alley to see if any of the store porters had been reckless enough to leave a dry-goods box out in the cold. The Elder filled his pipe and had a smoke, and in a moment of emotional insanity he dropped the red-hot clay into his coat-tail pocket. Combustion and ignition followed, and when the janitor returned the Elder was skipping over stools and benches like a boy getting away from a delegation of hornets. There was a strong smell of smoke and fire, but the Elder had no time to relate particulars. He sat down in the water-pail but it was waterless. He rolled over and over on the floor, but the smell grew stronger. It was not until a dozen members had come in and chased the old man into a corner and collared him that it was discovered that he was on fire.

When Elder Toots started for home he was a sadder man. He also had an old coffee sack thrown carelessly over his back to give him the appearance of a Roman brigand. The incident was duly announced to Brother Gardner as he came in, and when the meeting opened the old man said:

"Let dis lesson sink deep into your hearts. Do not cultivate sereneness. Sereneness will wade frew a mud-hole all de y'ar round when half an hour's work would bridge it. Do not be tranquil. De tranquil man am either a great villyun or too lazy to keep up wid de purceshun. Avoid absent-mindedness. It may do in a great man, but when it comes down to poo' folks like us, one case of absent-mindedness will knock our credit at de grocer's or butcher's higher dan a kite. Avoid sweet repose. De man who kin shet out dis busy world an' de sound of its machinery at de airly hour of seben o'clock in de ebenin', can't hev any money lent out on a chattel mortgage, an' has no ax lyin' aroun' de wood-pile fur any one to steal. Lastly, de world neber has any pity on de man wha burns off his own coat-tails. Let us now purceed to bizness."

MORE BASENESS.

"Gem'len," said Brother Gardner, as he held out an alleged two-shilling piece on the palm of his hand, " at de las' weekly colleckshun some one of ye drapped dis so-called quarter into de hat. It am not only a base counterfit to begin on, but it has free holes bored frew it. Now, de ideah of histin' such money off on dis Club am a little too dizzy, an'

SERENE TOOTS AS A ROMAN BRIGAND.

if de same coincidence incurs agin, I shell deliver a speech of indignashun lastin' an hour an' a half. One word moah: De member of dis Club who am totin' such stuff aroun' in his pockets had better look out."

Samuel Shin arose for the purpose of saying that the bogus quarter might have dropped from the ceiling as the hat went round, but just as he got his mouth puckered up he was told that there was no question before the meeting, and he therefore fell back on his bench.

PETITIONS.

The petitions read off by the Secretary numbered thirteen, representing six different States. Among the more prominent petitioners were James Comeback Dodge, of St. Louis, and Gen. Sardanapalus Smith, of Natchez. Mr. Comeback is the original inventor of the art of putting a crimson flush on a whitewashed ceiling and imitating cobwebs in the corners, and the General invented the jetty system at the mouth of the Mississippi river just three days after Capt. Eads did.

AN APPEAL.

A letter from Kansas City asked the Club to forward a contribution to aid the colored people in placing a spire 150 feet high on their church edifice, but Brother Gardner shook his head and observed:

"De time has arrove when de religun in a pusson's heart am gwine to be jedged by his words an' deeds, an' not by de steeple on his church. Folkeses who can't praise de Lawd in a buildin' widout any spire on de top, am not de sort to praise Him at all."

INSURANCE.

A letter from the Secretary of an Eastern Insurance Company made inquiry of the Club as to what per cent. of the colored people of Detroit carried life insurance. The letter also stated that favorable terms would be given such members of the Club as desired to insure.

"Dis life inshurance am one of de problems dat mix me up," remarked the President, "but I'll take down de names of anybody who wants a policy."

Elder Toots thereupon came forward and said he thought he'd take about three million dollars on his life, and Ezra Buck guessed he'd take five. This settled it with the others, who realized that no company could lose over $8,000,000 and come to time on other losses.

ABOUT DOGS.

The Committee on Internal Improvements submitted their monthly report at this meeting. It was devoted almost entirely to dogs, the committee having been instructed to investigate the newspaper statements that every colored family in Detroit owned an average of three canines. This statement first appeared in the New York Tribune many years ago, in an editorial written by Horace Greeley, and is constantly passing around the press. The committee made a thorough canvas of the city, and found that no colored family had over three dogs, while the majority had only one, and thirty-eight were keeping house and scrubbing along without even a cat. The report being adopted, the Club passed a resolution demanding that the Tribune should retract its statement in a double-leaded paragraph.

VISITORS.

The Committee on Reception reported that the Hon. Deflective Jones, of Augusta, Ga., and Edward Springhill, Esq., of Chicago, would both arrive in the city the present week to visit the Club, and a resolution was adopted to invite them to speak before the next meeting. The Hon. Jones has the largest possum farm in Georgia, and is coming North to secure machinery for making three-cornered bricks, and Mr. Springhill is selling a new sort of shoe-blacking, which kills corns as well as shines the leather.

DE CRANK.

Col. Ebenezer Canister then offered the following single-barreled resolution:

·*Resolved*, Dat dis Club has no sympathy wid cranks, an' dat it am de sense of dis Club dat more hangism would result in less crankism."

The resolution was passed by a unanimous vote, and Brother Gardner added:

"I feel strongly dat way myself. De man who kin pay out an' receive money, trade aroun' de kentry, do bizness an' keep outer de way of de butcher-carts, musn't shoot my ole woman an' den plead hereditary, heretofore, hereafter or any odder sort of insanity. De crank who can't resist de temptashun to steal must keep outer my tater patch or take de chances of my puttin' a han'full of shot inter his corpus. De crank who am not morally responsible fur his utterances will feel de weight of my fist de fust time he calls me a liar. De crank who am not financially responsible wants to keep right away from me de hull week frew. De crank who am impelled by Deity, Debit, or any odder power to do me bodily injury, had better be sartin of his aim, fur if he misses me I'll light down on him like a ton of de reddest brick he eber saw. I doan' go a cent on any insanity outside of a lunatic asylum. If a man am luny, put him among the lunatics. De fack dat he am not put dar am reason fur holdin' him legally responsible fur ebery act."

DE GONENESS.

As the triangle sounded the President slowly arose to a picturesque position and observed:

"Prof. January Sunbeam, of Mississippi, am waitin' in de ante-room to address de meetin' on de subjeck of 'De Goneness of de Past.' De Professor am not only known all ober de kentry fur his theories on astronomy, but he am de only man in America who kin skin a woodckuck in seben minits by de watch. Sir Isaac Walpole, you an' Giveadam Jones will put on your yaller kid gloves an' long-tailed coats an' escort the Professor into de Hall."

In about five minutes the stranger made his appearance and was greeted with a burst of applause, which upset the water pail and filled the shoes of eight or ten of the nearest members. On taking the platform, he was introduced by the President, handed a piece of slippery elm to keep his throat moist during his oratory, and he then bowed and began:

"My dear fren's, whar' am de past? Look fur it

under de bed, down cellar, up stairs, in de wood-box or whar' you will, an' you cannot find it. Why? Kase it am gone. It has slipped away like a streak o' grease runnin' across de kitchen floo', an' it will neber, neber return. (Sighs from all over the Hall.) Do you meet Plato as you go up de street? Do you fin' Cicero waitin' at de ferry dock? Do you hear of Diogenes hangin' 'round de Union Depot to work de string game on some greenhorn? Not any! Dey belongs to de past an' gone. Dey sleep in de dimness of odder centuries. Whar' am de glories of de Roman Empire? Whar' am Cæsar an' Brutus an' Cassius? Let de dust of de past answer. (Much blowing of noses.)

"My fren's, de past am not de fucher, any more dan day after to-morrow am day befo' yesterday. As time fades so does glory fade. To-day you may march at de head of de purceshun, yer hat on yer ear an' a red sash tied aroun' yer body—to-morrow ye may be in jail fur borrowin' somebody's woodpile to keep yer feet warm. (Sly and suspicious winks all over the room.) Do not prize de present too highly,—do not forget de warnings of de past. We cannot recall de past, but we can look back an' see whar' de grocer gin us short weight on codfish, an' whar' we took advantage of a cloudy day to pass a twenty-cent piece off fur a quarter. (Cheers and applause.)

"My hearers, we should not lib fur de past, but fur de fucher. What am it to us as we riz up in de mawnin' wedder Cæsar met his mother-in-law at de depot or forbid her his house? What am it to us as we retire to our humble couches fur de night wedder de orators of Athens greased deir butes wid lard or went bar'fut? As we sit on a box in de alley to consume our noon-day lunch, we car' not wedder Brutus dyed his goatee or was clean-shaved. (Cries of No! no!) But de fucher am big wid events. To-day we may be full of sorrow. If so, we hope dat de morrow will bring clam chowder. (Great smacking of lips.) If de present am full of biles an' chilblains an' heart-aches, de fucher may be as bright as a cat's eye shinin' out of a bar'l on a dark night. Neber look back on de past. It am as much gone as a three-cent piece paid out fur Fourth of July lemonade. Neber dispair of de fucher. When de heart is heaviest, de fire lowest, an' work de skeercest, you may find a lost wallet, or strike some butcher willin' to give credit. (Whoops of applause.) My fre'ns, I am dun. Thanking you severely for your infectious distraction, I 'rambulate to my seat wid oderiferous feelings of concentrashun towards each an ebery one of you."

During the wild excitement which followed the close of the masterly effort, Samuel Shin and Trustee Pullback fell upon the hot stove in an enthusiastic embrace, and seven windows had to be lowered to let out the odor of overdone mule steak.

ABOUT ART.

"Lale in de ebenin' de odder night," began the old man as Elder Toots quit coughing and the dust from Pickle Smith's boots settled down, "my cabin war surrounded by seberal leadin' citizens of Kaintuck. When dey had been invited in an' placed whar dey could all spit on de stove, dey denounced de object of deir wisit. De Hon. Saleratus Bloater, who am not a member of dis Club, arose an' said dat hisself an' odder cull'd citizen war aggitatin' de subjick of establishin' an art gallery in dis city fur de encouragement an' benefit of de African race, an' he wanted de inflooence of de Club in de enterprise. Gem'len, de queshun am open fur discushun, an' Sir Isaac Walpole hez de floo'."

Sir Isaac said that he had also been informed of the scheme and asked to favor it. In his mind's eye he saw a dozen colored men without overcoats, toes out to the frost and pockets empty, standing before a painting of some European palace, but he thought they would rather criticise a square meal of codfish and potatoes

Waydown Bebee believed in art and art galleries. An art gallery hung with smoked hams, loaves of bread and baked potatoes was his idea. He would rather hold a private interview with a peck of turnips under a shed than to stand before a statue of Apollo in an art gallery, but he would be guided by the majority.

"I stan' up heah widout any undershirt on!" said Squire Trotback, as he rose up like a telescope getting ready for business, " an' de man who emagines dat I prefer a lan'scape to an undershirt am frowin' away his time."

" An' my ole woman," said the Hon. Cabiff Jones, as the other sat down, " am at de present minit gwine about de house wid a boot on one foot an' a shoe on de odder, kase I can't afford to buy her two boots, though I'ze bin workin' ebery day fur de las' six months. She'd look sweet standin' befo' de pictur' o' 'Contentment,' wouldn't she? I fink I see her right dar!"

"Gem'len," said the President, as he gave the bear-trap a left-handed squint, "de day may come when we kin have all we want an' plenty to lend, but jist at de present time de cull'd folks of dis kentry need art galleries about as much as a pig needs wings. We will drap de subjeck an' progress towards progreshun."

A CORRECTION.

The Secretary read a letter from Haverstraw Miller, of St. Louis, asking what brought about the rupture between the Lime-Kiln Club and Gen. De Luc, of the Agricultural Bureau, and Brother Gardner replied:

"Why, dare hain't de least bit o' rupcher atween us. It was only yesterday dat I received a communicashun from de General axin' my way of keepin' bedstead casters safe from de frost doorin' de winter, an' my answer goes out by nex' mail. Shoo! now, but dis Club an' de General am workin' in de softest harmony togeder, an' if de public lets us alone it won't be a y'ar befo' we shall solve de queshun of growin' pink-colored cabbage-heads. Rupchur atween de General an' dis Club—neber!"

NOT IN PARTICULAR.

A communication from St. Joseph, Mo., inquired if the Club had yet adopted any particular color as its own, and this brought the President to his feet again;

"I can't say dat we really hez. Indeed, we am considerably mized up on dat head. Some of us run to sky-blue, some to pale-yaller, an' de younger members seem to hev a great hankerin' arter lavender an' vermillyun. Howeber, if de time eber comes when de queshun am brought to a wote, I 'spect dar would be a thumpin' big majority in favor of yaller striped wid scarlet."

BOUNCED.

Maj. John Smoothshod here offered the following preamble and resolution:

"*Wh'aras*, Dis Club hevin' been offishully notified dat Cyrus Washington Brown, of Nicksburg, Miss., an honorary member of de organizashun, hez been detected in an attempt to enter a grocery store by way of de back winder at midnight; an'

"*Wh'aras*, Dis Club believes in buyin' its groceries in de daytime an' payin' cash down; now, darefore,

"*Resolved*, Dat de name of de said Cyrus Washington Brown be an' hereby am drapped from de rolls forever, an' all good members of de Club am 'spected to turn up de nose of scorn at him wheneber an' whereber met."

The resolution was adopted without debate, and Cyrus can now wipe his weeping eyes on his elbow.

RE-ADOPTED.

Tne Rev. Penstock took the floor and said that he last year voted for a resolution to combine Thanksgiving, Christmas and New Years in one general holiday, and christen the same "Thankschrisyear's." He wanted to inquire if the Club still adhered to its ideas, and if so, what day it would observe.

Samuel Shin just missed knocking down the stovepipe as he arose to inquire if the Fourth of

July couldn't be voted back into the middle of January.

Trustee Pullback was in favor of a consolidation. He didn't have chicken now on any of the three winter holidays, and if they were combined in one, he might possibly scrape up a pullet.

The Hon. Gazeteer Larkins was sorry that he could not agree with the Senator from the Fifth, but he would rather have more holidays than less. He didn't always have plum pudding and chicken pot-pie for a holiday dinner, but those days always gave him a chance to sit around the stove and warm his heels clear through.

Several other members spoke for and against the proposition, and the Club then adopted a resolution combining the three winter holidays in one and naming it as above.

THANKS.

A firm in Boston forwarded an offer to supply the Club with enough oilcloth to cover all the benches and stools for winter at twenty per cent. below regular wholesale rates, and the Secretary was instructed to write a letter of thanks in reply and ascertain if he could, how many degrees colder oilcloth is on a cold day than regular ice.

The meeting then adjourned.

THE AIRY PERKINS.

AT this stage of the proceedings Sweetbriar Perkins stood up in the northwest corner of the Hall, flourished a red silk handkerchief, adjusted his lavender tie, and announced that he arose to a question of privilege. He had just returned from a trip to Ohio, and during a short stay at Cincinnati he had been refused permission, or rather the right, to eat at the tables with other guests. The waiter had seated him at a small side table, with no other company, and had even thrown out hints that he should have sought a cheaper hotel. Brother Perkins felt that the Club had been insulted through him, and he wanted to know what action would be taken.

"It will take no furder ackshun dan to reprimand you fur your impertinence," replied the President. "In de fust place you had no money to speak of, an' had no bizness in a fust-class hotel. In de nex' place you forgot your origin. You had no mo' bizness sittin' 'longside o' white ladies an' gem'len dan dey would have in luggin pails o' whitewash aroun' de street. I know all about de Civil Rights law, but it doan' count. De people who made it had no sympathy fur us. Not a man who woted fur it would sit beside us at de table or in a theatre. De law of proteckshun applies to a cow as well as a hoss—to a goose as well as a calf. Boaf am equal in law—boaf have de same rights in law, but do you see cows mixin' wid hosses, an' tryin' to equal 'em in pullin' an' walkin' an' trottin'? Am a goose veal bekase it has de same rights as a calf? Do calves try to fly bekase de air am as free to calves as to geese. If I should see a white man sot down to a table wid twenty black men I should dispise him, an' de black man who fo'ces his presence upon white folks should be taken by de neck an' bounced inter de fust hoss pond. Brudder Perkins, you am a leetle too airy fur a black man, an' about sebenteen shades too dark fur a white one, an' onless you make a change your fate is sealed."

DE GOOD OLE DAYS.

"What I am longin' arter," said Brother Gardner as Trustee Pullback ceased coughing and Samuel Shin finally got a rest for his feet, "what I am longin' arter am a sight of a good, old-fashioned man or woman—sich as we could find in ebery house thirty y'ars ago, but sich as cannot be found now in a week's hunt. It makes me lonesome when I realize dat our old-fashioned men an women are no mo'. In de days gone by, if I fell sick, one woman would run in wid catnip, anoder wid horseradish leaves, anoder wid a bowl o' gruel, an' tears would be shed, an' kind words spoken, an' one couldn't stay sick to save him. In dose good ole days de kaliker dress an' white apron abounded. An honest woman wasn't afeard to wash her face on account of de powder. Ebery woman wore her own ha'r, an' she wore it to please herself instead of fashun. Thick shoes kept her feet dry, thick clothes kept her body warm, an' dar was no winkin' and' wobblin' an' talkin' frew de teef.

"Dar was goodness in de land in dem good ole days. Dar was prayin' to God, an' de hearts meant it. De woman who wore a No. 6 shoe was as good as a woman wid a foot all pinched out of shape an' kivered wid co'ns. You didn't h'ar much 'bout beach o' promise cases an' odder deviltry. De man who parts his ha'r in de middle, an' believes he

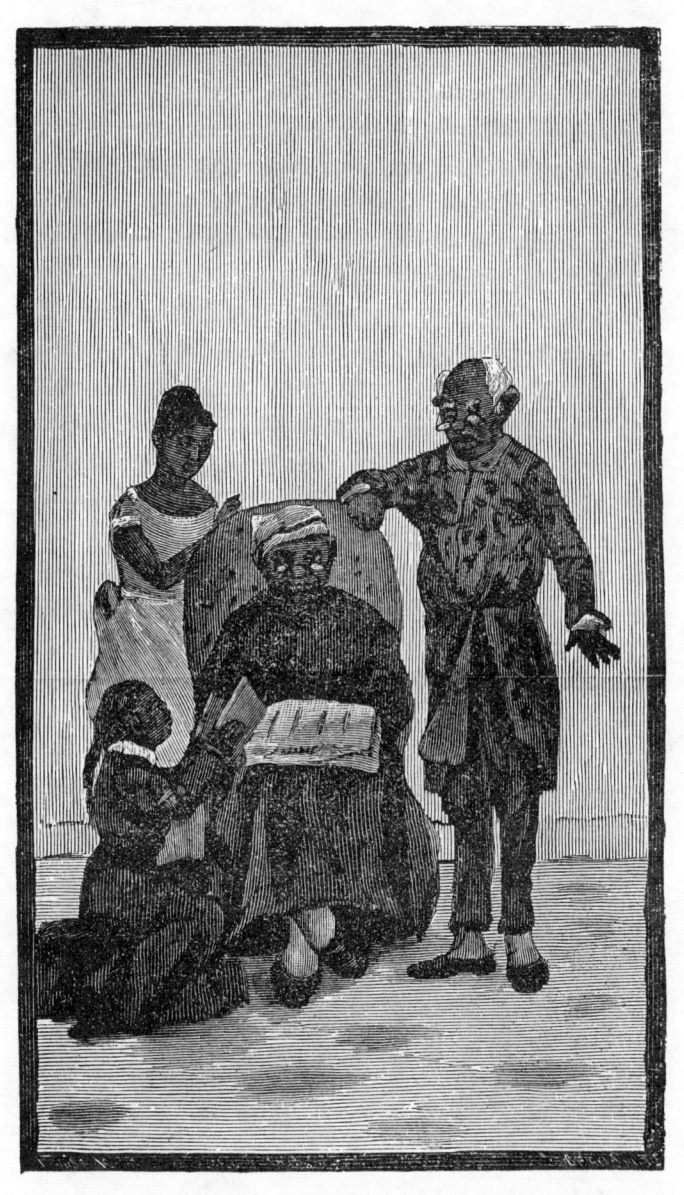

BROTHER GARDNER IN THE BOSOM OF HIS FAMILY.

mashes his wictims by de score wasn't bo'n den. People didn't let deir nayburs die under deir noses widout eben knowin' dat sickness had come to de family. Men worked hard an' put in full time, an' women foun' sunthin' to do besides gaddin' de streets to show off a small foot or a new bonnet.

"De world calls it progress. We must shut our hearts against our naybur, sacrifice all fur fashun, conceal our limps an' pains, appear what we am not, an' when we go to de grave fur rest we am forgotten in a week. Whar one woman looks to Heaben a dozen looks to fashun. Whar one man helps de poo' from kindness of heart a dozen chip in because de list of names will be published in de paper. When I sot down of an evenin' an' fink dese fings ober it makes me sad. I doan' know jist how wicked Sodom was, nor what deviltry dey was up to in Gomorrah, but if either town had mo' wanity, wickedness, frivolity an' deceit dat Detroit, Chicago, Buffalo, or any odder city in dis kentry, rents mus' have bin awful high."

SPRING DECORATIONS.

The Committee on Decorative Art announced their readiness to submit the regular monthly report, and leave being given, the Chairman stated that the advent of spring would bring many new changes. All kitchen ceilings will be given a sky-blue cast, with faint streaks of old gold around the edges. The popular shade of walls and fences will be an aristocratic purple, toned around the knot-holes with a rich pink. Outside blinds will be painted a dove-color and trimmed with second mourning. Rag carpet can be bordered with stripes of blue horse-blanket where the family desires to combine a light atmosphere with a dreamy effect. Old hats have long been considered en regle for filling the place of broken window panes, but decorative genius has found something new. Card board cats, printed in colors and made all sizes, are pinned to the sash so neatly that the passer-by is struck with admiration. Where six or eight panes are broken in the same window, and six or eight cats are pinned to the sash, the general effect is decidedly picturesque.

HOW UNCLE PETE DIED.

"It am my painful dooty," said the President as the meeting was called to order, "to announce de fack dat Brudder Kanaby passed from airth away yesterday arternoon. He was known to moas' of us as Uncle Pete, an' I believe he has passed away widont leavin' an inemy behind him. Who does not remember his white ha'r, wrinkled face, kindly voice an' good-natured smile? Who kin not remember his kin' words and good deeds? Who eber axed him fur help dat he did not get it?

"An' poo' ole Uncle Peter am no mo' among us! Some few of us war up dar' when he breathed his last, an' none of us will soon forgit how he passed away. When you see de cold, dead face at de funeral to-morrer you will see dat it carries de same kin' smile as in life. He died feelin' dat he was gwine home. He was only a poo' ole black man, not able to read or write, and all frew his life he had met wid sorrows an' misfortunes. Men had told him dat he had no soul. Men had told him dat dere was no God.

Men had laffed at him fur believin' dar was a hereafter fur weary souls. An' yit how did he die?

"When de poo' ole man realized dat de summons had come his smile was like dat of a child's. De prayer he made will ring in my ears foreber. In his heart, so soon to be still, he felt dat his long y'ars of faith war' 'bout to be rewarded. He had held fast through darkness and scoffin' an' trial an' dispair, an now de reward was clus at han'. Dar war' tears in our eyes an' we could not see, but we knew what he saw. If eber mortal eyes looked into Heaben, dat curtain was lifted to him. Wid his hands clasped—wid a heart puttin' its trust in God to de las'—wid a smile which showed nuffin' but faith an' trust dis ole man slipped from de lovin' hands around him an' jined de percession which am allus marchin' from de shores of airth to de gates of glory. As many of you as can make it convenient will attend de funeral to-morrer, and de Janitor will see dat de wacant cha'r am decked wid crape fur de usual thirty days."

OUR COLORED HEROES.

The President announced that it was time to bestow the semi-annual prize offered by the Club for the greatest display of heroism by any colored man in North America, and he called for the report of the committee. Waydown Bebee, Chairman of said committee, reported that he had several cases to mention, as follows:

1. The case of Harrison Dayball Carter, of Tennessee, who plunged into a burning building and brought out a baby in one hand and a gallon jug of whisky in the other. It could not be definitely as-

certained whether the jug or the baby incited Mr. Carter to his heroic act.

2. The case of Gen. Pompeii Jones, who put a string around a mad dog's neck and led him into a suburb of St. Louis. It had been charged that the General did not know that the dog was mad, and picked him up with the intention of being a dog ahead.

3. The case of Elder Theopholis Smith, of Georgia, who plunged into a raging flood to rescue a boy 10 years old. It had been asserted that he did not plunge until the boy's father had offered a reward of $100, and the committee could not come to any conclusion.

4. The case of George Washington Defoe, who descended into a well thirty-eight feet deep to rescue a man who had just cheated him blind on a mule trade, and who refused a reward of fifteen cents for his noble efforts. This case, in the opinion of the committee, was the most deserving, and on the question being put the Club was unanimous in voting the prize to Mr. Defoe. The prize consists of a silver-plated tobacco-box, with a compass in the lid, and the Secretary was instructed to mail it to the hero forthwith.

THE GLEE CLUB.

The Glee Club then tuned up and sung and played the following so beautifully that the Hall clock stopped dead still at five minutes to ten.

> De robin am chirpin'
> De blue-bird am singin'
> De voice of de blue jay am heard in de land·
> De wild ducks am flyin'

De ganders am sighin'
An' de big bunko man he am showin' his hand.

De mud's growin' deeper,
An' thunder's a comin',
An' de possum comes out of his log fur to see;
De warm rain's a fallin',
De spring calf am bawlin',
Ad' de white-washin' season has opened for me.

REPORTS.

The Committee on Astronomy reported a riot on the sun's surface, but advised everybody to go to bed at the usual hour.

The Committee on Ways and Means reported in favor of increasing the number of political offices in this country; likewise an increase of jails and prisons.

The Committee on Agriculture reported that it had contracted cider to be delivered in October at $1 per barrel.

The Committee on Sanitary Measures could not say that a barrel of soap-grease in the cellar of a house would create dampness in the parlor bed room, but the matter was being investigated.

The Librarian reported the number of almanacs of the date of 1882 on hand at 2,827, and more coming by every mail.

The remainder of the business of national importance was placed on ice, the water-pail turned bottom-side up, and the meeting slid down stairs, while the Glee Club sang: "Oh! Who Would Die This Summer?"

DE GOOD MAN.

The President ordered thirteen windows to be raised, the ice in the water-pail to be renewed, and all the dogs turned out of the room, and then said:

"When you cum across a man who has no vices nor weaknesses, drap him as you would a hot 'tater. De Lawd intended man to be mo' or less weak, wicked an' wretched. It was not de ideah to turn out a perfeck man. If it had been, we should have had neither religion, preacher nor Bible. Airth would have bin Heaben, an' dar would have bin no call to die.

"Natur' sometimes turns out a pusson widout guile, jist as she turns out one-eyed colts an' three-legged calves. Sich pussons soon become known as either fools or lunatics. It am agin natur's way to bring men into dis world wid an angel's wings already half grown. An' it am a leetle suspicious to find a too-good man. When you diskiver a human bein' who isn't lame somewhar'—who neber deceives, cheats, lies, envies, covets—who goes about satisfied wid de weather, craps an' himself—who won't bet, drink, go to de circus or look upon a hoss race, you have found a man to let alone. He am too good. Natur' made him fur an angel an' forgot to put him in Heaben.

"I like a man who has weakness an' sins. Den I know dat he am a feller-mortal who was put on airth to be saved. I like a man who has had sickness, heartaches an' grievous trouble. Den I am sartin of a man who has sympathy. I like a man who has bin foolish 'nuff to git drunk an' strong 'nuff to kick de temptashun ober a seben-rail fence. Den you know whar' to find him. He has bin dar an' knows what a fool he was. I like a man who has bin a liar, an' who hasen't entirely recovered from de injury. Den I know how to trade hosses wid him, an' I know what to believe when he tells me dat he has bin fishin'. If a goody-good naybur borrys my spade I doan' know when it will cum home, nor how much of it will be left. If a thief takes it for a loan I am pretty sartin to rekiver it in a day or two an' in good condishun.

"When a man tells me dat he has become so good dat he feels like bustin', I go right home an' put an extra padlock on my kitchen doah. When a man sheds tears ober de condishun of de far-off heathen, de heathen at home had better be keerful how dey lend him money. De man whose conscience won't let him go to a place of amusement, has bin known to elope wid anoder man's wife. De man who can't remember dat he eber used an oath or tole a lie has bin follered across de ocean an arrested fur robbin' widders an' orphans. De man who allus w'ars a smile am now sarvin' his third term in State Prison.

"Let me say to you in sumin' up dat de man who sins an' knows it an' wants to do better, am sooner to be trusted dan de man who neber sins an' feels dat he am good 'nuff. If you lie to a man, let it be a man who feels dat he am weak an' sinful. You will den have a pardner who am not a freak of Natur'. Let us now embarass ourselves wid de reg'lar order of bizness."

ABOUT PROGRESS.

The report of the Committee on Arts and Sciences being called for, the Chairman, Two-Ply Hastings, said that he had nothing new to announce. As to the query from Liverpool, England: "Are we progressing as fast as we might in Art and Science?" he would answer no. Science is still in its baby-clothes —Art still clings to the nursing-bottle. Science asserted that the world had stood for 10,000,000 years, but when you come to shake a $10 bill at a savant and ask him to cover it he loses faith in his assertions. Art had decorated cuspadors until any man with the instincts of a gentleman felt obliged to spit in his coat-tail pocket. Two-gallon jugs had been turned into such objects of *vertu* that drink for harvest hands must now be carried in the field in sedentary and unromantic wooden pails. But Art had only been awakened—only been measured for its first pair of shoes. The day was coming when every fashionable dwelling in America would outshine a circus band-wagon, and every kitchen woodbox would reflect scenery so wild as to frighten small children into fits. We are not progressing in Art and Science as fast as we might, and the principal reason therefor is the high price of yellow paint, whitewash brushes and wash-bluing.

The Committee on Agriculture reported fine weather for Canada thistles, and that sunflowers were coming out right smart.

The Committee on the Judiciary reported in favor of a law making it a penal offense for a butcher-cart to run over more than six persons per week.

The Committee on Foreign affairs advised the recall of twelve American Consuls, and the substitution of the same number of cheap stone dogs in their stead.

The Committee on Ways and Means reported in favor of substituting hymn-books in the Indian rations in place of flour, and after a sharp debate on what sort of binding should be used in case the change was made, the meeting went home by the shortest cuts.

NONE O' YOUR BUSINESS.

"WHEN a man axes me who libs nex' doah," began the old man as the triangle sounded to order, "I answer him Brown or Jones or White, or whatever de name may be, but when he goes beyond dat an' axes what salary de man airns, how often his wife changes bonnets an' how dey make seben dollars a week go furder dan I kin fo'teen, I become a clam. I has no business to know, an' when I do know I won't tell. I used to have some curiosity in dis direcshun, but I has got ober it of late y'ars. When I know dat a sartin man, receivin' a salary of $12 per week, kin give parties, hire carriages an' dress his wife in silks, it makes me glum. Dat is, it used to. I used to wonder why I couldn't do de same thing on de same money, but I nebber could. When de ole woman used to tell me dat sartin women had new silks, new hats, new close an' new shoes once a month de y'ar roun', an' we havin' to lib clus on de same money, it made me mad. Dat is, it used to. When I saw men who owed fur deir washin' struttin' aroun' like lords, while I had to work seben days in a week an' pay my debts, I felt like smash-in' frew de sidewalk. But I has got ober all dis When I meet a woman who kin dress like a banker's wife on de $10 or $12 per week paid her husband, I doan' 'low myself to eben fink about it. When I see a man buyin' twenty-cent cigars, sportin' a cane an' takin' champaigne, while his chillen at home am bar'fut, I try to believe dat it am all right. When a lady wid $300 worf of close on axes me to do a job of whitewashin' in a parlor whar de bes' pictur's come from a tea store an' de' bes' cha'r am under chattel mortgage, I doan' stop to wonder who she thinks she am foolin'. Nayburs ob mine who owe all de butchers widin a circle of a mile, kin pay fo' dollahs cash fur a libery rig on Sunday an' I shant criticise. Wives may go shoppin' ebery day in de week an' gin parties ebery night, an' my ole woman will keep de cabin jist de same. Since we quit wonderin' an' speculatin' ober dese fings we feel much better. We know fur a fact jist how fur we kin make money go. If odder folks kin lib like lords on a salary of $600 a y'ar it's a streak of good luck an' none of our bizness. My advice to you am to let sich fings pass. Dey are mysteries wid which we have no bizness, an' de mo' you ponder ober dem de less you will injoy what you have honestly airned by hard work an' saved by good economy."

CAN'T TELL YET.

A communication from South Carolina made inquiry as to whether the Lime-Kiln Club was in harmony with the various State Legislatures, and Brother Gardner replied that he could not return a decided answer yet. They were in harmony on finance, foreign policy and civil service reform, and all had faith that cold tea was good for weak eyes, but they might differ on other questions. He had prepared and intended to forward to the different legislative bodies the following resolution:

Resolved, Dat we refuse all free passes on railroads, discourage set speeches, oppose a long seshun, favor a reduction of salary, an' agree not to vote fur any private bills."

All those who adopted the above would be closely in harmony with the Lime-Kiln Club.

ABOUT EMBLEMS.

A communication from Oberlin, O., signed by Judge Burnett, Ben Colwell, Prof. Lane and other colored men of national renown, stated that the colored people of the Buckeye State had concluded to adopt the sunflower as their emblem, and the assistance of the club in making it national was solicited.

"I doan' take no stock in emblems," replied Brother Gardner as the letter was filed for answer. "De laziest crowd I eber knode had a beaver fur it's emblem. I have seen a dozen saloons wid bee-hives ober de doahs. A man may take a white dove fur his emblem an' yit keep his wife carryin' a black eye ten months in de y'ar. If de cull'd people of Ohio feel de need of an emblem de sunflower is as good as any odder. It's a flower which stays out all night widout goin' to sleep nex' day. You can allus tell whar' to find it. It grows faster dan de turnip, an' produces a bigger head dan de cucumber. Dis Club won't pledge itself to any perticklei emblem at present, but will continue to do white washin' at de same reasonable figgers, an' put a better shine on a stove fur twenty-five cents dan any odder Club does fur forty."

A HARD TASK.

The Committee on Pains and Anxieties, who were several weeks ago ordered to investigate the subject of warts, corns and bunions and report thereon, now announce that their investigation had been pushed as far as possible, with but few satisfactory results. They would report:

1. "De wart doan' amount to much onless it comes on de eand of de nose. We traced it back to de y'ar 740, an' den we got tired an' went home. Warts am sometimes a sign of a culchured mind, an' sometimes dey ain't. De way to git shet of 'em is to riz up at midnight fur three successive nights an' make faces at yerself in de lookin'-glass.

2. "De co'n wouldn't be noticed by any respectable pusson if it didn't grow on de foot. We kin trace it back to de drift period, an' we kin give a list of ober 10,000 distinguished pussons who hev had from one to fo' at a time. Dar am ober fifty cures for co'ns, not one of which am wuth shucks. One of de bes' remedies we know of am to hev boaf feet cut off at de ankles. In dat way you am sartin to git de bulge on 'em.

3. "De bunion am an invenshun to take de place of knockin' a man down wid a rail an' draggin' him all ober a hull county by de ha'r of his head. Arter a bunion freezes to you it can't be coaxed to go on a wacashun, nor bribed to let go an' tackle some odder mortal. It goes to bed wid you an' rises up wid you an' it neber lets you forget dat it am on han' an' fully prepar'd fur de bizness. Pussons hev got rid of 'em by gwine ober Niagara Falls, an' by walkin' on de railroad track."

SWEARING OFF.

"We am now about to cloze," said the President, as he looked over Waydown Bebee's head at the clock, "an' I want to say a word about swarin' off on New Y'ars Day. Doan' do it. De man of bad habits who waits fur a sartin day in order to swar off, won't reform wuth a cent. It is my opinyon dat we mus' take de comforts of life as we go 'long. If you like to smoke keep on smokin'. If you like to chaw, keep on chawin'. If you hev any pertickler expreshun which you use when you stub your toes agin a stone, doan' let go of it simply bekase a new y'ar has come. All dat am 'spected of you am dat you airn your money honestly, pay your debts promptly, use your family well, an' cast your inflooence on de side of right. I shall look fur you to do dis all de time, widout settin' any sartin day to begin. De man who has bin waitin' fur a hull y'ar fur de first of Jinuary to arrove so dat he can promise to brace up am not wanted among us. Dis Hall will be open to de public on Monday, an' I hereby extend a hot invitashun to de Common Council, Board of Educashun an' odder public bodies to come in purceshun an' drink sweet cider from an old-fashioned tin dipper. Let us now abscond."

CHAMPION POETS.

THE Committee in whose charge the prize poems on the watermelon have been given as fast as received since August 1st, reported that 126 poems had been altogether received, each one written by a colored man. The choice of the Committee had rested on the three following named efforts:

First prize—"Softly Stealing Through the Melon-patch," by Juneberry Smith, of Arkansas. Mr. Smith can take his choice between a hand-painted back-action autograph of Capt. Kidd, or $3 in money.

Second prize—"Down where the Melon Pined," by Killem Davis, of Tennessee. Mr. Davis privileged to a choice between a pen-wiper used by Oliver Cromwell when he signed the Declaration of Independence or a $2 bill with a corner torn off.

Third prize—"Bury me Whar' de Melons Grow," by Destructive Skivers, of Illinois. Mr. Skivers has the choice between an eight dollar note of hand against William Penn or a silver dollar with a hole in it.

While the Committee were limited to three prizes, and while they endeavored to select the best, the other 123 poets need not feel discouraged. There is room for all, and those who continue to court the muses must some day achieve success. Any one of the rejected poems would bring the highest cash price per pound even when the market was overstocked.

SOME OBSERVASHUNS.

"Doorin' my three score y'ars of life I hev observed some curus things," said Brother Gardner, as the thermometer showed 98 degrees and rising. "I hev observed, fur instance, dat de men mos' cousarned 'bout de welfare of de kentry am de men who do de least to prosper her.

"I hev observed dat de politishun who sots out to save de kentry am ginerally hauled up fur robbin' her.

"I hev obsarved dat de men who seem to hev de mos' sympathy fur de poo' neber wait five minits to foreclose a chattel mortgage.

"I hev observed dat good cloze an' impudence will pass fur riches an' educashun.

"I hev obsarved dat brag an' bluster am better weapons dan argyment an' truf.

"I hev observed dat a grand monument in a graveyard doan' hide de meanness of a dead man's relashuns.

"I hev obsarved dat charity kin make paupers almost as fast as a conflagrashun.

"I hev obsarved dat while all agree dat honesty am de best policy, not one man in a hundred hesitates to work a lead nickel off on a street kyar company.

"I hev obsarved many odder things equally strange and inconsistent, an' I am prepared to say to you:

"Mottoes doan' mean bizness.

"Maxims kin be forgotten faster dan written.

"Promises am a wheel wid one cog gone.

"Friendship will last as long as you kin afford to pay ten per cent. per annum. Let us now purceed to bizness."

THE FIRST TWINGES.

Colonel Anniversary Williams said he took the floor in the interest of 4,000,000 colored people. During the past three days he had felt that uneasy motion around his heels which precedes an outbreak of chilblains, and by this time next week he expected to have a full-grown mine on hand. This early outbreak of symptoms was sufficient to excite the gravest alarm, and he hoped the Kime-Kiln Club would come to the rescue by securing a remedy at whatever cost.

The Secretary was instructed to offer a reward of $50 for a certain remedy, and likewise correspond with the Agricultural Department and ask if Gen. Le Duc did not, some six or seven years ago, advise chilblained patients to wear cornstalks in their boots for a cure.

A DELICATE QUESTION.

A letter from a Fourth Ward Alderman in the City of Mobile, contained an inquiry as to how far a member of the Lime-Kiln Club was licensed to save property at a fire, and Brother Gardner replied:

"Dat am a delicate queshun to handle. If a member of dis Club should be aroused at midnight by de cry of fiah, an' should find dat de flames was devourin' de grocery on de co'ner, he would naturally feel like rushin' in an' helpin' to remove de sugar, an' coffee, an' codfish an' flour. In his excitement an' zeal, he might tote some of de stuff home to keep it from de flames. I doan' say dat de only safe plan am to sit on top de fence an' see de stuff burn up, but I warn all members of dis Club to keep so powerful cool in time of fiah dat a sarch warrant nex' day won't turn up a box of soap in de hencoop."

RESOLUTION OF SYMPATHY.

Giveadam Jones then offered the following one-horse resolution:

"*Resolved,* Dat dis Club extends its heartfelt sympathy to the people of each an' ebery State in which there am to be a Session of de Legislachure dis winter."

The resolution was adopted by a vote of 168 to 1, Elder Toots voting in the negative to spite Samuel Shin for waking him out of his first nap.

AGRICULTURE.

THE Committee on Agriculture submitted its regular quarterly report through the Chairman, Prof. J. Skyhoof, who is now in constant correspondence with the heads of all agricultural bureaus in the world. The report showed:

1. That the soothing-syrup plant can be successfully cultivated as far north as Michigan, and that the crop always averages fair to medium, no matter what the season.

2. Speckled cabbage is steadily growing in favor, and will eventually drive all other styles out of the market.

3. It costs no more to raise an acre of carrots than it does to raise an acre of old stumps, thistles, bobsleds, broken down wagons and used-up plow-points, and a roasted carrot will cure the worst case of earache in seven minutes by the watch.

The Committee recommended the use of windmills wherever there is any more wind than needed by local politicians, and have the fullest confidence that the Dairy interests of America can be greatly increased by milking the cows on the left-hand side.

RESOLUTION DEFEATED.

The Rev. Penstock offered the following resolution:

"*Resolved*, Dat de Lime-Kiln Club will use its inflooence on all possible occashuns to suppress de brutal and barbarous bizness of prize-fightin'.

Medicated French called for the ayes and noes on the resolution, and without further remark the roll was called and the resolution was voted down by a majority of thirty-six.

" While dis Club may not favor prize fightin'," observed the president, "it seems to hold dat if two brutes want to go out an' pound each odder to pieces it am cheaper to get rid of 'em dat way dan to hang 'em."

PETITIONS.

Among the the thirty odd applicants for membership were two of the most famous co'ored men in America—Gen. Napoleon Dodo, of Toronto, who first applied sour milk and mashed potatoes for the cure of chilblains, and Judge Slipback Cassowary, of Virginia, who invented three different attitudes for safely milking a kicking cow. Both of them have stood in the shadow of the Pyramids, floated on the Nile, climbed the mountains of Switzerland and been swindled at Niagara Falls. They are now ready to join the Lime-Kiln Club, buy a checkerboard and a corn-cob pipe and settle down for a life of domestic peace.

INDEMNITY WANTED.

The Secretary announced a letter from a Mrs. Wallaby Smith, of St. Thomas, Ont., demanding

$1,000 of the Club to indemnify her for the loss of her husband. Against her earnest protest he had decided to become a member of the Club, and while on his way to the postoffice to mail his application he fell over an embankment and broke his neck. The Club was therefore responsible for the accident, and the $1,000 could be forwarded by express or draft on New York. The Secretary was instructed to deny jurisdiction and responsibility, and to vigorously defend any attempt to deplete the treasury.

ONLY SONS AND A PROTEST.

"If I had an only son," began the old man as the lights were turned up and Biblical disputes suddenly ceased, "if I had an only son, an' he growed up as only sons are pretty sartin to do, an' he went off on a Sunday skule picnic an' got drowned, I should feel a leetle sorry an' a heap thankful. If I had an only darter, an' she growed up as only darter's allus grow, an' she run away wid a lightnin'-rod man an' was left in de po'-house, I should be a leetle sorry but not a bit surprised. De family wid an only son or an only darter needs no odder trouble. When you meet a man who carries his cigars in his hind pocket an' goes off behind de barn to take a chew of terbacker, sot him down fur an only son. When you meet a man who flusters an' brags an' secks to lord it ober odder people you have foun' an only son. When you meet a man who finks de world was made fur him alone you have met an only son. De only son am de man who takes up two seats in de **kyars—who crowds de chill'en at a festival—who** eats hisself sick when he pays two shillins fur all he kin eat. I doan' say dat he am to blame, but I do say dat de world feels relieved when he goes to his grave. Once in a life-time you may h'ar of an only son who hasn't turned de family out of doahs nor had all de nayburs fur a mile aroun' shoot at him an' offer to buy him a tombstone, but be keerful how you believe it.

"When you meet a woman who puts you in mind of selfishness out fur an airin', sot her down as an only darter. When you fin' a woman who expects de kyar to stop in de middle of a block—when you meet a woman whose husband am allus ready to dodge, sot her down fur an only darter. De only darter grows up to whine an' complain an' tyranize an' make de world mo' wretched fur people wretch-'nuff befo'. De odder day I was called upon to go ober to a naybur's an' box de years of an only darter whose poo' ole mudder lay upon a bed of sickness, an' I must say dat I kinder enjoyed it. Dat same ebenin' I was called upon to visit anoder naybur whose only son wanted to sell de family cook stove to buy him a yaller dog an' a single-barreled shot-gun. I had a short struggle wid de young man, an' he won't be out of bed fur a week to come.

"My exper'ence is dat a family which de Lawd has forsaken arter sendin' one chile, has woe an' sorrow in de household. Selfishness takes root dar' an' grows amazin' fast. Wickedness creeps in dar' an' neber lets go. De small-pox kin be stamped out —de yaller fever mus' give way to frost—de cholera only settles down heah an' dar', but de only chile am allus wid us, he or she meets us ebery day, **walks wid us frew life—brings upon us de larger** sheer of our miseries. Pity de fadder wid an only son—thrice pity de mudder wid an only darter. Wid dese few configgerashuns, frown out in a speerit of astonishment an' intensity meant to accomplish no desirability in perticklcr, we will now close de winders, put a leetle mo' wood in de stove, an' purceed to asphyxiate de transcedent order of de inviduous programme."

SETTLED.

Of course, the Rev. Penstock arose. He couldn't stand that motion. He inquired if it was the intention of the Chair to let those last remarks be spread upon the regular minutes of the meeting?

"It am," was the quiet reply.

"Den I protest. De language am unparliamentary an' foreign to de pint."

"Brudder Penstock, do you charge dis Cheer wid usin' foreign language?"

"No, sah! I charge de Cheer wid makin' bad use of de English language."

"Brudder Penstock, you jined dis Club fo' y'ars ago. You am a preacher of de Gospel, an' you has trabeled. You has bin down to Tennessee, Kentucky, Georgia, South Carolina, an' Alabama. You imagine dat you has seen de elefant an' tooken in de circus. On varus occashuns you has disinterrupted de harmony of de meetin' to k'rect de language of dis Cha'r, an' on varus odder occashuns you has intimated dat de purceedins lacked chic an' tone. Bekase you know what *sic semper cum digis solis pluribus curantea* means in English, you regard de rest of us as poo' ignorant black trash. Brudder

Penstock, you has reached de end of de clothes-line!"

"But, sah—but—"

"An' you must stop! I'ze bin 'lected ober all opposishun to run dis Club. You mus' not disinterfere wid me. If you persist in so doin' I gib you fa'r warnin' dat I shall lay aside Mr. Cushin's manual, walk down de aisle, an' move de prevus queshun in such a manner as will seriously interfere wid your feelin's. Drap back on your cheer, Brudder Penstock—drap back."

"Brother Penstock "drapped," but he is a man who can't be long suppressed.

DRED SCOTT DECISION.

"WILL Brudder Dred Scott Hastings step dis way?" blandly inquired the President after the votes were counted.

Brother Scott stepped up with a grin on his face as if he expected to draw a chromo, and the President continued:

"Brudder Hastings, fo' weeks ago you was tooken sick."

"Yes, sah."

"You called in de doctor, put a hot brick to yer feet an' sent word to our Relief Committee to file your claim for $3 per week."

"Yes, sah."

"Dat committee reported favorably on your case, an' de money was sent you—$3 per week fur two weeks. Your illness was said to be chills an' fever."

"Dat was it, sah."

"Just so; but what brung'em on? Brudder Hastings, I diskivered yesterday dat you got into a dispute wid a naybur about de aige of Moses when he died, had a fight an' was knocked into a ditch full of water. Dat was what started your chills an' fever."

"I—I—yes, sah."

"An' you lied to de Relief Committee when you claimed to have got wet comin' home from a funeral!"

"I—I didn't mean to, sah."

"An' you wilfully an' maliciously put up a job to rob dis Club of $6?"

"I'll pay it back, sah."

"No, you won't! You haven't seen de time in de last fifteen y'ars dat you had $6 to spar'. Dat money am gone, an' you am gwine to follow arter it! You kin take down your hat an' walk out of Paradise Hall fur de las' time. We want no men in dis club dat cares wheder Moses was seventy or 700 y'ars old when he died, an' we will not keep de name of a liar an' deceiver on our books. Walk out, Misser Hastings—walk right out."

Mr. Hastings walked and it was noticed that several parties near the water-pail looked as if they expected another bomb-shell to fall somewhere.

A GREAT GAIN.

"GEM'LEN," began the old man as the dust settled down a little, "I war called upon las' evenin' by de Hon. Joseph Jackson, of Kenedy. I spect dat man am one of de biggest cull'd orators in dis kentry, an dat what he doan' know am not worf knowin'. Arter we had talked an' talked, he squar'd off to me an' says he: 'Brudder Gardner, you hev bin runnin' dat Lime-Kiln Club eanemoas' two hull y'ars. De purceedins hev purceeded reg'larly, an' heaps of bizness hez bin split to pieces, but what hez bin gained? What good hez dat Club did? Who has been made gooder?' I could hev made de ole Canuck a speech fo' hours long in reply. What hez dis Club did? Two y'ars ago de cull'd men in dis town war pullin' an' haulin dis way an' dat way, cuttin' down on de prices of whitewashin' an' cuttin' up on de prices of stove-blackin'. Nobody seemed to know nuffin'. Our Samuel Shin didn't know 'nuff to peel onions, an' now he am de leader of a string band, belongs to de church an' hez a barber shop. Waydown Bebee couldn't even read an' was in rags; to-day he kin read an' write an' figger, wars good clothes, an' who keeps a better barber shop dan Brudder Bebee? Elder Toots, ober dar, was in de jug, his wife had run'd away, an' life was nuffin to him. Am dar a happier man in dis town now dan Uncle Toots? I kin show you forty men who hev l'arned to read. I kin show you big changes in home circles. I kin show you dat dis Club has paid off debts, re-united families, clothed children, helped de sufferin' an' put pride into low-down hearts. Isn't dat 'nuff? Am dar any member who could ax fur more?"

Speeches were made by Sir Isaac Walpole, the Rev. Penstock, Josephus Bottle and others, and every member of the Club seemed satisfied that the workings of the Club had been all that could be expected.

ABOUT KIND WORDS.

"I saw in de papers de odder day," began the old man, after carefully wiping the top of his head, "a leetle item 'bout speakin' kind words to our fellow-men as we trabbel de highway of life. Dat's easy 'nuff to do, an' a mighty cheap way of scrubbin' 'long, but I doan' want nobody to practice it on me. If I use dem right; dey will use me right, an' we kin trade kind words. If you meet a man in de gutter, doan' stand on de sidewalk an' tell him dat you am ready to bust wid sorrow, an' dat you solemnly wish he wouldn't do so any mo'. Stan' him on his feet an' start him fur home, an' let his wife an' de poker run de kind word bizness, or hunt fur a purleceman an' have de drunkard boosted for sixty days. If you meet a poo' man, whose wife am lyin' dead in de house, doan' wipe yer eyes an rattle yer chin an' tell you'd jine de funeral purceshun if you only had a mule. Walk right down inter yer west pocket fur half yer week's wages to help pay fur de coffin an' odder expenses. If you meet a feller-man who am out of wood an' meat an' flour, an' has a broken arm to excuse it, doan' pucker yer mouth an' tell him dat de Lawd will purvide. De Lawd doan' furnish purvishuns fur dis market. Instead of droppin' a tear of sorrow on de doah-step, step aroun' to de woodyard an' de grocer's an' lay down de cash to feed an' warm de family fur a fortnight.

"When I meet a leetle gal who has lost her doll-baby, or a leetle boy who has stubbed his toe, I take 'em up in my arms an' wipe deir leetle noses an' sot 'em down wid a handful of peanuts. When I meet a widder who am out of wood, an old man who has bin turned out doahs, or a workin' man whose home am under de shadder of death, I doan' lean on de fence an' look to Heaben fur relief. If I'ze got a dollar I lend it out. I lend it or give it, or make em take it, an' if Heaben does anyfing furder dat's extra. When you read dat it am easy to speak kind words, jist reflect dat it am also de cheapest way in de world to help a naybur. Turnips am quoted at forty cents a bushel; kind words have no value in de market. Let us now attack de reg'lar order of bizness."

A DANGEROUS FAILURE.

At this juncture the Keeper of the Pass-Word announced that Prof. Boliver Jackson, of Halifax, Nova Scotia, was present with his Back-Action, Three-Ply, Full-Jewelled Heel-Compressor, and would like to give an exhibition before the Club. Brother Gardner explained that the Secretary had had some correspondence with the inventor, and that the gentleman had come on at his own expense. There were colored people just foolish enough to feel ashamed of the long heels given them by nature to make their mark in the world, and this Heel Compressor had been invented to reshape the foot. He was perfectly satisfied with his own feet, but he would have the machine brought in and let any member of the Club try it. Prof. Jackson was accordingly admitted, and he placed his invention in the center of the room and delivered a short lecture on his long struggle to secure what the colored race had so long sighed for. He warranted it to work smoothly, evenly and satisfactorily in all respects, and Pickles Smith volunteered his feet to be experimented on. **Pulling off one of** his cow-hides he placed his right foot in the box, and the Professor began turning the crank and singing: "We Shall Never Meet Again." At the seventh turn of the crank the springs encountered a corn fourteen years old on Brother Smith's heel, and an explosion took place which knocked the Professor down, pitched Samuel Shin into the wood-box, and shot Smith headlong down the Hall on his stomach. Five of the lamps were extinguished, one of the bear-traps thrown down, and 117 new cracks appeared in the ceiling. It was a great wonder that no one was killed, as pieces flew here and there, and one cog-wheel weighing four pounds was hurled through a window and knocked a shower of shingles off an ice house. There was great confusion for two or three minutes, during which time the Professor leaped from a back window into the alley and escaped.

"Gem'len, what does dis prove?" asked the President, after order had been once more restored. "It proves dat de pusson who ain't satisfied wid de way Natur' did her work comes next doah to bein' a fool. Let dis be tooken as a solemn warnin' to let our heels alone, an' to banish all feelin' agin de white man kase he has straight h'ar."

THE AMENDE HONORABLE.

As soon as the meeting opened in due form Giveadam Jones secured the floor and stated that he desired to render justice to an innocent man who had been dwelling under a cloud of suspicion for the past week. It had been hinted around that the Hon. Burdock Cantelope, acting as Janitor during the absence of Samuel Shin at Long Branch, had embezzled a large sum of money. His account, as handed to the Secretary for approval, read as follows:

	1881.
1 quart oil	10
1 lamp wick	1
1 cup	5
Total	1,881 16

It appeared from the above that the Hon. Cantelope had used up $1,881 for which he could render no account, and the Committee on Finance were ordered to investigate, and empowered to send for persons and papers. After a long wrestle with the mystery it was discovered that the Janitor had added the year to his expense account and thus made himself a seeming embezzler. The investigation had cleared his character as white as bleached cotton at fifteen cents a yard, and the Finance Committee had given him a vote of confidence.

A MISS.

The Secretary announced the receipt of a telegram from the Hon. Burkweather Skipp, the "Web-footed Orator of the Wabash River," stating that he had missed the freight train and would not be on hand to deliver his lecture on "The Modern Abuses of the Stomach."

"Wall, we'll have to make de bes' of it, I 'spose," sighed the President. "I know de man perfeckly well, an' as he am deaf in one ear, has a squint in one eye, and stutters like a boy wid a marble in his windpipe, I doan' 'spose we has missed nuffin' dat we can't find when we want it."

THE DEFEAT OF KYFUSTUS.

DISMISSED WITH COSTS.

The Rev. Penstock presented a written appeal from the wife of Kyfustus St. George, stating that her husband was confined to his bed and she hadn't a cent in the house to get her hat re-trimmed for Sunday. The Reverend backed up the appeal in a speech that brought tears to the eyes of Gen. Scott, and jammed Samuel Shin in between the window and the wood-box so hard that it took two men to pull him out.

"Brudder Penstock, did you inwestigate dis case?" asked the President.

"I nebber investigate, sah, when I h'ar de voice of distress."

"Do you know what ails Brudder St. George?"

"I understood dat he was seized wid a chill, an' de arternoon I was in dar his pulse was up to fo' hundred, an' he was outer his head, an' talkin' bout wolves an' bars."

"Jist so—I see. Maybe I kin gin you some pints on de case. I war' out lookin' fur my ole hoss de odder evenin' an' I passed Brudder St. George's cabin. He an' his wife war jawin' as to which owned de dog, an ten minits later, when I returned, de dog was running fur de woods. Kyfustus was lyin' on de grass all broke up, an' his wife was settin' on de fence suckin' a lemon. Arter a man has been knocked into de middle of Jinuary wid an ole base ball bat he am quite apt to have chills an talk 'bout wild animals. I shall dismiss de appeal wid costs."

IT DOAN' PAY.

It having been officially announced that the Right Very, Very Hon. Phosphate DeBar, of North Carolina, was in the ante-room, the Reception Committee put on their white gloves and yellow neckties and proceeded to bring in the honorable gentleman In appearance he somewhat resembled George Washington, having the same generous feet and arch of eyebrow. As near as could be judged he was six feet high, had two hind pockets in his pants, never smoked a cigar costing less than five cents, and was the sort of a man who would fish all day and never swear if he didn't get a bite. When he mounted the platform and bowed to right and left he was welcomed with a cheer which broke four panes of glass and awoke Elder Toots from his first nap.

"DOES HAPPINESS PAY."

In a voice as full of music as a buzz saw cutting through a side-walk spike, the Hon. De Bar announced the subject of his remarks as above, and continued:

" Philosophers an' writers of all ages have told us dat de hight of human ambishun was to be happy. Pick up a book or newspaper an' you am confronted by de announcement dat one who am not happy might as well be dead. We am advised an' talked to an' written to an' urged to be happy, an' it am all nonsense an' has eber bin so. In de fust place no one kin be perfeckly happy. When you get posseshun of a great big watermellyon an' sit down in an alley to devour it all by yerself yer mouf waters, yer back sort o' humps up, an' you fondly emagine dat you am perfeckly happy. But you ain't. You haven't taken ober two bites befo' you remember dat de ole woman wants a porus plaster, an' de chill'en want shoes, an' de rent will be due on Saturday, an' a dozen odder fings cum to mind to knock yer happiness higher dan Gilderoy's corn-sheller. It's de same when you play poker an' win ten dollars. You feel happy fur de minit, an' you dance aroun' on one leg an' chuckle ober yer smartness. Den comes de reaxshun. You remember dat you owe about fifty dollars, an' dat de wood am out, de fiour-bar'l am empty, an' de chill'en have bin cryin fur bacon.

"In de second place, what's de use of bein' happy? [Sobs from Elder Toots.] Happiness doan' increase de price of blackin' stoves. You can't charge any mo' for whitewashin'. [Sensation behind the stove.] You can't git any mo' for beatin' a carpet. [Groans of despair.] Bein' happy doan' help our credit at de grocer's or butcher's. [Sighs.] What dey want is money an' not happiness. Show me a happy man who has any mo' to eat an' war dan an unhappy one. [Distressing coughs from all over the Hall.] It has bin said dat happiness am better dan riches. Doan' let 'em fool you! [Sensation.] De happy man am sent to jail quite as often as de unhappy one.

"In de third place, happiness am not healthy. It runs into liver complaint, consumpshun an' palpatation of de h'art. We am placed heah on airth to bet on de losin' hoss; to marry de wrong woman—to catch on to heaps of bad weather an' deadloads of tribulashun. Doan' go round lookin' fur a happy man. If you find one he'll be somebody so soft dat dey have to put him on ice. Our greatest an' best men am de mos' unhappy ones. Show me a man who has lost three wives by yaller fever, six chill'en by the cholera, three or four houses by fire, an' has himself bin sent to jail on false testimony, an' I will show you a noble Roman. [Cheers.] Thanking you fur your parsimonious imprecations, an' predictin' dat de time am not fur distant when de honor of bein' a member of de Lime-Kiln Club will be all de honor one man kin lug aroun' in hot weather, I now deliberate towards de importunity of de infringement, an' bid you good-night."

The close was received with wild applause, during which the sacred bust of Andrew Jackson fell from its bracket and was broken into seven pieces.

AS YOU FIND HIM.

"When I shake hands wid a stranger," said Brother Gardner, as silence fell upon the members. "I doan' care two cents wheder his great-gran' fadder was a Cabinet Officer or a cobbler; wheder his own gran'fadder sold silk or kaliker; wheder his fadder was a cooper or a statesman. De man I hev to deal wid am de man befo' me, an' not de dust an' bones an' coffins of his predecessors. He may size up well, or he may run to remnants; he may be square or he may be a bilk; he may be honest, or he may hev de right bower up his sleeve—dat am fur me to find out.

"I doan' propose to jine hands wid a stranger bakase his gran'fadder cum ober wid de Pilgrims. Neither shall I lend five dollars to one of my own color on de ground dat his uncle weighed a ton an' shook hands with three different Presidents. What a man am, an' wedder his fadder was a poet or a blacksmith, won't make him any better or wuss. Size up your man on his own personal shape.

" It doan' matter to you what sort of a head his fadder had, or how big his uncle's feet were, he am de man you am doin' bizness wid. De pusson who trabels from dis kentry on nothing but de record made by some relative half a century since, will land in jail as soon as in good society. When I hev any plug tobacker to spare, de man whose fadder didn't do anything but mind his own bizness an' purvide fur his own family, will git it quite as soon as de man whose fadder diskivered a comet or predicted airthquake.

" I want each an' ebery member of dis Club to stand on his own shape. If he am fast color dat's all we want to know. If he crocks or fades in de washin' he must step down an' out. De fack dat Samuel Shin's fadder was lected to de South Carolina Legislature doan' prove dat Samuel hisself knows beans from hoss-barns. Likewise de fack dat Giveadam Jones had an uncle hung fur stealin' corn doan' go to prove dat it would be safe to leave our brudder in a grocery store for half an hour while de clerk went out arter change. When a man boasts dat one of de family signed de Declarashun of Independence, doan' you take his note widout a good indorser. People who lay back on nothin but de glory of de dead or de statesmanship of some one who sot in Congress a hundred years ago am jist as apt to work off a bogus dollar on a sore-eyed railroad conductor as a man whose geological tree has a baker hangin' to ebery limb."

Giveadam Jones was on his feet before the President ceased speaking, and he wanted to know if the remark in regard to his absent-minded uncle was a personal fling at him. Samuel Shin likewise desired to know if the President had intended to hold his lack of education to the contempt of the world at large. Brother Gardner replied that he had used them simply to illustrate points, and but for a slip of the tongue he would have had the uncle steal the whole outfit of a national bank instead of three bushels of corn.

ON TERMS.

The Secretary announced a letter from New York asking if the Lime-Kiln Club was on friendly terms with Congress, and prepared to work in harmony with it during the coming session. Reports to the contrary were abroad in the East, and the friends of the Club were anxious to know how matters stood.

"So fur as my offishul knowledge goes, dis Club an' Congress am on de best terms," replied Brother Gardner. "While I am opposed to any ideah lookin' towards de consolidashun of de two bodies, I still believe dat de welfare of de kentry requires us to work in harmony. We are willin' to meet dat comparatively influenshul body half way in matters lookin' to de good of de kentry. To prove to de kentry at large dat dis Club does not desire to monopolize entire public attenshun doorin' de comin' winter, I will appint Waydown Bebee, Givedam Jones an'

Holdback White as a committee to confer wid an equal number of Congrissmen to agree upon a mutual course to be pursued fur de next six months."

The Secretary was instructed to forward a certified copy of this action to David Davis, and to request that gentleman to name his committee as soon as convenient.

NOT ONE CASE.

The President stated that he had been asked on several different occasions if the æsthetic lunacy had visibly affected the colored people of the North. His own personal observation had not furnished any evidence in the affirmative, but he would like to hear members express themselves.

Kyhaven Johnson said that a neighbor of his had run all over town to purchase a second-hand bedstead, and that she had finally secured one twenty-three years old, but he thought from the hot water treatment given it, that she did not prize it as a relic.

Trustee Pullback knew of a case where a colored man had paid seven dollars for a coat supposed to be twenty-eight years old, but it afterwards came out that he expected to find money in the lining.

Elder Toots said that his third wife had evinced a desire to pay seventy-five cents for an old earthern platter which had come over in the Mayflower, but when informed that if she did she would go without shoes all winter, she had said no more on the subject.

As far as could be ascertained from the best posted members, the colored element are entirely free from lunacy, and not likely to be affected this year,

A RARE GIFT.

After the election, Brother Gardner announced that he had received notice of the shipment to the Club of a rare gift to the museum, being a No. 8 shoe unearthed from the ruins of Troy by Dr. Schliemann. The sole of the shoe bears the letter " H," and is supposed to have belonged to Helen of Troy, as she is known to have worn a shoe of that number. The gift is from the Colored Art Association of Pennsylvania, before which society Brother Gardner will deliver an essay on "Ancient Bunions." The Secretary was instructed to return thanks, and the relic was orderd to be placeed directly over the bear trap.

HIS ODE.

Waydown Bebee then arose and presented the Club with the following original ode:

DE WATERMELLYON.

Oblong an' luscious—
 Black seeds or white
Lemme devour you
 Outer my sight.

Mottled or speckled,
 Thick rind or thin;
Devoid of all cramps,
 Colic an' sin.

Georgia or Jarsey,
 Speckled or spotted;
Dose who doan' like 'em
 Orter be shotted.

There being no further business in the ice-box the meeting adjourned for one week.

WAYDOWN BEBEE.

SARTIN PEOPLE.

"What I was gwine to remark," began the old man as he took an undissolved troche from his mouth and placed it on a corner of his desk, "was to de effect dat it am none of our bizness what our nayburs do, onless dey frow stones at our dog or toss deir oyster cans ober our fences. One great cause of so much unhappiness arises from de fack dat sartin people want to know all about sartin odder people. Frinstance, Deacon Turner's wife runs ober to my house an' tells my wife dat Elder Dorker's wife has got a new bonnet dat neber cost less dan $12. De Elder am workin' on a straight salary of $8 per week, an' he has a wife an' four chill'en. How can he save up $12 on sich a salary as dat? How did his wife git dat bonnet? An' what cheek fur a poo' woman who can't set table for seben nor ride on de street kyar once a week to flam out in dat manner! De wimin sot dar an' talk an' wonder an' get mad an' want ter pull har, an' I slip out an' go to pullin' weeds in de garden. Its nobody's bizness how she got dat bonnet, an' yit some folks feel sick bekase dey can't find out.

"My ole woman goes down town to buy three towels wid a red border, a spool of No. 60 white thread, an' half a yard of linen to make me some cuffs. She am as pleasant as a June mawnin' when she starts out, but when she returns dar am a hull cyclone in her left eye. She pens me up in a corner an' demands to know how de gals dat stan' behind de sto' counters fur three, four an' five dollars a week kin pay bo'd an' washin' and dress in silks and satins. I can't tell, an' de less I know 'bout it de madder she gets; an' bime-by dar cums a climax an' somebody gets hurt. If a gal can make fo' dollars a week go furder dan I kin make twenty, dat's none o' my bizness or your bizness.

"De odder day my ole woman cum home from Jedge Blank's an' said dat de Jedge's hired girl had gin 'em notice dat she was about to go to de kentry on her annual six weeks wacation. Mrs. Gardner was hopin' mad, but I was as cool as a red-hot crowbar. Why shouldn't a hired gal want to go to de kentry an' have a rest from breakin' dishes an' kickin' tinwar aroun' de kitchen? It improves her complexshun, braces up her form, shapes her feet, an' often results in her marryin' a millionaire. If de Jedge and his family can't afford to go, dat's nuffin to do wid de servant.

"Mrs. Kernul Dash was axin' my ole woman only last nite if she couldn't hunt her up a seamstress who'd be kind an' obleegin' nuff to do a few day's work at twelve shillin's a day. She won't git one. Dis am de season when de poo, overworked an' half paid seamstress packs her trunk, draws her money from de bank, an' hies to de seashore to secure de benefits of de ozone an' salt-water bathin'. Arter dey reach Long Branch it am hard to tell one of 'em from de wife of a banker or broker, but dat's none of our bizness. Let yer naybur save, squander, keep sober, git drunk, war good cloze or ole cloze—its nuffin to you. Let us now extricate ourselves upon de reg'lar order of bizness."

SOME VALUABLE RELICS.

Since the last meeting, the friends of the Club in various localities have bestirred themselves, and the

Janitor has been kept busy receiving and opening boxes sent by express. Some one at Elmira, N. Y., forwarded a padlock weighing four pounds, and warranted to be the padlock used by William Penn to fasten his smokehouse door. A friend at Fredericksburg, Md., forwarded the hat worn by Gen. Jackson at the battle of New Orleans. It shows seventeen bullet holes and any amount of old age, and will be highly prized by the Club. A party in North Carolina forwarded a four-gallon jug full of tar, to be used in greasing the hinges of the doors and stoves in Paradise Hall, and the Janitor kept his nose in the jug for the greater portion of two days. Some kind friend in Chicago forwarded the tin coffee-pot used by Martha Washington, and parties at Indianapolis sent on a beautiful cabinet photograph of the last negro murderer in that State. Paradise Hall has not only become a place of meeting for the Historic Club, but a museum and an art gallery of no mean reputation.

NO NAMES MENTIONED.

"Gem'len," said the President, as he looked down upon the bald pate of Brutus Stivers, "I believe dat de good times so long hoped for an' talked about am now on deck. I believe dat dar am a better show for workin' men to-day dan at any time since Jay Cooke went an' fotched dat panick on de. kentry. Wages am good, craps are big, money am plenty, an' you kin buy a swaller-tailed coat good 'nuff fur Sunday wear fur about five dollars. Yes, de good times am heah, but dat am no excuse fur de poo' man to hanker arter dose fings which belong to de rich.

"Last week I was told dat six different members of dis Club had dun gone an' rented lock boxes at de post-office. I won't menshun any names, but I want it understood dat I frown upon any sich piece of extravagance. I doan' believe dar's a nigger in dis city who gets ober one letter per week, an' de ideah of rentin' a box an' gittin, a key an' flourishin' around am all nonsense. De money paid out dat way orter buy shoes fur de chill'en, or 'taters fur de celler, an' we all know it. Las' Sunday I saw certain members of dis Club ridin' out wid livery rigs. I doan' call any names, but I know dat dose men doan' airn ober eight dollars a week at de best. Dar dey was, whoopin' aroun' an' heapin' on style, when dey could no mo' afford it dan I kin afford to whitewash de Capitol at Washington fur de sum of fifteen cents an' board myself. I tell you dat it doan' pay in de long run. You may fink it looks gorgeous to see a nigger airnin' eight dollars a week seated behind a speckled hoss hitched to a top-kerridge, but you am softly mistaken. It looks like somebody would be eatin' thin johnny-cake an' cheap 'lasses nex' Jinuary."

A VAIN APPEAL.

The contents of a formidable-looking envelope on the desk were next made known by the Secretary. The communication was from Casabianca J. Jones, an honorary member, residing in Philadelphia. While on the roof of a building to see a circus procession pass along the streot, he had fallen through a photographer's sky-light and sustained severe injuries. The photographer had refused to settle for personal damages, Casabianca appealed to the Club to stand by him and aid him to carry his case to the courts.

"I move dat dis Club extends its heart-felt sympathies an' forward de money to pay a lawyer," promptly responded Lord Byron Throgs from the back end of the Hall.

"Brudder Throgs," began the President, as he rose up and bent his gaze that way, "dar am no doubt in my mind dat you know all about de bizness of stuffin' sassage an' preparin' root beer, kase I has seen you at work; but when it comes down to a queshun of law, you may be as badly mistaken as de nigger who picked up a red-hot horse-shoe in de blacksmif shop. While it am de dooty of dis Club to purtect an' assist members, what do we know of de perticklers of dis case? De pints of law in de case am seberal. De lawyers would ax how high de buildin' was; if it was brick or wood; whose circus was passin' long; if dat circus had de only sea-lion in dis kentry; if de photographer was at home or down to de sea-shore; if Brudder Jones was standin' still or gallopin' aroun'; if he was gwine inter dat circus on a ticket or meant to crawl under de canvas, an' whar' would dis Club be when de jury got frew wid de case? We doan' take no ackshun till we git bigger perticklers, an' eben den we must go ahead as keerfully as a hen walkin a picket-fence."

A PROJECT KILLED.

Maj. Ahbury Congreeve gained the floor and the recognition of the Chair, and said he had a matter of great importance to communicate to the Club. He had long been of the idea that Paradise Hall should be connected with a gymnasium for the use of colored people only, and he was willing for one to take a liberal amount of stock in a project of the kind and become a liberal patron. He believed that muscular development meant long life, and it had pained him to discover that the colored people of Detroit had of late years entirely neglected muscular development, and that death was busy in their ranks.

"Gem'len," replied Brother Gardner, as he pushed up his sleeve, "I'ze got muscle 'nuff to frow a tramp ober two fences an' a row of 'tater-hills, an' I got it all at de wood-pile. Right in dis room are ober fifteen members who am above sixty y'ars ole an' in de bes' of health. We hevn't lost but one member by death in ober two y'ars, an' green apples was de cause of dat. We doan' want any better health, an' we doan' want any mo' muscle. If we do, we kin secure it at de wood-pile, in de garden, or by handlin' de brush. De man who keeps hisself clean, goes to bed airly, has solid food an' lets whisky alone, will live jist as long as de Lawd intended he should, an' dat's long 'nuff fur anybody. If Brudder Congreeve wants more muscle I kin git him a job of unloadin' a sand-scow. We will now strike de triangle, raise our voices in song, an' den walk de sev'ral ways to our homes, grateful dat catfish hev got down to six cents a pound, an' thankful dat de price of white-washin' remains firm an' de market steady."

ENDIN' UP.

A YALLER dog belonging to Samual Shin was dropped out of the alley window, Trustee Pullback got his feet into the wood-box, and the President fined Cadaver Smith four dollars for upsetting the water-pail into Elder Dunbar's brogans. Then he stood up and began:

"In lookin' ober de papers I see predickshuns dat de world am to come to an eand. Las' nite several cull'd pussons called at my cabin, deir brefs smellin' of onions an' deir eyes bulged out, an' dey want to know what dis Lime-Kiln Club am gwine to do about it. Dey was de scartest lot of niggers I've seen since de close of de war, an' I couldn't get dem out of de house till I'd cut a big watermelon lyin' on de ice fur breakfast. I laid awake all night finkin what dis Club could do in de case, an' long 'bout daylight I cum to de conclushun dat we couldn't help it. If de world wants to eand its gwine to do it in spite of us."

There was a decided sensation in the Hall. The Rev. Penstock said he'd like to draw his salary six months in advance. Waydown Bebee favored going to Canada until after the world had got through ending. Elder Toots awoke and moved the previous question, and Samuel Shin begged to inquire if the coming judgment day also included the white folks. If it did he was willing to take his chances; if not, he should demand that the Civil Rights bill be enforced at once.

"Gem'len," continued the President, as a look of silent scorn crept over his face, "I hezn't got much to say on dis subjeck. De world may eand up on de date menshuned, just as de papers predick, but my advice to de cull'd folkses of dis kentry is to wait ill dey smell sulphur mighty strong befo' dey own up liftin' any chickens off de roost! We will now include to bizness."

PETITIONS.

The petitions numbered twenty-eight, and included two men with a wooden leg apiece, and one man with a cataract on his eye and a touch of liver complaint. Electricity Bombshell, of Wayne, Mich., stated in his petition that he owned three dogs and wore a red woolen shirt and a coonskin cap, but if admitted to membership it must be on his own personal merits. A colored man who goes barefooted and walks in the middle of the road is no more favored in this Club than one who dresses in broadcloth and owns a ten dollar silver certificate.

FRAUDS.

A communication from Elias Tiffle Spencer, of Academy Corners, Pa., disclosed the fact that a young colored man of that locality, answering to the name of L. Y. Gardner, was making a pretty good thing of it by claiming to be Brother Gardner's eldest son. Also that another man of color and cheek was selling a rat trap in that state on the forged recommend of the Lime-Kiln Club, and by displaying a photograph of Sir Isaac Walpole. After the Secretary had finished reading the communication the President arose and said:

"Gem'len, if any member of dis Club had an ideah dat I had a son in Pennsylveany, I might remark dat my oldest son was a gal, an' dat she balanced an eight-pound pumpkin de day she was born. Dat's all de son I eber had, an' de poo' fing was tooken wid fever an' died befo' she was four yars ole. We has got some of de little dresses up home in de chist, an' sometimes when I go in softly by de back way I find de ole woman kissin' dem relics an' weepin' like her ole heart meant to nebber forgit dat she had bin a mother. Dis chap down dar am a fraud of de fifth water, an' I hereby offer a reward of $10 fur his arrest. As to de rat trap dat's another fraud on de Club, an' if we can cotch de trapper we'll put him whar de rats will step on him ebery minute in de hull twenty-four hours."

A QUERY ANSWERED.

During a brief interval of silence Judge Garnishee Johnson arose and asked the President if it would not be well to discuss the Bank Panics.

"It would be well, sah, if dar was anythin' to discuss, sah," was the bland answer of the President.

"But doan' you low dat a bank panic proves anyfin dat might be heeded as a lesson to de cull'd folks?" injuired the Judge.

"Yes, sah, I does," answered Brother Gardner. "It proves dat since de palmy days of de Freedman's Buro you nor no odder man has seen a nigger who had a dollar to deposit in a bank or a shillin' to lose by a bank panic. Sot down, Judge, an' rest yer back."

The Judge sot.

VOTED DOWN.

Henry Plumbago, a waiter in a hotel; and a fine dresser, has for some time past had a sore on one side of his nose and a mole on the other, and he is continually making mistakes, and scratching the one when his intentions were to scratch the other.

Patience ceased to be a virtue at this meeting, and he introduced a resolution that the Club purchase for the use of members twelve hand-glasses.

"What was dat?" asked the President, as he rose up and glanced down the Hall.

Henry re read his resolution, but in a very weak voice, and the President replied:

"Gem'len, de wery minit dis Club begins to emagine dat one of us needs anythin' more scollopy dan a coarse comb, a crash towel an' a hunk of bar soap to keep us lookin' purty, den all orgranizashun will be lost, all interest die out, an' de public will cease to remember us. I take de liberty of puttin' that resolushun in my hind pocket, an' now let de triangle strike, an' de convention draw apart for one week."

THE CASE OF SMITH.

There was a look of business in both eyes as the President found room for his feet on the platform and blandly observed:

"Will de Hon. Injun Rubber Smith please walk dis way?"

There was a startled movement all through the Hall, and Pickles Smith swallowed three of five beans he was holding in his mouth and came near choking to death. Mr. Smith advanced. His left eye was closed and his nose was swelled to twice its natural size. He slumped along to the platform and squared himself before the President's desk, and Brother Gardner cleared his throat and said:

"Brudder Smith, I find by consultin' de dickshunary dat you jined dis Club about seven months ago. On numerous occashuns you hev hearn it talked ober heah dat none of de members should put demselves for'd in pollyticks. We know, an' we have talked it in dis Hall, dat de cull'd race of dis kentry doan' know 'nuff to 'leckshuneer an' run campaigns, an' dat de white folks beat us ebery time we want offis. It hez bin understood by all, dat members of dis Club would go to de poll-evils an' wote as dey thought best, say nuffin to nobody an' go home an' tend to bizness. Didn't you understand it dat way?"

"I speck I did." was the sullen reply.

"But at de 'leckshun de odder day you riz up airly in de mawnin', rushed aroan' to de polls, hollered for dis candydate an' abused dat one, an' long in de evenin' you got into a row an' was so badly pounded dat you had to be car'd home on a doah. What hev you got to say to all dis?"

"I 'spects I'd better resign," replied Smith.

"Brudder Smith, you hez struck de key-note,' continued the President. "Dis Club accepts your resignashun wid de utmost cheerfulness, an' de Seckretary am instructed to draw his pen across de name of de Hon. Injun-Rubber Smith an' write in red ink below it: 'Resigned on 'count of his political engagements.' Mr. Smith, you kin now retire an' devote all yer twenty-four hours of de day to gettin' some white man 'lected to offis an' bein' called a fool fur yer pains. Good night, sah."

Smith retired.

"Am it necessary fur me to say anyfin furder on dis subjeck?" asked the President, as he looked up and down the Hall.

"It are!" solemnly replied Elder Toots, who had been dreaming of stealing hens and awoke just as the police were about to overhaul him. He was trotted out and fined nineteen cents for disturbing the peace. And he dropped down with a sigh as l arge as s nail-keg.

A DEFICIENCY.

Judge Sunflower Truax, Chairman of the Committee on Foreign Relations, here announced that he had a delicate mission to perform. He had been requested by the new Janitor to state that there was a deficiency in the cash accounts of the old Janitor. The Treasurer's book showed that the Janitor should turn over to his successor the sum of thirteen cents, whereas he had only turned over eight. Brother Gardner requested the ex-official to step forward and explain, and he stood up and said:

"I tole de new Janitor all about it, an' he had no bizness to raise dis fuss. Dat five cents was lost down a crack in de flo' out in de ante-room, an' de Treasurer should report it as cash on hand."

"Kin dat five cents be sawn down dar under de flo'?" inquired the President, and being informed that it could, he appointed a committee of two to "sawn it" and report. The result was the acquital of the old Janitor of the serious charge of embezzlement. The committee reported that they could see the nickel under the floor, and that it could be recovered any time a carpenter was called in.

CORRESPONDENCE.

The Secretary reported that he was in correspondence with Profs. Watson, Swift, Peters and others on special points in astronomy. The Lime-Kiln Club does not believe that the moon is inhabited; it does not believe that there are other worlds than this; it does not believe that the world can revolve on its axis unless the axis has something to rest on; it does not believe that it is 93,000,000 miles to the sun.

"We may be way behind de aige," observed the President, as he cast his eyes across to a map of Europe, "but we want to be suah we are right befo' we go ahead. If it am only fifty miles to de sun what's de use of our believin' dat its ten thousand times furder?"

ANATOMICAL.

A letter from Cincinnati, written in very cautious language and signed only by an initial, made inquiries of the President of the Lime-Kiln Club as to the average number of deaths in the Club, and suggesting that the writer and the President might make a good thing by standing in with some medical college and disposing of the cadavers. Great indignation prevailed all through the Hall at the reading of the communication, and a resolution was passed authorizing the Secretary to write out and post upon the door a notice offering $20 reward for the arrest of the writer of the letter.

VALUABLE TIME.

"How many members of dis Club know de value of Time?" asked the President, as he looked up and down the Hall and took a left handed squint at the bear trap.

Some of the members shook their heads and sighed as they remembered how they had wasted time hunting for watermelons which were not there, and after a moment the old man continued:

"I refer to de odd minits an' half hours we all git aroun' de house. When we come home arter a day's work we drap down to rest our backs befo' supper. We hev a leetle time in de mawnin', sometimes a quarter of an hour at noon, an' all dis time added up wid a piece of chalk makes four or five hours a week. Doorin' de past week I hez found dese few hours de most valuable of all. Wheneber I hez foun' a chance to drap down I hez had a book handy. My spare minits fur one week figger up three hours an' a half, an' I learned de follerin' new facks neber known to me afore, viz: Dat fleas neber go in droves; dat if de sun should strike dis world it would upsot all de houses; dat sunflower tea am good for de mumps; dat de moon hez a certain inflooence on rats; dat de smallest star in de sky am bigger'n de City Hall, an' dat you kin look a housefly outer countenance by closin' de right eye. I hez fully l'arned de value of time heretofore wasted in pokin' de firee or spittin' on de stove, an' I'ze gwine to make use of it. Sich members as will pledge demselves to do de same will raise de right hand."

Every right hand came up, and Trustee Pullback was distinctly heard telling Pickles Smith that the first five minutes he could spare should be devoted to finding out who invented the blue mop-handle, and why it was generally preferred to the red.

REMITTED.

Good old Sir Isaac Walpole descended from the platform and asked the privilege of making a few personal remarks. Leave being granted, he referred to the case of Samuel Shin, who was fined $1,100 at a previous meeting for sacrilege. He had known Mr. Shin for several years, and had always respected him as a citizen and a brother of the Club. Samuel was hilarious at times, but such was his nature. He acted on the impulse of the moment, and while not always right, no one would charge him with intentional wrong. He was in steady employment and was now saving about sixty cents per week, and it would take him over forty years to pay the fine imposed. While the speaker would not for a moment question the wisdom which imposed the fine, he hoped that the Club would let mercy and charity prevail in their hearts and give the sad-hearted brother one more chance.

The Hon. Kickapoo Johnson thereupon introduced a resolution remitting the fine, and it was carried by a hearty and unanimous vote.

GUESS IT HAS.

The Secretary announced a communication from the Secretary of the State of Kansas, asking the Club if education and a higher state of civilization had had any influence on the natural courage of the black man.

"De Seckretary kin answer back dat we guess it has," said the President. "Only dis mawnin' I saw one white man chasin' two black ones as hard as dey could jump, an' dey seemed to feel dat dey couldn't jump half fast 'nuff. Answer him dat readin', writin' an' grammar, an' so on, has inflooenced de cull'd man to back up agin a shed when he wonts to fight, an' de furder off de shed am de better he likes it."

VOTED DOWN.

The Secretary's desk further yielded up a well-written letter, signed by six colored ladies of Niles, Mich., asking the Club to take under consideration the proposition to establish a branch lodge for women, to be known and called "The Daughters of the Brush." The letter gave a dozen reasons why such a branch lodge would result in good, and the question being brought before the Club for discussion, a lively debate ensued.

The Rev. Penstock favored the proposition. He said that Queen Victoria was never heard of until she joined a lodge.

Waydown Bebee also favored it. He thought a Saturday night lodge meeting would give hundreds of gates and miles of sidewalk a rest.

Paradise Doolittle was opposed to any such scheme. He thought women ought to be content to stay at home and play the piano and eat frosted cake.

Judge Cranberry also opposed the idea. While he was away to his Club his wife sat in a red rocking-chair and read "Lady Audley's Secret," and no sensible woman could ask for more.

The question being put to a vote, it was defeated by forty-eight majority.

THE SPELLING REFORM.

The Committee on the Judiciary, to whom had been referred the question of a reform in spelling for the colored race of the land, made a full and exhaustive report. Below are given a list of words and the changes in the manner of spelling them suggested by the committee and adopted by the Club:

Old way.	New way.	Old way.	New way.
Apple,	Apul.	Clothes,	Cloze.
Wagon,	Wagn.	Dough,	Do.
Depot,	D-po.	Rough,	Ruff.
Chasm,	Kzm.	Cæsar,	C-zer.
Borrow,	Borer.	Gorgeous,	Gorjus.

The above are only a few samples of the words submitted. It was also suggested and adopted that the following abbreviations be made use of:

N. G.—"No good."
T. B.—"Go to Halifax."
R. S.—"I'll see you later."
A. B.—"Lend me five dollars till Saturday."
C. S.—"I'll put a head on you."
L. S.—"I'll see you in Chicago first."
P. T.—"I don't want a nomination, but I'm in the hands of my friends."
XX.—"And don't you forget it."

THE CLOSE.

The hour of closing having arrived, the old man rolled up his eyes and said:

"Gem'len, remember dat de loudest voice doan' sink de deepest inter de heart. Big words may shut de odder man up, but dey won't convince him. One kind word am worf more dan a pleasant day, while a pound of crackers an' about half a pound of cheese will put more heart inter a poo' man dan all de promises eber made on de hind platform of a street kyar. We will now pass out inter de cold an' crewel world an' seek to our separate homes."

ON THE FENCE.

THREE or four minutes before time for sounding the triangle, a boy with a pair of boots five sizes to large, and a hat big enough to cover four heads of cabbage, climbed the stairs and encourtered the vigilant Tyler in the ante-room.

"Boy, you fly right down dem sta'rs, or I'll make a bar'l of soap outer dat body!" shouted the Sentinel.

"I guess not, sah, kase Ize got a letter heah for Sir Izook Poletall," replied the boy.

"Werry well, den. Now you squat ober dar on de wood-pile till I takes dis 'pistle in to de Seckretary, an' if you try to look inter de lodge-room, one of de biggist kind o' gosts will jump out an' bring ye sich a box on de ears as you nebber heard tell of."

It was a note addressed to Sir Isaac Walpole, and it was from Brother Gardner. He stated that he was then sitting on a rail fence three miles in an air line from the City Hall, defending a load of corn stalks and ten bushels of corn from the attacks of three white men, who had stolen and carried off one load before he arrived. The note concluded as follows:

"De highest duty of a man am to protect his own from de hands of de despiler, an' it may be dat I shell hev to sot here all night. Go ahead an' open an' run de meetin' to de bes' of your 'bility, not forgettin' dat Pickles Smith will b'ar watchin', an' dat Elder Toots allus falls off a bench to de left when he gits to sleep."

SIR ISAAC

Took the Presidential chair, read the epistle to the members and signaled for the triangle to bring order. His first move was to call off the names of the Committee on Agriculture and request them to proceed without delay to the spot where Brother Gardner held the fort and assist him against the common enemy.

PETITIONS.

The petitions numbered only eight, the lightest number for several months, but easily explained on the ground of ᾿lection and the general excitement attending. The only "big gun" in the eight was Warsaw Jones, LL. D., of Lynchburg, Va., who has preached in thirteen different states, and who originated the theory that all living creatures descended from the persimmon and defended it through three rough and tumble fights before the Boston Academy of Science.

ELECTION.

T. D. Williams, June Hastings, H. Clay Lukens and Paine Turner were shaken up in the bean box and shown to be worthy of membership.

THE OYSTER.

The Committee on Catfish and Turtles, to whom had been submitted the query: "Can the oyster be domesticated and made obedient to the commands of man?" were called upon and reported as follows:

"In de fust place, de ister am not purvided with legs nor teef, an' he wouldn't be worf ole bones to drive a cow outer de back yard. In the nex' place his eyes am sot too fur back in his head to permit him to rush frew a brush fence in an air-tine. He hasn't de back-bone to stand up to a row, nor de wings to fly away from one. He can't see in de night, an' he am too lazy to see in de day-time. His gineral build and his average habits proves, to dis committee, dat nature nebber 'tended him to act as a watch-dog nor occupy a bird-cage. As a fish he am a sudden failure. As a grasshopper he can't hoe his row. We turned him ober an' ober, took him in from all sides, an' arrove to de conclushun dat he am fillin' his mishun when he am stewed, fried, or taken on de half-shell. Dis committee darefore asks to be discharged from de furder considerashun of de subjeck, an' will ebber pray."

Elder Hardfoot Stoher objected to the report on the ground that it might encourage poor people to buy oysters instead of pig's heads and spare-ribs, but it was accepted while he was in the middle of his remarks.

THE SICK.

The Committee on the Sick and Relief reported nine cases of illness among the members, three of them very serious. Four of the cases were chills and fever, three had a tendency to rheumatism, and the other two fell off a wood-shed. The Committee had ascertained that the last named members had climbed upon the shed to see a fight going on in a wood-yard, and "through a dispensashun of Providence had been anticipated to the ground below."

"I am de oldest man in de Club," said Sir Isaac in reply, "an' I hez yit to l'arn dat Providence eber mixes herself up wid a fight in a wood-yard. De queshun of relief will, darefore, be jumped ober to de nex' meetin', when Brudder Gardner kin handle it as he sees fit."

A FAILURE.

During a discussion in the Club some time since on the question of preserving fall vegetables, Trustee Pullback annonnced that pumpkins, after being treated to two coats of varnish, could be kept for several years. The Chairman of the Committee on Agriculture was instructed to treat several pumpkins in this manner and report progress to the Club. At this meeting he announced his readiness to report, and said:

"De next time dis Club wants to waste any varnish it had better pour it down a rat hole. It took jist a quart to a pumpkin, 'ceptin' what de chill'en drank up. De fust week dar' was no great change in de pumpkins, but doorin' de second week two of 'em showed signs of de measles, one turned wrong side out, an' de odder two kinder keeled ober to de norf. At de end of de third week de sanitary purlece knocked on de doah an' tole my wife dat if we didn't get dat smell outer de house dey'd send me to de workhouse fur eighteen hundred years. De varnish bizness am a fraud an' a snare, an'it takes a heap of soap to wash it off de fingers."

SNUBBED.

Caraway Fitzjohn here secured the fioor and asked leave to read a ballad entitled "The Lost Schooner," composed by himself and dedicated to the Lime-Kiln Club.

I object," said John Quincy Davis in a prompt manner.

"Sustain de jeckshun," came from all parts of the Hall.

"Brudder Fitzjohn, am dat ballard written in red ink?" inquired the Chairman.

"No, sah."

"Dat's one serius objeckshun. Whar was dat schooner losted?"

"On de Red Sea, sah."

"Dats too far away from home—altogeder too far. What was she loaded wid?"

"De ballad don't say, sah."

"Den we don't keer to hear it read. You hez left out all de main points, Brudder Fitzjohn, an' I hope you'll forgive me when I tell you to stick to de razor an' let poetry take care of itself."

THE LIBRARY.

The Librarian reported that he had now 1,100 volumes on hand, including over 1,000 almanacs, and he suggested the need of more shelving at once. He further reported that his corner had been well patronized since the evenings had become longer, and that he could make good use of the works treating on higher philosophy and modern anatomy.

NO DINNER.

The Rev. Penstock got Elder Toots to wake up and introduce a resolution to the effect that the Club give itself a Thanksgiving dinner in Paradise Hall on the proper day, paying all expenses out of the treasury, and he then jumped up and made a seven minute speech in favor of the project. The idea seemed to take all over the Hall in a flash, and not feeling equal to the occasion Sir Isaac rose up and said:

"De moshun to adjourn am car'd."

DISTINGUISHED MEMBERS OF THE CLUB — SIR ISAAC WALPOLE AND SAMUEL SHIN.

"No moshun—no moshun!" yelled twenty members.

"An' we will darefore repudiate to our homes," he continued.

"Queshun! queshun!" they yelled.

"Gwine home takes de precedence ober all odder queshuns," softly replied the old patriarch, and he put on his hat, closed the books and beat the Thanksgiving dinner question out of sight.

DE CIRCUS.

As the triangle sounded the call for order, all Biblical discussions came to an end, and Brother Gardner wiped off his mouth and began:

"De season of de circus am come. I heven't seen de illustrious han'-bills on de walls yit, but de horn am tootin' only a few miles away, an' in a few days de unbendin' elefant, de musical hyena, de wrigglin' snaix an' de lemonade stand will be in our midst. Doorin' de past week I has recepted sev'ral letters from different parts of de kentry axin' if dis Club favors gwine to de circus, an' last nite two brethren of de church arrove at my cabin to ax me to use my inflooence to prevent de circus from destroyin' de Sunday skule bizness. Now, I has my own personal opinion 'bout dese fings, but I'd like to h'ar from de members of de Club in gineral."

There was a pretty solid chunk of silence after the President sat down, but Sir Isaac Walpole finally got up and said:

'Waal, now, I believe I kin remember of gwine to de fust circus dat struck de State of Old Virginny, an' I reckon none eber showed up in Detroit an' got away from me. I'ze bin right dar, frens, an' I'ze got half a dollar laid by fur de next one. I belongs to de church, I rings de bell fur prayer-meetin', an' I'ze tryin' to live so as to reach dat good place above whar' de weary am at rest, an' fo' de Lawd! I doan' believe dat gwine to de circus has eber rubbed de hide off in one single spot. De man who can't go a circus wid a clean conscience, an' come home de same way, had better set out an' diskiver a kentry for himself."

Several other speeches of like character were made, and the President arose and said:

"Gem'len, let it stan' as de opinyon of de Lime-Kiln Club dat gwine to de circus am twice as respectable as sittin' on de fence an' makin' up faces at de Bengawl tiger in his cage, am a heap better dan beatin' a wood-yard man outen three dollars by movin' in de night. We will now implore de reg'lar bizness of de meetin'."

SICKNESS.

The Committee on the Sick reported that Skylark DeSoto, a member living across the river, had met with a serious accident, having been thrown off the back of a mule. He had applied for relief, and the Committee desired instructions before drawing any order on the Treasurer.

"De queshun am, is dis Brudder 'titled to draw on de relief fund?" replied the President.

"In de fust place, why was he on dat mule's back? Didn't he know he might as well have been on de brink of Niagra? Was he racin' dat mule? Was he racin' de beast aroun' town to show him off? Lastly, was de Brudder sober or drunk? Sich questions should be settled befo' relief am granted, an' de Committee will proceed to Kennedy an' pump de wictim for furder informashun."

A PRIZE.

The Rev. Penstock, who had just returned from the home of his childhood in Toledo, here arose and said he would like to utter a few remarks. Leave being granted, he said he had for a year past been excited in mind over the wholesale waste in oyster cans. Every one of the millions of cans was worthless as soon as emptied of its contents, and he found them rusting in alleys, on vacant lots, beside the curbstone, and wherever he went. His philanthropic interest in the welfare of America, as well as his ever-present desire to encourage genius, had led him to offer a prize of one terrier dog, one hand-sled, one snow-shovel and two dollars in cash to any American who would invent a way to utilize the old cans. The subject had been broached to the Club on a previous occasion, but nothing had been done to encourage the inventive faculty, and perhaps nothing would have been done but for the enthusiasm of Penstock, whose active mind is ever busy with plans to better the dwellers in this great world.

FERTILIZERS.

A communication from the President of the Texas Agricultural College made inquiry as to whether the Lime-Kiln Club made use of any special fertilizer in its agricultural experiments.

"I 'spose I'ze got about as big a garden as any of us," replied the President, as the letter was filed, "an' I 'spose I'ze tried about as many different fertiloozers as any man heah 'ceptin' Sir Isaac Walpole. I'ze put on lime, ashes, salt, saw-dust, old bones, bottles, chips, an' heaps of odder things, but long ago I diskivered dat an old bed quilt, a towel or two, wid free or fo' ole straw hats chopped up fine, an' de hull spread out ober de ground will grow de biggest crop o' melons dat you eber saw. De vines climb right up like a gopher, spread out like city taxes, an' when de melons start to grow you can't stop 'em wid a two mule tean."

RESOLVED.

Judge Peachblossom, who has heretofore kept wonderfully quiet, presented a resolution to the effect that the present rates for whitewashing be increased twenty per cent, but the President rose up and replied:

"I am an old man. I hev seen de melyon crap come an' go nigh onto sixty-five times, an' it has taken me all dese long y'ars to learn to let well 'nuff alone. Too much charge am as bad as too much whitewash. It am now time to repress de meetin' an' go down on de market an' git a forty-cent watermelyon for a quarter."

SCRIMSHAW BAKER, LL. D.

It having become noised around that a stranger from the west would deliver a speech before the Club, Paradise Hall was filled to the last bench, and business started off with enthusiasm.

PETITIONS.

The petitions for the last two weeks counted up thirty-eight, of which Halifax and Winnepeg each sent one, and three came from California. Of the total number thirty-three were careful to state that they owned dogs, and a large number carelessly intimated that they didn't like chickens. Two of the petitions from the south were accompanied by odes written in red ink and worked up to an intense climax. Such petitioners as desire a copy of the constitution and by-laws will please forward ten cents.

PASSED AWAY.

The President announced that he had received a communication from Fort Scott, Ks., giving the particulars of the death of Ebeneezer Flintlock, an nonorary member of the Club, and added:

"Gem'len, de letter states dat he passed away in de softest manner, an' dat his last request was to hev de Club notified of his departur'. I didn't know him personally, but I feel it safe to say dat he was honest, reprehensible, industrious, cutaneous an' well meanin'. P'raps he did't cut no great spread in de world, an' maybe he couldn't deliver a Fo'th of July speech widout mixin' up cocked hats wid gin cocktails, but what he wore he paid fur, an' what he ate he airned by de sweat of his brows. De Secretary, assisted by de keeper of de B'ar Trap, will hang an emblem of sorrow to de knob of de inner doah an' keep it dar for de space of fo'teen days, an' we will now jine in singin':"

> "Beneaf de sod a brudder sleeps,
>   To wake no more—to wake no more—
> Till past de ribber swift an' deep
>   He's landed on de odder shore.
>
> No pain or sorrow kin he know—
>   No words kin reach him in his grave;
> But up in Heaven he'll find dat rest
>   Which Heaven gives to e'en a slave."

The song was well sung and made a deep impression on all the older members. What, therefore, was the surprise of the convention to hear Samuel Shin attempt to add a chorus to the last verse by switching off on "Whoa, Emma!" He was immediately walked to the front, and amidst looks and expressions of indignation he was fined eight hundred dollars and costs. He pleaded anxiety of mind about an overdue water-tax as an excuse, but it was no go, and for some weeks to come he will probably be the most sedate attendant at Paradise Hall.

THE PHOTOGRAPH QUESTION.

At this point the Rev. Penstock, his face illumined with a smile like the background of a Swiss chromo, secured the floor and announced that a proposition had been made to the Club through him. It was that a photograph should be taken of the interior of Paradise Hall with a weekly meeting in full blast, and in return for the privilege each member was to be presented with a copy free.

When he had taken his seat there was a great hitching around, and Trustee Pullback and Enos Skimmerhorn were seen posing themselves as if ready before the camera. By and by the old man rose up and said:

"Gem'len, dar hain't de smallest doubts dat some of us am so awful purty dat we hadn't orter lose any time in securin' our fotograffs at any price, but out of respect for de feelins of doze who hain't any beauty to brag about, we'll wait awhile before consentin' to de proposishun. I an' de ole woman was tooken once, and I tell you it was de worst kind of a give away on our feet. I can close one eye an' imagine what a fotograph of dis Hall would be, an' I doan' want any of it."

AGRICULTURE.

The Chairman of the Committee on Agriculture had a brief report to submit. In answer to a communication from Gen. Le Duc asking for a sample of Michigan catnip grown in the shade of a red picket fence, he reported that he had collected a quantity of leaves and bottled them so that they would retain their fragrance. He stepped forward and handed the President an eight-ounce bottle and resumed his seat. Brother Gardner lifted the bottle shook it, pulled the cork and smelled of the contents, and as he read the label he indulged in a grin that revealed his back teeth. At that moment the Chairman came forward in great haste and exchanged the bottle for another, whispering:

"We doan' hev 'em in our beds, but de folks nex' doah am fairly car'd away by the pesky critters."

"WHERE IS THE LIMIT?"

The Committee on Reception now donned their wide collars and white gloves and proceeded to the ante-room to return as the escort of Scrimshaw Baker, LL. D., better known in the west as "the

Bald Eagle Orator of the Rocky Mountains." After being formerly introduced and indulging in a few preparatory remarks he began one of the best speeches ever delivered in Paradise Hall. The subject, announced above, was handled between drinks of water with a flow of logic like the current of some mighty river sweeping to the sea, and every hit was received with a grand yell.

"When de saw-buck was invented," said the Orator, as he cast a sly glance at Elder Toots' bow-legs, "some folks imagined dat de limit was reached, but it was only twenty-nine days before de world was convulsed wid de news dat de buck-saw had sprung into life. After de buck-saw came de horse-radish grater, an' upon de heels of dis came de glorus news dat genius had given us de far-soundin' tinkle of de cow-bell. [Cheers.] Some men wanted to fold deir hands an' die, finkin' de end had come, but genius plumed her beak an' lo! we had taller candles. [Wild whoops.] Light shone in dark places, but it was no time to stop. Wid one wild swoop of her raven wings genius left at our doahs a jug with a handle an' de wheel-barrow. [Cheers and yells.] So it has gone. We didn't stop wid de clothes-pin but sprung for'd to de ha'r-pin, de stove handle, de jack-knife, de dictionary, ice cream, lager beer, an' odder splinters of genius too many to menshun. We shall nebber stop. What am new dis y'ar will be ole de nex'. Genius will not be content wid replacin' de bed-cord by springs, or de stage by de locomotive, but will go on an' on an' on, until buttermilk kin be drawn from ebery hitchin' post, an' seven-cent sugar scooped in from de roots of ebery lamp-post,

In de language of one of Rome's grandest Senators, '*Pluribue, sylubus unum cum dig!*'"

Cheer after cheer shook the Hall as the speaker closed, and Waydown Bebee introduced the following:

"*Resolved,* That the uniformed thanks of dis Club are sagely due to de great Orator of de West fur de incarcerate effort he has made this evening to entertain, interest and instruct dis Club, an' we do hereby offer him de freedom of Paradise Hall during his stay in our middle."

The resolution was carried with a bang, and after the Glee Club had sung a few selections from Mozart the convention adjourned.

MISSING.

"GEM'LEN," began the President, as the meeting opened, "look around dis Hall an' tell me if you observe the well-known figger of de Hon. Mackerel Johnson. He was present at de last meetin' an' spit all ober de stove, but whar am he now? Ober dar am de sky-blue bench on which he sits an' watches de adventures of de meetin', but he ain't dar now."

A hush fell upon the members. Previous to the opening they had been discussing the origin of the nutmeg-grater, and had failed to notice the absence of the Brother.

"Gem'len, it am my painful dooty to denounce de fack dat de Hon. Mackerel Johnson am now lyin' on a bed of pain an' sorrow," continued Brother Gardner. "A day or two ago, while engaged in puttin' on free different kinds of frescoing wid his whitewash brush, he fell from be scaffold an' laid dar behind de kitchen stove like one struck dead. No bones was broken, but two surgeons rubbed him up an' smoothed him down, an' stuck plasters on him, an' said it would be weeks befo' his system would rally from de shock. I was up dar an' washed his feet an' fed him gruel wid a spoon. He was very low, but he knew me an' winked his left eye. I call dis case up as a warnin' dat in de midst of gittin' rich an' livin' on de top shelf we am liable to be pulled down by de roots or cut down from de top. Even if we hev pumpkin pie, fried eggs, bacon an' 'taters on de table all at once, we must be prepared to leave dis world on two minits' notiss. I see you all befo' me in boundin' health an' frisky speerits, but on your way home you may be shot by an Alderman, fall into a sewer, or pass a house whar de young ladies am indulgin' in archery. Dis world am full of trap-holes, fallin' trees, runaway horses, mad dogs an' butcher-carts, an' de wise man will work for cash down an' be ready for de crash when it comes."

PETITIONS.

The number of petitions was fully up to the average regarding "Hons." "Colonels," and "Esquires," and one fact was particularly noticeable. Nearly every applicant was careful to state that he owned a dog and a shot-gun, thus saving the Investigating Committee much research and trouble. Among the petitioners was Melinda Ann Buxford, of Troy, N. Y., who stated that she either wanted to join the Club or borrow thirteen shillings to pay for a winter hat.

"I move—" began Pickles Smith, half rising from his seat, when the President motioned him to "squat" and said:

"De season of de y'ar fur movin' am dun passed. De Seckretary will reply to de effeck dat her communicashun am placed under a fo'-pound weight on de red table."

AN APPEAL.

The Committee on Hills and Harbors was called upon for a report, and the Chairman advanced and verbally reported that the Committee had been instructed to bring in a list of forts, cities and streets named after famous colored men. The Committee had spent three months in research, and had not been able to find one single instance where anything bigger than a dug-out had been named in honor of any colored warrior, orator or statesman. The Committee recommended that the Club appeal to the government to do justice to the colored race in this matter, and a lively discussion followed.

Waydown Bebee thought the government should name at least three forts after prominent colored men. If the government refused to do so, then let the enlistment of colored troops be discouraged.

Pickles Smith arose with his mouth full of dry crackers and said the—yum—day was not far—yum—distant when the name of the City of—yum—Washington would be changed to Africanus, and don't you forget it!

Trustee Pullback moved that Brother Smith be fined fifteen cents for unparliamentary language.

Buttercup Hawkins supported the motion in a triumphant voice.

The Rev. Penstock arose to a personal privilege, when Camphor Davis hit him with a potato.

The Elder Toots awoke and cried for "order!" and Samuel Shin took advantage of the confusion to tear down the stove-pipe.

Waydown Bebee was about to call for the previous question, when a ripe tomato hit his ear and he changed his call.

Confusion prevailed in all corners. Lexington Knox fell over a bench with a terrible crash, and the water-pail was knocked out of shape as it fell off the bench. The meeting went to pieces in a minute, but when terror reigned supreme, one blast from Brother Gardner's horn restored order and quietness. He stood up, surveyed the ruins, and quietly said:

"De chair hez no words of consolashun or reproach. Human natur' am more streaked dan a citron, an' it will hev its own way. De Treasurer will pass around de hat."

The collection amounted to over twelve dollars, and sorrow and remorse could be read in every countenance. When the cash had been counted Sir Isaac Walpole offered a resolution appealing to the government to recognize the colored race in the future by naming public posts, light-houses, capes, bays, etc., and the same was adopted.

COMMUNICATIONS.

Under this heading, the Secretary read the following from Mississippi:

BROTHER GARDNER.—I take the liberty to inclose to you a copy of the constitution of the first lodge in modern times of the Independent Order of the Improved Jaw Bone. I have the honor to inform you that you were enthusiastically and unanimously elected the first honarary member of our order. If you will give it a place in Paradise Hall, we will send you the skull and cross-bones of a Boston music teacher, sung to death by our long-range Samson last week. With distinguished respect, I subscribe myself,

JNO. SMITH.

Founder of the order, and at present Most High Old Samson.

In further explanatian, the writer sent a printed slip reading:

We, the undersigned, for the purpose of more effectually troubling each other and making life intolerable to our neighbors, do hereby organize ourselves into a league, both offensive and defensive, and under the extremest of penalties subjecting ourselves to the rules and regulations of the following:

CONSTITUTION.

1. This league shall be known as the I. O. I. J. B.
2. The regular meetings shall be known as "Massacres," and all irregular meetings as "Disturbances."
3. The motto shall be: "No peace for the wicked."
4. The officers shall be elected at each meeting, and serve for one week, and shall consist of the M. H. O. S., the M. H. O. D., the L. R, S., or L. R. D., as the case may be, and their duties shall be: The M. H. O. S. shall preside at all Massacres, and impose fines for violations of the rules, and confer degrees on candidates, etc., etc.,

The Secretary was directed to say in reply that the I. O. I. J. B. had the best wishes of the Lime-Kiln Club for its future prosperity, and as the hour for closing approached, Brother Gardner arose and said:

"Brudders, in pacin' off our var'us ways to our var'us homes, let us remember dat de biggest windmill doan' pump de most water. De man who walks right along, takin' in de mud wid de good roads, 'ceptin' de weather as it comes, an' thankfully chawin' away on husks when he can't get corn, will git dar jist as soon as anybody, an' feel jist as much at home when de horn blows."

JUNIUS HENRI BATES.

THE hum of industry greeted the ear of the President as his head showed above the stairway. Elder Toots was telling Trustee Pullback how he was struck by lightning in 1854, Elder Button was reasoning with Samuel Shin on the offence of lying, and the Hon. Ensign Elevator had a drink of water down the wrong pipe and four or five persons were slapping him on the back. In a brief moment tongues and feet ceased to clatter, the triangle sounded, and the regular weekly meeting of the Lime-Kiln Club was duly opened for the transaction of business.

MATRIMONIAL.

"Will my friend Junius Henri Bates please step dis way?" blandly inquired Brother Gardner, as he arose and looked down the Hall.

Junius Henri advanced. He is a young man of twenty-three, distinguished for the noble manner in which he wears his very wide collars, and his good taste in selecting pale blue neckties. He has been a very quiet member of the Club for some months past, keeping his theories in the background and his feet well advanced. In a kind, fatherly way the President continued:

"Junius Henri, it am freely reported frew dis Club dat you am about to take a wife. Doan' turn red in de face, my friend, fur de informashun gibs us pleasure, an' ebery member will be ready to wish you all de happiness man kin take. We am your bes' friends heah, an' darefore I take dis occashun to say a few remarks barin' down on de occashun. No doubt you love de fair gal. Dat's c'rect. True lub excuses a big mouf an' a bad breff. True lub an' steady wages will make plenty of cake an' pie whar befo' dar was euffin but cole taters. Take a wife wid de expectashun dat you kin an' will support her. Figure on leavin' off rough ways an' rough talk. Doan' 'spect dat de Gods above am gwine to buy yer wood an' flour an' meat. Doan' 'spect dat yer life will be all sunshine. Doan' figger dat ye won't have disputes an' words atween ye. Lawd save ye, boy! my ole woman an' me calls names an' pulls ha'r ebery now an' den, but we make up in an hour an' forgit all about it. Be a good man an' a true husband. Keep off de co'ners an' away from de saloons. Make up yer mind dat ye've got de werry best woman in dis world, an' dat ye can't nebber do too much fur her. Dat's all, boy, an' dis Club will be only too happy to be on hand when de occashun comes off."

ABOUT "BOOMS."

The Secretary read a communication from Mt. Lebanon, La., hinting that now was the time for the Lime-Kiln Club to come to the front and "boom" for some of the various politicians.

"Does de honorable President understand de meanin' ob dat word?" inquired the Rev. Penstock, as he drew himself up.

Brother Gardner surveyed the speaker with proud disdain for a minute, and then replied:

"Do I know what a boom means? Sit down, Brudder Penstock, an' doan' forgit as long as ye stay on airth dat I knowed all about booms afore you was born! 'Deed, sah, I was boomin' down frew de cotton, able to do a man's work, afore you had teef big 'nuff to munch hoe-cake. A boom means to git up an' dust. To step to de front door an' yell. To climb to de top shelf an' whoop. To swing yer hat an' shout fur de perlece. To git up in de middle of de night an' sing de praises of a man who has an awful achin' fur offis. Booms! Booms! 'Scuse me, but dis Club has no pollytishuns to fear an' no candydates to favor."

SILENT CONTEMPT.

Elder Toots here suddenly awoke and offered a resolution to the effect that the Club adopt the principles maintained by the lamented George Washington, but Pickles Smith was the only member who seemed to even hear his words, and Pickles squelched him with a paper wad between the eyes.

SIGNS.

The Committee on Atmospheric Influences announced that they were ready with a report, and leave being granted, the Chairman submitted a well constructed report regarding the coming winter. The Committee had been guided entirely by signs, and their reasons for predicting a hard winter were:

1. The thickness of the corn-husks.
2. The unusual number of overcoats in pawn.
3. The anxiety of women to get winter bonnets.

BROTHER GARDNER AND REV. PENSTOCK.
Bro. Gardner "Do I know what a boom am?"

THE LIME-KILN CLUB.   195

4. The way the frogs have gone down for deep water.

5. The hesitancy with which young men climb out of bed in the morning.

6. The unusual number of dog fights to be observed by a colored man who keeps his eyes open.

The report was accepted and filed, and the Chairman sat down with a sigh of relief.

A SHORT SPEECH.

The keeper of the bear-trap sent word from his post in the ante-room, that Jonas Buckhampton, the great American traveler and Alabama statesman, was waiting to be introduced to the Club. The Committee on Credentials were ordered to bring him in, and the President gave him a formal introduction to the Club.

"I shall incline to indulge in a very condensed speech on dis occashun," he began, as he advanced to the front of the platform. "Has any member of dis Club eber perceived de Catacombs of Paris? I war lately dar. To some it am a festive sight, redundant wid joy an' enthusiasm. To odders it brings de pensive tear an' makes de chin wobble. De majority of you may have de impreshun dat catacombs refer to cats an' combs. Ah, my frens, dat's whar ye are lame. Dar's no cats dar—not a cat. Dar's no combs dar, onless ye carry one in yer satchel."

The speaker paused to drink a pint of water and wipe of his chin, and then resumed:

"Jumpin' from the Catacombs of Paris to de Paramids of Egypt, let me ax if any member of dis Club war eber dar? Dey am a grand sight. Men seems no bigger dan a calf compared to dem. Who built dem? Who 'rected dem? Who bossed de job of gettin out de stun, mixin' de morter an' layin' up de blocks? I can't tell. I axed several persons 'round dar, but dey couldn't tell."

Here he took another dipper of water and then went on to say:

"Let us pause an' ax ourselves who invented ha'r ile an' sticken'-plaster, an' let us take a piece of chalk and figger up how much benefit dey hev been to de world. Dats about all on dis occashun, my frens, and I trust dat de impulsiveness of dis Club will constantly detract from de plethora of its immensity."

For half a minute there was an awful silence, and then, as the orator was leaving the room, Samuel Shin fell over backwards off his bench and laughed till Trustee Pullback jabbed him with the brad-awl fixed in the toe of his boot. Samuel was walked out and lectured on the enormity of his offence, and but for his previous good character he might have been fined two or three thousand dollars.

"De plethora of immensity won't hurt us if we stick to our bizness," remarked the President, and order was restored and the business of the meeting went on.

BE WHAT YOU ARE.

When the notes of the triangle gave warning of the hour for closing, Brother Gardner said:

"My frens, de man in disguise am de chap who doan' take comfort. Be what you am, an' nobody else. Doan' pucker yer moufs to make 'em look small, nor pinch yer feet to lessen de bulge. Tryin' to pull on a No. 7 kid glove ober a No. 10 hand am on a par wid spendin' all yer money fur bacon an' den jawin' de ole woman cause ye hevn't got taters. Dat's all jist now, an' we will git under our hats an' impeach de meetin' fur a week."

COMMUNICATIONS.

Jason S. Strong, of Jackson, Fla., made written inquiry for the names of such members of the Club as were prepared to spend January, February and March in that land of flowers, as he desired to show them every courtesy and make their stay pleasant.

The Rev. Penstock heaved a sigh as big as a sawmill.

Sir Isaac Walpole smiled in a way becoming his position.

Waydown Bebee caressed his red neck-tie and grinned until his mouth seemed about to absorb his ears.

"Gem'len of de Club, how many of you am gwine down thar?" asked Brother Gardner as he looked up and down the Hall.

Samuel Shin arose to his feet after an embarrasing silence.

"You gwine down dar to sport around an' fatten up your health!" exclaimed the President as he surveyed Samuel. "Misser Shin, you sot down! If you worry frew de balance of de week widout freezin' your heels you'll be doin' extra well, to say nuffin of gwine down to Floryda."

Samuel sat down with such a bang as to jar the whole Hall, and during the rest of the evening he sat with his feet in Parsnip Hasting's plug hat, just to be mean and obstinate.

VISITORS.

The Committee on Reception reported the arrival during the week of a small colored gentleman and a very large bundle of something tied up in bed-ticking. The name of the man was given the Committee as Vice-Admiral Standhope, of the Italian navy, visiting this country to inspect naval affairs. The Committee might have accepted his statements had the stranger been less exacting in his demands. He wanted to march to Paradise Hall behind a band and a flag, put up at a hotel with a frescoed kitchen and be assured a private box in the opera house every night. The Committee consulted with prominent citizens as to the stranger's claims of official position, and the result was a movement on the part of the Admiral which placed him in Canada just five minutes ahead of a policeman.

The Committee further reported that they had been warned of the arrival of Joseph Q. Flatheart, of Elmyra, N. Y., who would spend a day or two in the city and present the Club with a new recipe for removing paint and grease from gold-bowed spectacles and piano legs.

COMMITTEE ON THE JUDICIARY.

This Committee had been instructed to gather statistics relative to the past and present habits of the American people, and report as to whether the present generation is an improvement on the last. The Chairman reported that they had traveled scores of miles, interviewed dozens of people, read several books, and had sought to thoroughly investigate the subject given them. He reported that there had been considerable change in the habits of the people. A great many people now cut pie with a fork, instead of taking the whole piece in the hand and biting off what they could handily chew at once. Women who used to do their own washings and grew healthy over it, now kept three servants and endeavored to look pale and languid. Men who used to be satisfied with a house-dog, and a poor one at that, must now keep at least three trotting horses and be three months behind in settling up with the grocer and butcher. Boys who would have been tucked away in their trundle-beds at dark thirty years ago, were now met on the streets at 11 o'clock at night, smoking cheap cigars and talking about "the old man's" childishness. Other changes were mentioned, but the Committee could not say whether the innovations had greatly increased the number of murders or added to the population of prisons.

"As to de improvement spoken of," continued the Chairman, "dis Committee am divided. Some of us believe dat de good clothes an' good grammar to be found all aroun' us to-day am a powerful boost on de present ginerashun, while odders put deir finger on de list of scandals, robberies, murders an' skips to Kennedy as an offset. De Committee hez, darfore, concluded to report dat de kentry am doin' as well as could be 'spected, an' dat de present ginerashun can't help what it doan know."

BEYOND THE VALE.

"As I war gwine to remark," said Brother Gardner, as Samuel Shin ceased poking the fire, "we does not know what a day may bring forth. At de last meetin' all was joy an' peace, an' ceptin' dat we 'spected anodder polar wave, we felt dat life was full of pleasant spots an' clam chowder. To-day—jist one short week—it am my prehensive dooty to inform you of de death of our honorary brudder, Judge Clingstone of Memphis, Tenn. From a letter received yesterday, I learn dat he cum to his last hour by fallin' off de roof of a house. What he was doin' on dat roof am not for me to say. De fall broke his neck, an' de doctahs couldn't save him. He was 56 y'ars of age, an' his appetite was good. He jined to dis Club about ten months ago, an' he has taken a very lurid interest in its prospects eber since. He had arranged to wisit us in de spring, an' delibera lecture in dis Hall, on 'How to Live to a Good Ole Age,' but death steps in, an' whar am Brudder Clingstone? What am de common sense of de meetin?"

A RESOLUTION.

Sir Isaac Walpole said that he was deeply grieved to learn that the Judge had passed away, and he suggested a resolution of respect.

The Rev. Penstock thereupon introduced the following preamble and resolution:

"*Wh'aras*, It has come to de knowledge of dis Club dat Judge Clingstone am no more wid us in dis cold vale; darfore,

"*Resolved*, Dat de acute sympathies of de Club in gineral an' of each member in pertickler, am hereby handed to de widow an' de fadderless, an' dat a black ribbon shall be hung on de triangle for de space of thirty days. It am also furder

"*Resolved*, Dat members of dis Club am hereby warned not to climb upon de roofs of houses at dis or any odder season of de y'ar."

The "common sense" of the meeting was adopted, and the President called for the report of the

INTERPOSED.

The Hon. Thomas Juneberry wanted the proceedings "interposed," and the Rev. Python Jones was cordially supported by the instruments as he ascended the platform and sung as follows:

>Some folks am on de exodus,
>An' some am on de walk;
>Ah-ha—oh yes!
>True es gospil!
>An' some am on de talk.
>
>I knows of certain cull'd men
>Too lazy fur to work;
>Ah-ha! Poo' scrubs!
>Hope dey'll freeze!
>De nigger mus' not shirk.
>
>De nigger who works will git de moas' pay,
>Way down! Way down!
>An' dey'll hev de mos' money when it comes Saturday—
>Way down! 'Suah's yer bo'n!

"NOT MUCH!"

A communication from Baltimore asked the Club to take some action regarding the increased consumption of tobacco, and to throw the weight of its influence against any use of the weed by citizens of any color. It stated that over twenty different fatal diseases could be distinctly traced to the use of tobacco, and that millions of money was annually wasted in purchasing the fell destroyer.

Brother Gardner asked for a general expression of opinion, and the following are fair samples:

Judge Crossgun—"Ize chawed terbacky for forty y'ars, an' Ize gwine to chaw her till I die."

Deacon Jackson—"Take away de Fo'th of July, but leave me plng terbacky."

Trustee Pullback—"It keeps de spirits up, cools off de system, braces de nerves, an' I only wish I could chaw on boaf sides of my mouf to once."

Independence Jones—"De man who would take away my pipe would pick my pocket."

Sir Isaac Walpole then presented a resolution to the effect that the Kime-Kiln Club had no emnity against tobacco, and the same was adopted and filed.

ON RELIEF.

The Committee on Local Relief reported that the closing in of winter had created considerable distress among the poor, but a great majority of the members of the Lime Kiln Club were pretty well fixed, as most of them had laid in supplies, and many of them were in steady employment. The Chairman of the Committee reported that he had been waylaid and struck on the ear with a frozen cabbage because he had refused to introduce a resolution granting $20 to enable a woman to make the first payment on a melodeon.

The Rev. Penstock at once arose and introduced the following, which was at once seconded and adopted:

Wh'aras, It has been demonstrated dat human life am not safe onless you cum down wid twenty dollars to help buy a melodeon; and—

Wh'aras, De practice of music seems to inspire malice an' murder in de human heart, to de exclusion of mercy an' pity; darfore—

Resolved, Dat we petishun de present Legislachur to foreclose on a law to de effect dat all musishuns shall furnish bonds in de sum of $5,000 each for deir good behavior.

The Secretary was directed to draw up a petition and see that each member of the Club signed it, and there being no further business before the meeting, it adjourned for one week.

MARY JANE'S PETISHUN.

THERE was an unstudied picturesqueness in the attitude of the old man as he got rid of a cinder in his left eye and began:

"Gem'len," began the President as he gave his nose a last wipe with a red cotton handkerchief, " I hole har in my hand a petishun from Mary Jane Bascomb, of Chicago, axin' dis Club to use its inflooence to suppress extravagance among de cull'd people of de land. I hez been givin' dis subject much thought of late, an' I find dat de last few y'ars hez developed sich streaks of extravagance among black folks dat it am high time some ackshun was taken by an organizashun like dis Club. A few y'ars ago de average cull'd woman war satisfied wid calico dresses an' articles to match, but now whar am she? Why, gem'len, right in sight of my ole cabin, am no less'n a dozen black women who walk out wid deir bombazine dresses trailin' way back, ten shillin' parasols lifted on high, an' hats on deir heads which nebber cost less dan twenty shillin's. An' dis, too, when deir husbands am skeercely airnin' a dollar a day. I hear of fam'lies buyin' ice cream on Sunday, strawberries ebery day frew de week, an' talkin' bont rentin' a boz in de post-offis. I see cull'd men sportin' blue necklies costing fifty cents, an' actually puttin' on kid gloves Sunday mornin! I know of cull'd families in dis town which hev cane-seat chairs in de parlor—yes, gem'len, right in de parlor, an' like a nuff a stuffed cha'r 'long wid 'em! De clean, white floor am kivered wid a carpet—yes, wid a carpet, an' on de walls am chroemeos refnlgent wid gorgeousness! What did our grand fodders an' our 4-fodders do? Didn't dey live an' grow fat an' die honest folks an' nebber have any sich richness? I tell you dat we am livin' too fast. We hez got to hole back. When an honest, hard-workin' cull'd man must hev a stuffed chair to sit down on, a walnut table to eat his meals on, an' reg'lar hinges to de front gate, same as de rich white folks, den you look out to see crime increase an' de measles go whoopin frew de kentry."

MORE HONORS.

Before taking his seat the President read a letter from the proprietor of a hotel for colored folks on Jersey Flats, New Jersey, inviting members of the Club going to or returning from Saratoga to make his house their home at ten per cent. discount from regular rates. In case the Club came in a body he would make a still greater reduction and throw in buttermilk free.

COMMUNICATIONS.

The following communications were read by the Secretary in a voice full of deep emotion:

To the Hon. M. B. GARDNER, President Lime-Kiln Club:

RESPECTED SIR—As Chairman of a "committee" appointed at an "adjourned meeting" of the "chartered and incorporated"

Society of "True and Loyal Brothers of the Seven League" to solicit funds for the further aid and establishment of said "society," do do herein present to your honorable body our petition for "financial aid" in order to prepare, erect and complete a thorough first-class "walking rink," with all the modern improvements (bay windows, hot and cold water, etc.), for the purpose of developing the latent physical powers of the colored race in this, our glorious and happy land. The early remittance of a fifty dollar check will meet with a hearty approval on the part of the undersigned; and am authorized to say that in such an event a "memorial window," with a *southern exposure*, will be erected to the honor and glory of your honorable body on the final completion of this colossal monument of modern architecture. To this will be added a glorious consciousness of having nobly responded to the call of suffering "colored humanity," myriads of whom are daily dying in darkest ignorance of the science and enlightenment of this, our nineteenth century. Heed the cry of the widow and the orphan, which is wafted on every breeze o'er our fair Southern land, echoed in the glens and vales of the Indian nation and borne on this tidal wave to our "migrating brethren" in the wilds of Kansas where gathering renewed force it thunders reverberate on the shores of the Artic Ocean, and with free hearts and willing hands put your shoulders to the wheel.

Most Sincerely Your "Expectent" Servant,

ERASMUS BAILY DEWITT,
Chairman.

"Gem'len," said the President, as he slowly rose up after the reading and took a long squint at the Sacred Bear-Trap, "when de time arroves dat dis Club favors de walking-match bizness I want to be in dat land whar all de populashun use wings stead of legs to git from place to place. De difference 'tween a loafer on de corner an' one in a rink am so mighty small dat an ole man like me am all mixed up, an' we will now drap de subjeck."

THEIR ANSWER.

Last week the Committee on the Judiciary and Buckwheat Interest were asked to report in one week on the conundrum of the Attorney-General of Iowa: "What do you consider the first duty of a man who finds a sack of flour in the road on a dark night, with no one around to see him shoulder it?" The Committee, through its Chairman, the Hon. Benign Crabtree, submitted the following answer:

"De undersigned got to-gedder an' took in de queshun, an' dar war only ten minits in arriving at a delushun. Dat delushun am to de effeck dat sich a streak of good luck doan' happen once in ten thousand years, but when she does happen it am de duty of de finder to take de fiour home an' eat it up to keep it from being struck by lightning."

DISSENTERS.

Trustee Pullback and Deacon Sunshade hoped the report would not be adopted. It was their firm conviction that the find should be advertised in all the morning papers and held thirty days for a claimant. If none appeared at that time the property should be turned over to an orphan asylum. The Club. however, adopted the report by a large majority, and when the vote was announced Samuel Shin's feet made so much hurrah that the bear-trap fell from its hook and cut a bad gash in the scalp of Lord Cornwallis Jones, who was dreaming he was flirting with an octoroon on the ferry boat.

THANKS AND MODESTY.

THE Janitor's face wore a more pleasant look than for weeks before as he flourished his dusting-cloth around and proudly pointed first-comers to a box behind the President's chair. Some kind friend at Marietta, Ga., had forwarded the Club a horse-pistol, once the property of Thomas Jefferson, a biscuit cutter used by Martha Washington, a grindstone on which Andrew Jackson sharpened his knife before paring down his corns, and a coon-skin cap which John Brown had worn.

THANKS.

"On behalf of de Club I return thanks for dese artikles of intelligence an' historic assumption," said Brother Gardner when the meeting had opened. "Two y'ars ago de only artikle of refinement an' culchur in dis Hall was dat b'ar-trap hangin' up dar. Look ober de walls now an' behold what a change! Two y'ars ago none of us could appreciate de red an' yaller streaks in a chroemeo. Now we neber git tired of drinkin' dem in. Progreshun hez been de word from de fust send-off, an' let progreshun be our motto in de days to come. De Janitor, assisted by de culchured Seckretary, an' bossed by de eminent Treasurer, will adorn de walls wid dese furder relics at de speediest convenient occashun."

MODESTY, THOU ART A DIAMOND.

The very first letter opened by the Secretary as he turned to his desk, caused a grand flutter of excitement in the Hall. It contained a communication from the President of a well known college conferring upon Brother Gardner the title of LL. D., and upon Sir Isaac Walpole that of A. B.

"Fo' de Lawd, but jiss listen to dat!" yelled Trustee Pullback, as he rose up and swung his hat. There was a grand yell from every member present, and during the excitement Samuel Shin managed to get in his work on the stove-pipe, knocking it down for the fifth time in three months. When the excitement somewhat subsided, the President arose and said:

"Gem'len, I am tooken by surprise. Had a pocket-book wid fifty dollars in it dropped frew de roof, de cold chills couldn't creep up my back any faster. But surprised or prepared, dar am but one course to take. I shell decline de title."

A groan of anguish resounded through the Hall.

"Gem'len, you forgit dat titles am only worn on de sleeve," continued the President. "We hev seen judges put off de bench for corrupshun. We know aldermen who kin be bought for money. Doctors of divinity hev stolen horses, and bachelors of art hev robbed smoke-houses. I has tried hard to win de title of an honest, hard-workin' man, who kin behave like a gem'len at all times an' in all places, an' dat's title 'nuff fur me. I am pleased at de compliment, an' am pleased to see de Club take it as an honor, but I must firmly decline to lengthen out my name."

"Gem'len an' brudders," began Sir Isaac as he rose up, "I am an ole man. Ize gettin' so tremblin' an' feeble dat I kin hardly walk about, an' I know dat de time am not fur ahead when dey shall hear my knock at Heaven's gate. I hev tried to do right by all, an' dat feelin' am worf a fousand times more to me dan all de titles all de colleges in de land kin kiver me up wid. Tell 'em dey hev my thanks, but dey kin tie de title to somebody who needs it afore he kin git trusted at de grocery."

NINE HOSSES AN' A DOG.

"Gem'len," said Brother Gardner, as Wendell Philips Pratt got away from the stove after burning his knee on the hot iron, " some of de members of dis Club hev risen to de importance of ownin' a hoss an' a dog. So fur as de dog am consarned I doan' keer, kase he am expected to pick up a bone heah an' a cold tater dere, an' scrub around an' keep fat, but de case am different wid a hoss who am tied up or hitched up all day an' all night. I war lookin' round de odder day, an' I found dat out of seven hosses owned by members of dis Club five war so poor an' pale an' sorrowful an' cast down dat life war a burden to dem an' dey didn't care a cent whedder school kept or not. Now, it am my opinyon dat de man who can't even feed a hoss on bran an' dried apples an' make him puff out an' look decent had better sell out an' put his capital into a cart, which doan' hev to be rubbed down or fed or watered, an' which doan' get de eperzootic jist when you want to use it de moas. Last Sunday I saw nine shades an' a dog bein' drawed around by a hoss owned by a member of dis Club, an' de smallest nigger in de lot was bigger dan de hoss. Sech exhibitions of puttin' on style are not only bad on de hoss, but white folks stop on de corners an' cry out: ' De Lime-Kiln Club am gwine up to Fisher's!' I doan' call eny names, but I am gwine to remark dat if de seven hosses, owned by members of dis Club, doan' git moar oats an' hay an' less Club somebody will be walked up heah an' talked to, an' de Club will pass a resolushun to do its sleigh-riden on a hand sled."

ELECTION.

The following eminent gentlemen were put through the bean box with neatness and dispatch: C. Columbus Herrington, of Georgia; Thomas Carlyle Stub, of Pennsylvania; Juan Scott, of Illinois; Thomas Benton Smith, of New York; Thurlow Weed Hopkins, of New Brunswick and Judge Summer Todd, of Ohio. Mr. Scott claims to be the only colored man in this country who can go upon the stage and act the part of "Hamlet." He has had a brother in the Louisiana Legislature, another in State Prison and is otherwise prominent. Mr. Stub's character was vouched for by three Pittsburgh bankers, one of whom added to his recommend:

"I think he'd subscribe fifty thousand dollars to the Washington monument as quick as a wink, if he only had the cash to spare. His greatest failure is his innocence, and the fact that he won't swear when he stubs his toe."

IN MEMORIAM.

Samuel Shin here got the floor, rising to a question of privilege, and inquired if the Club were expected to pass resolutions of grief whenever a Legislature adjourned. He had been informed that over twenty different Legislatures were now in session, and the Club should be prepared with some sort of resolution that could be applied to each body as it broke up in the spring.

"Brudder Shin, dar's brains in your head as well as fat," replied the President. "De queshun am well taken an' de idea good. De Committee on de Judishery will retire an' report a resolushun wid pathos in it."

THEY DID.

The committee cooled their heels in the ante-room five or six minutes ond then returned and reported the following:

"*Wh'aras*, De Legislachur of de State of ——— was composed of all de best talent dat could be foun' in town or kentry; an'

"*Wh'aras*, De body was unanimously in favor of reform, economy an' public wellfar', an' not a speech was wasted doorin' de hull seshun; an'

"*Wh'aras*, Such anodder body kin never agin be collected togeder, for want of talent; now, darfour,

"*Resolved*, Dat de corpse has our heartfelt sympathy, an' de widder an de fadderless our assurance dat what am deir loss am de kentry's gain."

The preamble and resolution were adopted, and the Secretary was instructed to make out as many copies as there are legislatures in session, and hold himself ready to forward to each at the proper time.

REMARKS.

It may be here remarked that no member of this Club is looking for the next Presidency, or wants further renown than what a good, square job of whitewashing will bring him in. The Rev. Penstock used to be a little anxious to spread himself over more or less territory, but of late he has seen the error of his ways and hardly ever interrupts the meeting

AGRICULTURE.

A letter signed Jonas Parker, dated at Scottsville, O , and making inquiries concerning the present buckwheat crop, called forth the following report from the Committee on Agriculture:

"Dis Committee yesterday visited fo' hardware stores an' a butcher shop to ax 'bout dis vary buck wheat crap, an' de reports in each case war to de effeck dat de crap am on de hum. All de prospecks pint to buckwheat cakes fur breakfast till de cook am tired in de elbows."

RATHER EMBARRASSING.

A Chicago statistician, of curious turn of mind made inquiry by letter as to the exact length of the shortest pair of feet in the Club. As the Secretary read the letter, sixty four pair of feet were suddenly drawn under chairs and benches. The sixty-fifth pair, belonging to Elder Toots, were too large to be hauled away all at once, and they therefore stood out like Jay Cooke's kitchen expenses.

"Dat am a leadin' queshun," replied Brother Gardner, as he looked around the Hall. "It am my private opinyun dat de length of a man's feet do not properly come under de head of public staytisticks, an' de Seckretary needn't bodder hisself to answer de letter. Among de home industries built up by de organizashun of dis Club am the rapid sale of No. 14 butes an' brogans, but furder dan dis I hev no partickulers."

WASHINGTON'S CAMP CHAIR.

Some friend in Milwaukee had forwarded to the Club the Camp-chair used by Gen. Washington at

Valley Forge, and the present so excited the Janitor that in building a fire for the weekly meeting, he put his hat in the stove under the kindlings and tried to hang a bundle of shavings on the hat-rack. The Janitor is a well posted man on American history. As the members gathered, he put the chair on the Secretary's desk and explained:

"It seems as if I almost knode dis chair, kase I've read of it so often. Right on de arm heah you see de syllables 'G. W.' George Washington cut 'em dar wid his own hand. He wasn't proud an' stuck up, but yet he liked to rest his back in a good chair. Seated in dis cha'r in front of his tent he bossed de offisurs dis way an' de sojers dat way, an' not a kick from de mules an' hosses 'scaped dat vigilunt eye. Dis cha'r went inter camp wid him, fought, bled an' died wid him, an' den was taken out West to brace up. It am a free gift to dis Club, an' though the b'ar trap an' de coffee mill an' de paintin's an' de odder relics am more or less waluable, dis ole man am gwine to see dis cha'r right frew de campaign or die in de attempt."

NO SORE HEEL RELIEF.

"Gem'len," said the president, as he picked up a bundle of letters marked "important," "I has often bin axed doorin' de past y'ar if members of dis Club who am laid up wid a sore heel am 'titled to de benefits of de relief fund. I has neber till to-day bin quite satisfied on dis pint, but now I am about to decide it. If a man falls sick, dat's sickness, an' he can't help it. If he breaks his leg. dat's an axident sent by Providence. If he gits hit on de head by an icicle, dat's luck. But de man who deliberately sots down an' lets a sore heel fasten its jaws upon him am either too lazy to breàthe or too smart to belong to dis Club. I darfore decide right heah dat eny an' all claims for sore heel relief filed wid de Seckretary will be used to kindle de fiah."

MISSING LINKS.

Some weeks since petitions were received from Gen. Scott Boodles, of Alabama, and Elder Whitehead, of Virginia, and the committee to whom they were referred were not ready to report back until this meeting. Their work had been very thorough. They had ascertained that the General was last year locked up for having thirteen dead chickens under the bed, and the Elder was known to have three wives and strongly suspected of hiding two more in the woods. The Committee therefore reported adversely on the petitions, and the same were ordered to the waste-basket.

"SUNDRIES."

In the weekly report of the Treasurer it was discovered that he had fourteen cents charged up under the head of "sundries," and when he had finished his reading the President observed:

"While I am free to say dat our respected Treasurer injoys my full confidence, I neberdemoar' regard it as my dooty to ax him to 'splain dat item a leetle clusser. Nuffin in de bizness of dis Club must be kivered up wid big words."

"Why, dem fo'teen cents went for sundries," explained the official.

"Sartin—sartin; but does dat mean railroad ties or spring overcoats?"

"I paid out nine cents for candles an' be balance for matches."

"Wery well—dat's perfeckly plain to de Club. After dis occashun, to save axin' queshuns, de brudder had better put de word 'sundries' in de woodbox an' specify each item. Matches an' candles am mighty handy to hev aroun' de Hall, but 'sundries' haint worf storage room."

ON DE MULE.

The Secretary announced that he held in his hand a communication from Kentucky, asking the Club if mules was a favorite animal in this neighborhood and how the climate seemed to affect them. The President was about to refer the matter to the Committee on the Future of our Country, when Cinnamon Johnson rose from his seat and desired to be heard. Leave being granted, he said:

"I was bo'n 'longside de mewl. I knows him from his nose to his hind hoof. Ize driv him an' he has driv me. De mewl in de Norf am not a success. De climate am right 'nuff an' de feed am good 'nuff, but de roads an' de streets am so narrow up heah dat you can't git a good swing to a fence-rail when you want to hit a mewl."

HE JURY SYSTEM.

A communication signed by six lawyers of Mobile desired to know if the Club had ever discussed the jury system, and if so, what decision had been arrived at. Brother Gardner explained that the question had never been called up, so far as he could remember, and he sat down to give members a chance to express their sentiments.

The Rev. Penstock was of the opinion that a man who stole a dog could never be convicted by a jury, and he believed that the day had come when either juries or dogs must go out of existence.

Trustee Pullback rather favored the jury system. But for a jury of six good men he would once have gone to jail on the charge of 'crooking' six hens, because a few heads, legs and feathers were found in his back yard.

The Hon. Reason Castaway had several times been on the jury, and it was his opinion that if they were better provided with watermelons, grapes, pears, small beer and gingerbread, they would arrive at more just and reasonable verdicts.

Waydown Bebee rather favored the jury system. He was once in court on charge of lugging off a wheelbarrow belonging to another man, and the judge looked so kind and fatherly that Mr. Bebee did not call for a jury. The result was that he was not only convicted of taking the wheelbarrow, but of loading it with potatoes before he started.

Several other individuals expressed their opinions favorable or unfavorable, and the President wound up the discussion by saying:

"It seems to be de gineral sentiment of dis Club dat de jury system am all right, whar it finds a veraict in favor of de defendant."

VOTED DOWN.

The Rev. Penstock offered a resolution to the effect that his desk be furnished with a twelve shilling inkstand, but the Club voted down the proposition almost unanimously, the President saying:

"Benjamin Franklin he used an old pepper-box fur an inkstand nigh onto fo'teen y'ars, an' I doan' believe dat any member of dis Club am a bigger man dan he was."

POETRY

Waydown Bebee got the floor and stated his belief that American poets were languishing for the want of encouragement and support. In this country, he remarked, the man who jumps ten feet or swallows a sword is looked upon with the greatest admiration, while the man who composes a poem or an idyl must walk in the middle of the road to prevent people barking his shins. He believed that poetry softened the heart, reformed the wicked and cheered the weary, and he truly hoped that the Lime-Kiln Club would take a step in advance and hold out encouragement to those poetically inclined.

Elder Bacon Jones and several others expressed favorable opinions, and when the discussion had ceased Brother Gardner said:

"I isn't much given to poetry myself. My ole woman sometimes takes a piece of chalk an' dashes off a verse or two on de wood-house doah, but I run mo' to biled dinners dan to poetry. Howsumeber, it may be well to encourage de poets, an' it may be well for dis Club to walk up to de head of de class in sich a movement."

DE BALANCE OF TRADE.

When the venerable pate of the President appeared at the head of the stairs Waydown Bebee and the Hon. Pope Harrison were engaged in an animated discussion on the subject of the balance of trade, Samuel Shin was looking at the stove-pipe to see what effect his falling over the stove had had upon it, and Trustee Pullback was slyly perusing a circular sent him from the east with an offer to furnish him with counterfeit money for fifteen cents on the dollar. There was a general scattering for seats, and during the confusion Elder Toots, who had almost fallen asleep on a stool, was upset and stepped on and mashed so flat that the buttons on his vest were found to be nine inches out of plumb.

"Doorin' de last few days I hez often been axed to 'splain what de balance of trade was," remarked Brother Gardner as the notes of the triangle died away. "A-cordin' to Waydown Bebee it means de cash dis kentry takes in fur de mules it ships abroad. A-cordin to de Hon. Pope Harrison, it means de board bills left behind in Washington by members of Congress when dat body a-jurns. Boaf of dese extinguished gem'len am barkin' up de wrong tree. De balance of trade, my frens, hez nuffin to do wid buyin' codfish at seven cents a pound, or stove blackin' at ten cents a bundle. It hez nuffin to do wid de water melyon sezun nor de persimmon crop. If I sell Judge Cokernut Jackson more taters dan he sells me, den de balance of trade am in my favor—purvidin' I eber git my pay. No member of dis Club hez any call to git excited ober de balance of trade queshun. It won't keep us in meat an' taters, an' it won't pay de preacher. Our bizness am to keep gwine right ahead wid de purfeshun of putin' on whitewash an' shinin' up stoves, an' de more we 'tend to our work de less danger we run of gittin' dizzy-headed ober de queshuns which floor de smartest white men straight from de shoulder."

BANKS AND WOOD PILES.

THE Committee on Banks and Banking, who have been very quiet for several months past, announced to the great surprise of the Club that they had a report ready. Being told to proceed, Windfall Cooper, the Chairman, submitted a well-written report, advocating the organization of one or more night banks in every town and city. All day banks now close at 4 P. M., and after that hour no business can be transacted with them. The Committee held that there should be other banks to open their doors from that hour until 9 o'clock A. M., and cited several instances where strangers had been obliged to travel around for half an hour to get small change for a quarter in order to pay a boot-black. One might have ever so good an opportunity to buy or sell a dog after banking hours, but no check could be cashed. The Club voted to adopt the report, and after some discussion it was resolved that the organization use its influence to bring about a new state of banking affairs.

A RECESS.

A recess was here taken to permit the President to go down stairs and meet a man who wanted to borrow $5 and leave a wheelbarrow as security, and the Glee Club improved the time by singing and playing a new melody by Samuel Shin, entitled: "De Crops." The first verse is as follows:

"De summer's gwine fast away,
De fall am almost heah;
De crops am jist a whoopin' up,
Each darkey's heart to cheer.
Sing hey, darkeys—
'Taters mighty big;
Squashes lyin' all around,
An' turnips dance a jig."

SPECIAL REPORT.

The Special Committee of three, to whom was referred the question as to whether a member of the Club could conscientiously live all winter next door to a school house with a big wood-pile attached, announced that they were ready to report.

"We hez looked at dis queshun from all de pints of de compass," began the Chairman as he got his balance. "On dis side of de fence am a member of dis Club an' his family. On de odder side am a big wood-pile an' de school house janitor. Dat's de situashun. In de fust place de member didn't put dat wood-pile dar'. In de next place de wood-pile had nuffin to do wid his movin' in. Dey am perfeck strangers to each odder. We doan' say dat de janitor won't miss mo' or less wood dis winter, but we hez 'nuff confidence in our brudder to believe dat, in de fust place, he will buy his own wood; in de next place, de man who lives 'longside of a big wood-pile an' steals any mo' dan he kin crowd in de stove to once am weak in de top story."

The report was placed on file, and the President remarked that he would take the matter under consideration for a few days longer.

NO ALLIANCE.

The Secretary of the "Society for the mitigation of the Condition of the Heathen in Africa," having its headquarters at Canton, O., forwarded a certified copy of the following resolution passed by that Society àt a late meeting:

"*Resolved*, That the Lime-Kiln Club of Detroit be requested to hereafter act in concert with this society in its future great work of bettering the social and moral condition of the African heathen."

The Secretary passed the resolution over to Brother Gardner, who read it over to himself and said:

"I 'spect dar be hethuns in Africa, an' I 'spect we orter feel much obleeged for dis invitashun to jine dat society in its great work, but if de African hethun waits for dis yere Club to whoop up de nikcels to lift him on de top shelf of society, he won't git dar for a fousand y'ars to come! De Seckretary may write back dat we doan' 'ciprocate worf a cent on de African bizness."

A LOAN WANTED.

The Secretary announced a letter from Julius Hannibal Scott, of Morristown, Tenn., asking a temporary loan of fifteen cents, and promising to refund it at the earliest opportunity. Samuel Shin was about to arise and offer a resolution granting the loan, when the President waved him down and said:

"Dis Club makes no loans of less dan $15,000, on account of de trouble of makin' out de papers an' puttin' letters in de post-office. De request of **Misser**

Scott will darefore be classed under de head of 'neglected communicashuns.'"

ABOUT ODES.

The Hon. Binghampton Jones here arose to a question of privilege. He said that he was daily pained and yet forced to realize the fact that the colored people of America had no national ode. The white man had the "Star Spangled Banner," "Pinafore," and "The Man From Pike" to select from on Fourths of July, and the Presidential ovations, but the colored man could call no song his own. He had given the subject serious consideration, and he hoped that the Lime-Kiln Club would at once move in the matter. It might not have a poet among its members capable of producing a great national colored song, but it could influence other poets to begin work and rest not until song or ode or chant or anthem was finished.

"It may be," began the President, as he rose up to reply, "dat de cull'd folkses of dis kentry am forgettin' who dey are, but I reckon not. It may be dat de hull race am ready to frow overboard all de happy songs of ole slave days an' take up wid some new fangled music dat runs up to de high C's, but I can't believe it. Brudder Jones complains dat we have no ode. Ask Sir Isaac Walpole, Waydown Bebee, Judge Tompkins or Elder Toots if dey eber heard de melody of "Gwine Back Home to Die" floatin' ober de ole plantashun at sunset, an' ask dem what man could make a sweeter song. Fur fifty long y'ars we hev bin singin' melodies that no other race of people kin sing, an' now we are axed to frow 'em aside an' begin on a whoop an' eand on a growl. We can't do it, an' we won't do it! You may pile up odes as high as dis Hall an' yit our race will turn away from dem an' sing:

> 'Ize growin' ole an' weary now,
> I cannot work no more—'

Sit down, Brudder Jones, an' meanwhile let de triangle sound an' de meetin' be upsot fur one week."

DE OLE MAN MOSHER.

"Last night, jist as de ole woman was grindin' up de butcher-knife to cut her corns, dar cum a knock on de doah," began the old man, as Paradise Hall grew quiet. "It war de ole man Mosher, an' I could see right away dat he didn't feel in whoopin' speerits. I reckon you all knows de ole man, an' you knows he am hard-workin' an' honest. Well, he was ober dar to see about his son Hunyadus. Dat Hunyadus am a powerful bad boy an' I knows it, an' de ole man he sot down an' tole me dat de day had arrove when he could no longer control de boy. Yes, he sot dar on de edge of de wood-box an' cried like a chile cause dat Hunyadus had cum home an' cussed around, an' axed for money, an' declared he'd bust de hull family or hev it. I axed him how ole de boy was, an' he wiped his nose an' said sixteen. I axed him how much de boy weighed, an' he looked up at de ceilin an' said about a hundred and twenty. Den I pushed de tea-kettle furder back on de stove an' I went fur de ole man like a steamboat 'sploshun. De ideah of a boy like dat runnin' de house made me mad all de way up an' down, an' I tole Mosher if he didn't go home an' flop dat Hunyadus outer his butes an' den mop him around till he cried quits, dat he must nebber darken my gate agin. He got up an he went, an' I was clus behind him. Dat boy was still in de house, bluffin de ole woman around an' kickin' de dog under de stove, an' de opportunity was all dat could be axed fur. De ole man bounced in, waltzed up to de wayward chile, and de way he made de fur fly tickled me all ober. When I left de winder Hunyadus was wipin' de tears away wid one hand an' eatin' cold pancakes wid de odder, an de ole man had sich a smile as I hevn't seen on his face for ober seben years."

After the applause had subsided the President continued:

"Treat your boys kindly an' like a good fadder should, but when a son gets de big head an' emagines dat he kin run de caboose widout help from de ole folks, an' dat he am master of his days an' nights, sot right down on him like a bag of sand fallin' from de roof-top! Let him know who owns de cabin an' who brings in de purvishuns; an' hang onto his wool long 'nuff to convince him dat you am not too old to know what sort of store-clothes look de best on a poor man's son."

THE ONLY RELIABLE.

THE Committee on the Judiciary, who had been asked to investigate and report as to the best trade for colored boys to pursue submitted the following:

"De Committee am devided on dis subjeck. De barber trade am looked upon wid affeckshun by some an' wid distrust by odders. De waiter trade jist suits part of de Committee an' repels de balance. Driving a coal cart am recommended by some and rejected by de rest. De majority of dis Committee am, however, of de opinyun dat, while de waiter bizness an' de barber trade may make de moas money in a rush, dar's no weapon like de whitewash brush fur standing right by you all de y'ar round. It doan' eat anyfing, it doan' take up any room, an' it am always on hand when you want it. Whitewashin' was interdooced in dis kentry in de y'ar 1493, an' it hez been growing fonder in de affeckshuns of de public eber since. It improves de ceilins, whitens de walls, an' makes old fences look like new. Ebery respectable family shouldn't be widout it. Taking all fings into considerashun, de biggest part of dis Committee am darfore of de opinyun dat de whitewash trade am de moas reliabul one open to de colored youfs of de land."

The Rev. Penstock took exceptions to the report. He said that every colored boy in the land could be made a preacher of just as well as not, and those who didn't take to preaching would naturally turn to astronomy, philosophy and other scientific pursuits.

Elder Toots, Trustee Pullback, Windfall Cooper and others supported the majority report, and it was finally adopted as the sentiments of the Club.

A MISSING LINK.

It was announced at the last meeting that Col. John Pinchbar, of Missouri, would probably deliver a speech before this meeting, but he failed to come to time. He, however, forwarded his speech in writing, which Brother Gardner looked over and remarked:

"Dis speech seems to be on de subjeck of rag carpet. De Kernel takes de ground dat rag carpets am fadin away befo' de busy march of progress, an' it am my opinyun dat de Kernel had better fade too. De rest of de speech will be laid on de shelf."

GIFTS FROM THE WEST.

The Secretary apoligized for disturbing the routine of the meeting, and stated that he was in receipt of a fine crayon likeness of Abraham Lincoln, not yet unboxed, accompanied by some very appropriate poetry, both the gift of "Kit," of Wyoming. The poetry was at once read to the Club:

THE OLD DARKEY'S HOPE.

[Respectfully Dedicated to "Brudder Gardner."]

Dese eyes is gettin' old an' dim, dis wool's jes' like de snow,
  An' dese poo' ole legs kin sca'cely move along,
Befoh anoder wintah comes de ole man's gwine to go,
  Whar de angels sing de halleluyah song.
De joy dat rises in dis breast am hid from mortal view,
  It's a feelin' white folks cannot understan',
Foh when I gits to Heaben's gate, an' Peter lets me froo,
  I kin take ole Massa Linkum by de han'

Fo' many long an' dreary yea's before de sogers come,
  I toiled beneaf de sun in Tenessee,
Oh, how us darkeys shouted when we heard de beatin' drum,
  'Kase we knowed fur suah we'se gwine to be free,
An' when de proclamation come we all got down to pray.
  An' axed de Lo'd to bless dat holy man,
An' I knows dat when I finds him in dat Heaben so fa' away,
  He'll let de ole man take him by de han'.

While wand'rin' froo dis weary world Ize of'en, of'en found
  My cup of sorrer filled clear to de brim

THE LIME-KILN CLUB.

An' Ize of'en wished I war at rest down in de col', col' ground,
  Fo' I nebber feared dat King of Terrors grim.
But soon de veil will roll away from off his dreary spot,
  An' I'll see de beauties ob de promised lan',
An' I know dat all de pains of earth will be done gone fo'got
  When I feels de clasp ob Massa Linkum's han'.

Den soun' yo' trumpet, Gabriel, an' call de ole man home,
  Fo' Ize tired a libin' in dis world ob pain.
I wants to git to Heaben, whar no mo' in grief I'll roam,
  An' nebber suffeh pain an' woe again.
An' when I gets inside de gate Ize gwine right out to hunt
  All ober glory's bright an' happy lan',
An' when I sees dat good ole man I'll march right up in front
  An' take ole Massa Linkum by de han.'

COMMUNICATIONS.

Under this head the Secretary read a letter from Doctor William Henry Johnsing, of Hornellsville, N. Y., asking the Club to accept a painting representing several chickens in the roost. The Rev. Penstock at once arose to a question of privilege. He thought the offer was a direct insult to the Club, and he hoped it would not be accepted.

"Brudder Penstock, I doan' see de insult," replied the President. "Dis am only a painting, an' you couldn't take dem chickens off de roost if you should try all night."

Mr. Penstock sat down amid a general laugh, and the Club voted to accept the painting.

ACCEPTED.

The Club by a unanimous vote decided to accept the offer of Louis C. Briggs, of Charlotte, Mich., to deliver before it some time during February a lecture entitled: "How I Got Left in Lansing." Mr.

Briggs was a candidate for the position of boss of the cloak-room during the present session of the Legislature, and while he didn't miss the train and have to wait over he was "left" all the same. It is understood that his lecture will explain how thirteen State Senators pooled their influence against him and supported a colored man who went out there from Jackson with a new brand of stomach bitters and a pocket full of cigars.

REPORTS.

The Committee on the Judiciary reported that the following petitions had been drawn up, numerously signed, and forwarded to the Legislature:

1. Petition for a law to permit the killing of brush boys attached to barber shops, and to make it a penal offense for any barber to ask a man to have his hair cut from December 1 to April 1.

2. Petition for a State Observatory for the use of colored people; also, that at least one-half of the Lighthouses around the Michigan coast be named in honor of Colored Generals who fell during the late war.

3. Petition for a law to permit colored people equal facilities for securing front seats at the Fourth of July fireworks, and for the better protection of dogs belonging to colored men.

The Rev. Penstock was selected as a representative of the Club to proceed to the Capitol and urge upon the body the importance of these contemplated acts, and the meeting then adjourned.

SIGNED "X."

"Gem'len, an onpleasant dooty am forced upon me by de pressure of circumstances," began Brother Gardner as the Hall grew quiet. "De odder evenin' as I war reclinin' on de kitchen lounge, a rap was heard at de doah, an' de follerin' note was put in my hands:

"'Brother Gardner.—If you will follow the bearer of this, you will discover a number of this Club engaged in a very disreputable business.' 'X.'

"I followed de boy. In a barn in an alley off Hastings street de diskivery was made. A member of dis Club was dar, engaged in puttin' up a dog-fight, an' abont forty specktators were on hand to see de fun. I looked frew de cracks an' seen de hull performance. De dog owned by de Lime-Kiln man licked de odder canine in about ten minits, an' five dollars changed hands. But de blush of pride didn't come to my cheek on dat account. If dar ever war a time when I liked to see a dog fight it war way back in de forties. It am a cruel, bad bizness, too low for decent men to encourage or engaige in, an' it am now my painful dooty to ax Brudder Philbrick Gladstone to stand up an' let himself be seen."

HE STOOD.

The member mentioned slowly arose. The proceedings were a perfect thunder-clap to him. As he reached his feet and found sixty or seventy pair of eyes turned upon him, he would have resumed his bench if the thoughtful Jan. Harrison hadn't been behind him with a darning-needle.

"I—Ize heah, sah!" he gasped, as he turned to the platform.

"De Brudder will step seben or eight paces dis way," said the President.

He walked slowly forward, his knees playing a tune and his color fading to the complexion of French wall-paper, and when he was in position the President arose and said:

"Brudder Philbrick Gladstone, you hez heard de charges. Am you guilty or innocent?"

"I war dar, an' I owned de winnin' dorg," was the reply.

"Well, de sentence am dat you hand ober de five dollars to de library fund of dis Club, an' dat you sign a pledge neber to engage in such low bizness agin. In case you refuse to hand over an' sign, your name will be crossed from de roll, an' dis hall won't see you any more."

The Brother handed over the cash without hesitation, signed a written pledge, and as he returned to his seat he had to unbutton his vest to give play to his heartfelt emotions. He will doubtless be found in the front rank of philanthropists and humanitarians after this.

FROM THE PEOPLE.

A petition signed by forty-eight colored people of Texas was presented to the Club, in hopes that it might use its influence with the Agricultural Bureau at Washington for the introduction of a species of string-beans which would curl to the left when climbing a pole. All beans now climb to the right, notwithstanding one man out of every seven is left-handed. It is hoped that the Commissioners will give this subject immediate thought and investigation. The petitioners would further request him to introduce a different style of cucumber. One in the shape of an apple, with a third rind and some sort of handle to, would soon drive the common vegetable out of market.

"WELL, HARDLY——."

A letter from Selma, Ala., written "in haist," made inquiry if it was considered unlady-like in a Northern colored woman to go barefooted in summer. The Rev. Penstock at once arose and said that no true lady, no matter what the color, would ever appear in society without shoes and stockings on, even if in a hurry to catch the last hack at a funeral.

Sir Isaac Walpole said that going barefooted saved a heap of shoe-leather, and so far as he was concerned, he thought none the less of a lady for it, providing she hid her feet under the bed or behind the wood-box when strangers called.

General Flatbush said his wife had gone barefooted every summer for twenty years past, and he couldn't see but that her standing in society was as good as ever. It gave the feet a chance to spread out and cool off, and he didn't know but that it improved a lady's gait. Without giving the subject at least three weeks' steady thought, he wouldn't like to venture an opinion which might kick the shoes off of a half a million colored ladies in one hot day. The question was therefore laid on the table for future discussion.

THE LIBRARY.

The Librarian reported the receipt of ninety-six additional almanacs, and a work on the logwood industry of Brazil. He suggested that a raise of salary for the coming year would be very acceptable, as his work had increased more than one-half, and this suggestion gave rise to a sharp debate. After the storm had passed over, Waydown Bebee offered the following resolution:

"*Resolved*, Dat when de laborious labors of any posishun in dis Club git to be more'n de officer kin walk off wid, he should resign de same an' make a trip to de sea-shore for his health."

The resolution was adopted, and the Librarian sat down and unbuttoned his vest and had nothing more to say.

ANOTHER INVESTIGATION.

Col. Amandus Johnson wanted information. He said that the price of New Orleans molasses had remained at exhorbitant figures for seven years past, although dry-goods, groceries and wages had been going down to hard pan, and he now wanted satisfaction as to why this thing was thus. Kerosene, whale oil, castor oil and vinegar were way down, and yet New Orleans molasses was up. It was a question which directly interested all colored folks, and he hoped the Club would take steps to solve the mystery. The President, after some further discussion, appointed a Special Committee to investigate and report, and the meeting adjourned.

LET 'EM DIVORCE.

"I HOLD heah in my hand," began Brother Gardner, as he waved the missive aloft, "a letter from a cull'd clergyman in Tennessee, axin' dis Club to use its inflooence to secure more stringent divorce laws in de varus States, an' to sot its face agin de procurement of divorce, except fur de very gravest reasons. Dis Club will do nuffin of de kind. On de contrary, it will wote solid to furnish all facilities fur parties desirous to be onhitched wid promptness an' dispatch. Nuffin comes nearer perdishun dan an unmated an' unmatched couple tryin' to lib togeder as man an' wife. I hold dat no couple who doan' lub each oder —who don't agree an' can't forgive—who won't excuse—should lib togeder ten minits. If we git a house we doan' like we sel it. If we git a hoss we doan' like we trade him off. If we doan' like de nayburhood we move away. If we doan' like our nayburs we let 'em alone. How, den, kin you spect husband an' wives to put up wid ugliness, meanness drunkenness, profanity, extravagance an' all dat am hateful in de human heart.

"Let 'em divorce. God intended husband and wife to lub, cherish, forgive an' be all in all to each odder. Whar dey can't be sich it am a thousand times better dat dey be devorced. No man or woman who had lub in deir heart eber yit applied for one or eber will. If a divorce could be had by simply payin' a fee of fifty cents no husband mated wid his wife would think of separashun any more dan he does now. People cheat an' deceive when courtin'. Married life brings out de faults which dey hid. It has allus bin so, an' will be so to de eand, an' when husbands and wives quarrel an' hate, a law to make 'em continue to lib togeder am unjust an' wicked. Let us now attack de regular order of bizness.

SOMETHING WAS UP.

SOMETHING was up. Just what it was no one knew but Brother Gardner's countenance wore an unusually severe expression, and Sir Isaac Walpole was observed to have on a clean shirt, while Elder Toots, for the second time in his life, had stove-blacked his broad brogans and had his vest buttoned all the way up.

"Gem'len, I shell now have de unjellified pleasure to introduce to you one of de moas cornspicus black men in dis kentry," remarked the President as his eagle eye wandered down the shady aisle. "De Committee on de Judishury will now act."

The committee acted. Led by the Hon. James Pullback, they disappeared in the direction of the ante-room, to reappear after a moment escorting a distinguished stranger of middle age.

JUDGE K. C. B. DAVIS.

"Gem'len, I hev de honor to present to de Lime-Kiln Club my ole friend an' companyun, Judge Davis, at present of de State of Georgia," said the President, as the stranger reached the platform.

The reception given the Judge was fully equal to the enthusiasm of farmers over the late rains, and those hit with chunks of falling plaster preserved their goodnature in a wonderful degree.

A SPEECH.

The Judge explained that he was on his way to Lake Superior to see his aged father, and he had halted here for a couple of days to make the personal acquaintance of every local member of the Club, and to petition it for membership. He had noticed the high stand taken by the Club in matters affecting science and art, and he was greatly pleased.

"Science," added the Judge, as he stepped on Waydown Bebee's corns, "am above us, below us, an' all around us, an yit de great majority of men doan' seem to realize de fack. What builds de fiah in de stove, 'cept science? What biles de tators in de kettle 'cept science? What furnishes our clothes, our homes, an' eben our graves, 'cept science? Gaze on de sun. But for science who'd know whether dat shiny orb war ober in Kennedy or 90,000,000 miles in de sky on a bee line? Gaze on de moon. But fur science, who among us would know its infiooence on de water-melon crop? Look at de stars. Before de advent of science who could tell Venus from Aunt Betsy, de Norf star from de big dipper, or de dog stars from de cat stars? Science made de steam engine, de kivered cars, de wheelbarrow, de whitewash brush, an' de several odder articles which hev made dis nashun what it am to-day. Science frows bridges across great rivers; it brings up water from de deep well; it puts out fires; it gives us de finecomb; it makes de plug hat an' de paper collar; it brings us de glorus Fo'th of July; it mixes peas an' beans wid our coffee so dat we can't tell what it tastes de moas of, an' but for science de man wid de toofache would be nowhar."

After taking a very lean drink of water and absorbing a troche to offset it the speaker continued:
"We will now turn to art. We see art in ebery fing around us, from de pictures on de milk-carts to a pile of clam shells in de front doah yard, an' yet dere am souls who can't respond. I know men who might stand fur a hull hour in front of a tea store chromeo representing sunset in Wisconsin or sunrise in Noo Jersey an' not see nuffin to expand deir souls an' turn deir thoughts into better channels. I've seen white men stand before a bust of Cæsar an' find fault wid de squint of de left eye, an' I've seen black men stand befo' a fence all painted off wid red an' blue an' yaller, an' look fur nuffin but nail holes. Take science away from us an' we wouldn't know why we grease de wheelbarrow. Take art away from us an' we might as well live in canal boats. I am glad to see de intress dis Club takes in boaf subjecks. Your reports on astronomy hev reached ebery corner in de land, an' your picturs an' relics in dis Hall am proof dat art, left in your care, will grow an' flourish till no maker will dare offer a broom to de public widout de handle am painted blue. Wid dese few suggestions an' aggregations, I will now clothes."

THE SICK.

The Committee on the Sick reported that Jared Comstock, a local member, was sick abed with bilious fever, and his heirs had applied for relief.

"I war spectin' dis report to come up," remarked the President in answer, "an' I want to show dis Club a few articles clusly connected wid Messer Comstock's case."

He thereupon slowly unrolled his handkerchief and displayed a slice of a large Cucumber, a piece of cocoanut, a piece of bologna and the half of a hard-boiled egg, and continued:

Down at de market de odder day I got my eye on Brudder Comstock. He had jist bin paid tur a job, an' he was gwine inter luxuries in de moas extravagant manner. Dese pieces war left on his plate arter he got through stuffin'. I saw dat man devour fo' cowcumbers, most a hull cokernut, six eggs an' three bologneys, sayin' nuffin' of apples an' radishes an' a big hunk o' pie, an' now he has de cheek to ax dis Club to aid him from de relief fund!"

FINED.

The Rev. Penstock at once came to the front with a resolution to suspend the Brother from the Society for the period of six months, but Waydown Bebee moved to amend to fine him and double his dues for three months. The amendment being accepted, the resolution passed, and the President placed the fine at ten dollars and costs.

·VHITEWASH.

The Secretary laid before the meeting a communication from the Board of Health of Jersey City, asking what sanitary benefits the Club had noticed from the use of whitewash, and the members were invited to relate their experience.

Sir Isaac Walpole said he knew of a case where a certain family were always having the mumps. One coat of whitewash on the kitchen ceiling, at an expense of only forty cents, drove the disease away and made the family one of the healthiest in the city. The cure was so marked, and the benefits so apparent, that the man afterwards hired Mr. Walpole to whitewash the parlor, and cheated him out of his pay.

The Hon. Primrose said he once knew a family who were greatly troubled with headache and cold feet. After spending fifty dollars for patent medicines they hired him to whitewash a bed-room, and all was joy and peace. He had to take his pay in old clothes-lines, but the cure was there just the same

Waydown Bebee stated that he was once consulted by a family troubled with the ague. He advised a coat of whitewash on the fence, and only seven pickets had been whitened before the man was able to get up and walk to the window to see a dog-fight, and in an hour the wife was down town overhauling goods.

The Rev. Penstock knew a case where a family cured consumption by whitewashing the barn, and of another where a citizen had his chambers whitewashed on Saturday, and found fifty dollars in cash on the street on Monday.

The Secretary was instructed to answer the Board to the effect that every barrel of lime used as whitewash offsets the labors of at least three doctors, and that no respectable family should be without it.

N. B.—The prices for whitewashing in Detroit will remain the same.

THE LIBRARY.

The Librarian reported that he had during the past month received twenty-seven almanacs, five cook-books, one horse book, one medical book, and

1,000 tracts on "How to Reach Heaven." The tracts had been distributed among colored families in Detroit, and he was sorry to say that family fights increased by one half within a week.

THE MUSEUM.

Pickles Smith, who has charge of the reception of relics and the care of the museum, reported that some fiend had entered the room by climbing over the roof and carried away one of the two skulls of Oliver Cromwell, sent to the Club from Boston. He had placed the case in the hands of detectives, but thus far no clue had been obtained to the identity of the guilty parties. The Secretary was instructed to offer a reward of $5 for the return of the relic, and in case it could not be recovered, to procure a skull of some of the rest of the Cromwell family.

The Janitor took the pail and dipper and passed from man to man, and "yums!" and "ohs!" of gratification followed in his footsteps. When every throat had been cooled, and almost every hand held a slice of squeezed lemon for future benefits, the President again arose and said:

"Dis Lime-Kiln Club am heah assembled to honor, in its poo' an' simple way, de mem'ry of one of de greatest men de world has eber knowed. De great an' good George Washington has long bin dead, but his name kin neber die while America lives. [Cheers] Kings have spoken his name (Cheers); queens have written it (yells), an' it has ascended to Heaven along wid de prayers of little chill'en. [Cheers and applause.] To be sho' he was a white man, but when he saved dis kentry he saved ebery cull'd pusson in it as well as de white folks. [Awful applause.]

He couldn't help bein' a white man, an' he would have accomplished no less had he bin as black in de face as Rhubarb Spooner, an' had feet like Harper Jackson." [Continued cheers, during which the bear-trap fell down.]

The President sat down in an exhausted condition, and Sir Isaac Walpole arose and said:

"Let me grow old—let me hev chilblains all summer—let me sit in de dark an' shiver in de cold—let me bury my ole wife an' wander frew de world sorrowful an' alone—but neber let me forget de name of Washington, or cease to remember dat if he had bin any han' to play base ball, he'd have played it wid a cull'd man as quick as a white man." [Cheers and applause.]

MORE SINGING.

The members of the Glee Club could not sit still under the excitement of the hour, and upon receiving a wink of encouragement from the President, they jumped in on the following:

"Blow de horn! Beat de drum!
H'ar de bugle blowin'!"
Fifty million Yankees here,
An' still de kentry's growin'!

CHORUS.—Let dat canawl alone, Misser Lesseps.

"Soun' de bones! Shake de hoofs!
See de people smilin';
Everybody's on de rush,
An' bizness am a bilin'.

CHORUS.—Kase if you don't you'll get hurted."

DIDN'T PLAY WITH HIM.

Pickles Smith got the floor as the last beautiful strain of music died away, and said:

"I didn't play wid George Washington when we war boys, but dat wasn't my fault. If he'd cum'd ober to our plantashun, he'd hev foun' me to hum. Neberdeless, Ize willin' to admit his greatness an' goodness. [Cheers.] My grad'fadder war named George Washington Smith. [Cheers.] My fadder war named George Washington Smith. [Cheers.] My oldest brudder am named George Washington Smith. [Cheers.] My second son am named George Washington Smith. [Cheers.] Ize got about fo'teen uncles, an' cousins an' aunts named George Washington Smith. [Cheers.] It's a name our family feels proud of an' means to stick by. [Cheers.] All honor to de man who shouldered his plow an' went fo'th to mash the inimy!" [Furious cheers and long continued applause.]

ELDER TOOTS REMEMBERS.

Good Elder Toots said he had no desire to occupy the valuable time of the meeting (Cheers), but he could not help but remember of once having driven a mule (Cheers), past Mount Vernon, the sacred spot where lies the dust of Washington. [Terrific yells.] Hs therefore believed that he keenly realized Washington's greatness and goodness. [Cheers.] He did not know how others felt, but as for him, he wanted liberty or death—and another dipper of lemonade.

The hint was acted upon at once, and the beverage circulated around the Hall, and the Glee Club walloped the following:

"THE GREAT G. W."

He am dead!
A chief has passed away;
His race am run—
His life am dun,
His form am wid de clay.

But lives his name
In ebery freeman's heart;
A thousand years
Won't dry de tears
Dat at his name mus' start

A DUTY DONE.

As the nsual hour for adjourning approached the President folded his arms across his heaving bosom and said:

"I believe dat dis Lime-Kiln Club has did its full duty by George Washington, Mrs. Washington, de American flag, dis glorious Republic, an' seberal oder pussons an' fings, an' we will now disband an' approach our homes. Let no man forgit his dooty to his kentry, an' yit in remembering dat dooty, let no member forgit dat de Lime-Kiln Club comes fust an' kentry next, an' what am left should go to hiz fam'ly. We now stand disrupted."

A WORD TO CRANKS.

"Am dar a crank present in de Hall to-night?" softly asked Brother Gardner, as the meeting opened.

Not a voice answered.

"Have any of you seen a crank around town dis last week?" continued the President.

Not one had, or at least no one admitted it.

"Two weeks ago de kentry was full of 'em. You could find 'em on de street kyar, at de depot, around de hotels, an' eben in church. All of a sudden you can't scare up a single crank. De bizness has got to be unhealthy. De plea of insanity doan' go down wid de jury as slick as it did. De time when one man kin put a knife into anoder an' make de jury believe he was bo'n dat way an' couldn't help it has about expired. De crank must go. He must quit shootin', stabbin an' stealin' an' being heard of in de land. When de crank fust brought forward de ideah dat de Deity was behind him an' urged him on it was sunthin new an' novel, but dat ideah am played out wid de rest.

"My frens, let de cantankerous bizness alone. Doan' call stealing by any odder name. If your hands itch fur money dat belongs to some one else, take it an' skip, an' when de law overhauls you doan' sot up de plea dat an' angel from Heaven urged you on. Legal farces hev had deir day in dis kentry. Insanity, kleptomania, sudden emotion, drunkenness an' loss of memory will be poor excuses before fucher juries."

PETITIONS.

Among the many petitions on the Secretary's desk was one from Prof. Eben Shin, Past Grand Mogul of the B. O. K. & S. H. M. Society, of Berkley, Va. The Professor has for the past two years sought by every means in his power to break down the influence of the Lime-Kiln Club in the South, even going so far as to claim that Brother Gardner was a robber, Sir Isaac Walpole an escaped convict and that Waydown Bebee had fled from justice in Alabama. When Giveadam Jones went to Norfolk to deliver his great lecture on "The Nothingness of Space," the Professor insulted him at the depot in the presence of over 3,000 citizens. He now sees the error of his ways, and humbly seeks to be counted with the faithful.

There was also a general smile of satisfaction when it was announced that January Jones, of Selma, Ala., had returned to his dish of crow. Three years ago Mr. Jones withdrew from the Club because it refused to endorse a petition of his asking the government to provide the colored people of this country with fish-line and coon dogs. He started an opposition lodge in Alabama, but it went to pieces in three weeks, and January himself got into Georgia only an hour ahead of the Sheriff. He has lately returned to his native place, settled with the owner of the mule, and now desires to be restored to membership in the Lime-Kiln Club.

THE SICK.

The Chairman of the Committee on Sick reported that Brother Walk About Grandy had been knocked down on the street by a hack and would be laid up for two weeks. The Treasurer was ordered to forward him relief to the amount of $3 per week, and the Committee were instructed to see that no part of it was used to purchase ox-tail soup or white sugar.

The Committee further reported that Brother Greenbrier Claxton had fallen down stairs and driven his eyebrows clear up to the roots of his hair, but they had no recommend to make. The President said that falling down stairs did not come under the head of accident, and the matter was laid on the table to see if the eyebrows wouldn't settle down to their place.

THROWN OUR FOR CAUSE.

The following candidates were unfavorably reported on for causes named:

Kenawha Smith, of Maryland, charged with being caught in a bear-trap at the door of a neighbor's smoke-house. His excuse that he mistook the smoke-house for a school-house at which there was to be a spelling school that night, was decided to be too thin.

Cemetery Hastings, of Indiana, charged with feeding his wife with powdered chalk when she had the ague and making her believe it was quinine. His defense was that the chalk cured her, but the Committee were afraid that if the action were overlooked he might next compel his wife to believe that a chip on a cabbage leaf was quail on toast.

Sincerity Flats, of South Carolina, charged with assisting to put out a fire in a grocery. He worked so zealousy that next day a constable discovered twenty-eight cans of peaches, a box of soap, ten pails, two hams and twenty-one bed-cords hidden away in Mr. Flat's cabin. His defence was absence of mind, but the Committee refused to consider it, holding that while an absent minded man might possibly carry home such articles as enumerated in the charge, he would hardly take up the kitchen floor to hide them.

THE TORPEDO CHICKEN.

Further reports were submitted regarding the torpedo chicken, lately invented in Mobile. A specimen chicken had been procured by the Committee, and its workings exhibited, The invention is not as deadly as at first supposed. It is loaded with four ounces of bird shot and two of powder, and placed on the roost. When it is reached for a catch is thrown out of place, a powerful spring set in motion and a hammer strikes and explodes a percussion cap. The shot are thrown out in every direction, and within ten seconds after the explosion a dark figure is seen galloping down the alley and in a husky voice is heard inquiring: "Fo' de Lawd, but what has de white folks got hold of now?" The Committee closed its report as follows: Havin' pushed de investigation an kivered all de groun', we beg leave to be discharged from furder considerashun of de subject, an' to respectfully inquar' of our respected President: 'Kin dis torpedo chicken be suppressed?' If not, what shall we do? An' we will eber pray."

"As to de suppressin' de inwenshun I see no way to accomplish it," replied Brother Gardner. "As to what shall we do, I have been serusly reflectin' fur de last ten minits, an' it am my solemn belief dat de best thing de cull'd race kin do am to cultivate a taste for some odder sort of meat."

THE WEATHER.

The Committee in charge of the meteorological disturbances for the coming week reported the following probabilities:

SUNDAY—Look out for Thunder.

THE LIME-KILN CLUB. 247

MONDAY—Hot enough for old maids to go barefoot.

TUESDAY—Shocks of earthquake felt in several localities, and old sinners begin to repent.

WEDNESDAY—Opens with a tornado in four acts, each act worth the price of the whole performance.

THURSDAY—Calm as a sleeping babe, but the beasts of the field sniff the air, paw the ground and seem uneasy.

FRIDAY—This will be known as the dark day. Heaven as black as tar; moaning in the air; fowls terrified; grocers forget to put peas in their coffee; fish don't bite worth a cent; all marriage engagements declared off.

SATURDAY—Sort of a grand climax, with thunderclaps loud enough to raise a debt outlawed for fourteen years. Clears off toward evening and beer gardens get ready for the arduous labors of the Sabbath.

THEY COME.

Among the fifteen or twenty petitions was the following:

NORFOLK, VA., December 10, 1881.

BRO. GARDNER.—*Dear Sir;*—I have been instructed by a unanimous vote of the Anatomical and Scientific Society of Colored Men of Virginia, headquarters at this place, to make application to your Club for membership as a body. We number fifty-one baldheaded members, each one of high moral character and standing solid on his pins. In case our application meets with success, we will pay our dues for a year in advance, close our hall and labors here, and forward to the library of the Lime-Kiln Club several beautifully preserved specimens of shin-bones of deceased poets, comic lecturers, and the man who spits on the floor of the street car. With confidence,

VERTEBRÆ JONES,
Secretary of the A. and S. Society.

Pickles Smith arose for information as to what anatomical meant. If it was anything in regard to polishing stoves, the would-be members should bind themselves not to cut under rates.

Trustee Pullback seconded the motion, provided there was any motion to second. He knew of colored men who were blacking stoves for fifteen cents apiece, and making no extra charge for wheeling off two or three barrels of ashes. After several others had spoken to the same effect, the President said:

"I allus gits astronomy, anatomy an' antimony all mixed up, but Ize sartin suah dat none of 'em refer to blackin' stoves. I think we kin take our chances on votin' dis society in, an' thus increasin' our list of distinguished members."

ELECTION.

The Glee Club struck up: "We'll Swim or Sink Together," and as Sir Isaac Walpole passed the bean-box down the aisles, no living man could have told that he had ever made a running jump over a fence seven feet high to get away from a dog which seemed fourteen feet long. The following members were elected in cold blood and with malice aforethought: Old Lime Jones, Elder Tucker, Anxiety Hastings, Glad Tidings Taylor, Zeke Anderson, Heroic Brayton, Texas McFadder, Prof. Kipp and Wintergreen Brown.

NOT EXACTLY WILLING.

The Secretary further announced a communication from the Rev. Jasper, of Virginia, asking the Club to indorse his theory that the sun moves, but Broth-

er Gardner said that the time was not yet ripe. In
years gone by, some one had started the theory that
the sun stood still while the earth moved around it,
and the majority of people had come to accept that
theory as a fact. It might be radically wrong, and
yet the man who brought forward any other theory
would be scoffed at and called a crank. His advice to Rev. Jasper was to hang to his theory and
wait.

HE CAN'T GO.

A communication from Norwalk, O., signed by
such leading citizens as George McGee, Sandy McCoy, Ben Van Camps, Amos Hopkins, George Hanshaw, Friday Hodge and Charles Augustus Hopkins, stated that the colored population of that city
were very much agitated over the question: "Do
sidewhiskers dignify a colored man's position in
life?" Three dogs had been poisoned, two windows
smashed in and the lives of three men had been
threatened, and yet the question had not been settled. A public meeting had been called for the 28th
inst., and it was hoped that Brother Gardner would
be present and throw his influence one way or the
other.

He stated in reply that he could not go, nor could
he furnish either side any advice by letter. He had
seen colored men with sidewhiskers who inspired
him with awe. He had seen others who reminded
him of Darwin's theory. There was dignity in any
sort of whiskers, but what is the use of dignity if a
man had to wipe his nose on a vest-buckle and button his Sunday coat with a shingle nail. It was a
local affair, and must be settled among themselves.

THE SICK.

The Committee on the Sick reported that Judge Alanthus Griggs, a local member in good standing, was confined to his bed and had asked for his allowance from the relief fund.

"What am de matter wid de Judge?" asked the President.

"Sprained his back."

"How?"

"By jumpin' ober a hitchin' post on a bet of ten cents."

"Bein' dat he sprained his back by jumpin' ober a hitchin' post, he kin now obtain relief by fallin' off a house," concluded the President, as he blew his nose and sat down.

The Committee also reported that Darkweather Smith was likewise confined to his bed with bilious colic and needed relief. It being ascertained that he let himself loose on four pounds of grapes to see what he could do, the President decided that it was not a case coming under the provisions of the relief fund.

MORE RELICS.

The Librarian reported that he was in receipt of the hat worn by Cornwallis at the Yorktown surrender, sent on to the Club from Williamsburg, Va. Also a pair of sheep-shears, owned by Martin Van Buren, forwarded from Boston.

THE MEDAL.

The Secretary announced that the annual Lime-Kiln Club medal to be given to the colored man performing the greatest **deed** of heroism during the year, was already in his hands for the year 1881. The medal is of silver and bronze, about the size of a trade dollar. On one side is a picture of a mule, and on the other that of a persimmon tree with a 'possum hanging to a limb. The inscription reads: "When our heroes die our country will die."

REPRIMANDED.

The Janitor was called from the ante-room and asked if he had made any special study of the radition of heat, as requested at a late meeting by a unanimous vote of the Club. After considerable hesitation he replied to the effect that when the stove began to cool off he had to radiate around in the alleys after dry-goods boxes and apple barrels, and on several different occasions had narrowly escaped arrest. He was advised to continue his specialty, and thoroughly post himself on the science of heat, and the meeting then awoke Elder Toots by rolling him off the bench, and adjourned.

DE SUN DO MOVE.

THE silence in the Hall was so thick that it could have been cut with an editorial jack-knife as the President calmly arose and began:

"I hold hear in my hand a letter from Philadelphia, axin' me if I believe wid the Rev. Jasper, of Richmond, dat de sun do move? Sartin I do. I know de white folks claim dat it am de airth which am movin', while de sun stands still, but right dar we split. Joshua was about as nigh bein' an angel as any white man will eber git, an when he ordered de sun to stand still he knew what he was talkin' about. It would have been just as easy fur him to hev commanded de airth to stand still, but he didn't do it. If Joshua didn't know his bizness de rest of us might as well hang up.

"An' now, you cull'd folkses, mind what Ize gwine to say. Doan' let de 'stronomy bizness keep you awake nights. De sun am up dar by day, an' de moon an stars am up dar by night. De Lawd put de sun dar to thaw de ice off de back doah-step, make cucumbers grow an' fotch up de grass an' de corn. It didn't do any wuss when astronomy was unknown, an' it wouldn't do any better if ebery family in de kentry had a telescope four hundred feet long. De moon was hung up dar dat folks might see to move by night when de rent got too high; dat lost cows could see to find dar way home, dat folks could see to chop wood and empty bar'ls of ashes on de street; dat wimin comin' home from prayer meetin' could avoid de nail heads stickin' up in de planks, an' fur varus odder reasons. You jist take de sun as he runs, an de moon as you find it, an' de less you worry about 'em de more meat an' taters you'll have in de winter. De poorest cull'd man I eber knowed was an ole black man down in Virginny who was always wonderin' if dey had a reglar lock on de gates of Heaven, or only a latch string. While his nayburs war plantin' he was wonderin'; while dey war hoin' he was theorizing; while dey was reapin' he was ragged an' hungry. Let de sun move or stand still—let de moon be made of old silver or green cheese—let de stars be ten miles or 10,-000,000 miles away—keep de whitewash brush gwine an' de buck-saw in good order an' you'll be all right."

GATHER THEM IN.

The Secretary announced a communication from John W. Calhoun, President of the West Virginia Liver Complaint Association, asking the Lime Kiln Club to receive them as a body. After an official existence of six months they found themselves out of wood and candles, behind in their rent, afflicted with corns and chilblains, and of no further use to high-toned society.

On motion of Pickles Smith, who stated that he was personally acquainted with Mr. Calhoun, the Liver Complaint Society was absorbed by unanimous vote.

RECEIVED.

The keeper of the Sacred Relics roported that he had received from Samuel Blood, of Nashville, a set of wooden blocks forming a puzzle called "13—14—15," a game very popular about 6,000 years ago. He had already returned thanks, and sent the donor a cure for hydrophobia.

He likewise reported the reception of an old carbine, used by Grace Darling when she went out to the rescue of shipwrecked sailors. Just how she shot 'em out of the water with it the sender did not say, but the thanks of the Club had been forwarded, and the old arm hung on the west wall.

VOTE OF CONFIDENCE.

The Committee on Internal Resources reported that it was in receipt of intelligence from various parts of the country to the effect that the supply of melons and green corn promised to equal the ordinary demand, and on motion of Pickles Smith the following resolution was unanimously adopted:

Resolved, Dat dis Club has fnll confidence in de agyculchural resources of dis kentry, but at de same time we would advise all members of dis Club to plug dar watermelyons befo' passin' ober dar money.

A COMING SHADOW.

The Secretary announced a communication from Mrs. Amanda Hopeshot, of Cairo, Ill., containing intelligence of the death of her husband by his own hand, caused by his failure to secure admission to the Club, and her determination to begin suit for $5,000 damages unless a check for $300 was forwarded by return mail.

The Secretary was instructed to return a reply to the effect that the Club could not consider itself morally or pecuniary responsible, and a hint was thrown out to the Treasurer that it might be policy to hide all his funds in an oyster can and bury the can under about four feet of back garden.

STANDARD PRICES.

Giveadam Jones announced that he had received replies from New York, Boston, Philadelphia, Chicago, and sixteen other points, and that the standard prices of the Lime-Kiln Club for whitewashing and stove-blacking, were being accepted all over the country. No uniform price can be made for cleaning up back yards. In the New England States back yards all run to clam-shells, peach-cans, and old hoop-skirts, during the winter. In Tennessee, they lean more to old boots and pint bottles. Down in Texas the remains of horse-thieves and tramps must be carted off with the oyster-cans and old hats, without extra charge.

UNDER CONDITIONS.

The Presideut stated that he had received the following personal letter:

oston, February 1, 1882.

BRO. GARDNER:—Is there anything wrong in playing a game of cards. Very truly, CRANBERRY JONES.

"When Elder Lightfoot an' his wife come ober to my cabin," replied the President, "an' we sot down fur a game o' euchre, we feel as innocent of wrong as a two-year old child foolin wid a revolver; but under certain odder condishuns a game of cards may result in great evil. If a pusson stacks the keerds, dat's wrong; if he puts de joker up his sleeve, dat's wrong; if he plays a lone hand, dat looks suspicious; if he winks at his partner to take it up or turn it down, it isn't a squar' game. Ordinarily speakin' dar's nuffin' wrong in a game of keerds—uuless you git all de nine an' ten spots, an' de odder man holds'all de bowers an' aces."

NEARER HOME.

The Janitor reported the breaking of five panes of glass in the back windows during the week, but he had been unable to locate anyone with his shot-gun. Also, that the rats were eating the legs off the safe in which the Club funds are stacked away.

The Librarian reported the receipt of three dozen almanacs, and a pamphlet entitled "How to Be Beautiful."

The Keeper of the Bear-trap reported everything clear in the West, and the meeting was brought to a close.

BEAUTIES OF THE BALLOT.

"I would like to spoke a few words to Telescope Perkins, if he am in de Hall'to-night," said the President, as the meeting opened.

The brother wiped off his mouth and advanced to the platform, and Brother Gardner continued:

"Brudder Perkins, I met you at 8 o'clock in de evenin' on 'lecshun night."

"Yes, sah."

"You war what de white folks call slewed."

"Ize mighty sorry, sah."

"You were full of glory. You felt dat you had saved de kentry. Your clothes war all mud. Your breaf smelt of skunks, an' you had to jump up and down an' whoop to keep from bustin' yer biler."

"Lots of white folks was doin' de same, sah."

"Sartin—sartin. You, an ole ex-slave, unable to read or write, was only followin' in de footsteps of intelligent, eddecated white men. Brudder Perkins I war walkin' round on 'lection day, an' I saw some curus things. I saw citizens who would not swallow ten drops of whisky if life depended on it wote fur men who hev sold de pisened stuff ober de bar fur years. An' dat was savin' de kentry.

"I saw men who would turn a servant gal out doors on a winter's night, if dey heard a scandle 'bout her, walk up to de poles an' wote fur men who rent from two to half a dozen houses to women of bad character. Dat was gwine it straight!

"I saw men whose wives am breakin' deir hearts ober de wayward course of beloved sons, walk to de winder and stick in ballots fur candidates who am in cahoots wid blacklegs an' de steady patrons of gambling houses. Dat am de glory of politics!

"I saw Christian men, who pray agin vice and shed tears ober de wickedness of society, wote fur candidates whose private lives am one long night of debauchery and corruption. Dat was standin' by de party.

"I saw ministers of de gospel cast wotes fur drunkards, libertines an' outlaws of society. Dat was supportin' de principle.

"I saw de honest, decent men arrayed on one side, an' de thugs, thieves an' loafers on de odder, an' de honest, decent men war swept away like chaff befo' a gale. Dat was an illustrashun of de beauties of de 'lective franchise!"

"But I won't do it agin, sah," pleaded Brother Perkins.

"You kin sot down," quietly remarked the President. "Dat same night I heard Aldermen bawlin' like mules bekase some favorite candidate had pulled frew wid de aid of money an' whisky. Citizens who wouldn't let you in at de front doah rolled in de mud dat night like hogs. Men who hev sons to bring up met an' shook hands an' rejoiced ober de 'leckshun of candidates who know de way into ebery saloon an' poker room in Detroit. Blame you, Brudder Perkins—blame you for follerin de example of leadin' white folks! No, sah! Go an' sot down an' feel proud dat you come so nigh bein' an eminent citizen!"

SIGNS OF SUCCESS.

The Committee on Improvements signified their readiness to render their monthly report, and the Chairman stated that they had made a careful canvas of the city to see what progress was being made in bringing about the new time-table, in which the next hour after 12 o'clock noon will be called 13 o'clock. They found the new system in use in several stores and factories, at two breweries and three wood yards, and other establishments were preparing to adopt it. The Committee received plenty of assurances that the public would take kindly to the change, and that the next generation would never suspect that the clock makers of this one were too stupid to be able to count above twelve.

MORE HONORS.

While Brother Gardner was called into the anteroom to throw a half-drunken man down stairs the Secretary read the following:

Paris, Ky., Aug. 27, 1881.

Brother Gardner:

Dear Sir—At the last meeting of the Big Four Literary and Philosophical Society of this city you were elected an honorary member for life, and the Secretary instructed to request you to prepare and deliver an address before us, on the first Wednesday evening in October on the subject of: "The Good Time Coming."

I am, sir, very truly,
Dragoon Parker,
President B. F. L. and P. S.

GENIUS INVOKED.

The Secretary of the Board of Trade of Milan, Ohio, forwarded a communication in which he asked whether a person suffering with chilblains could pull off his boots and scratch his heels in church or the theater without outraging public sentiment.

"Dat am a queshun which has gin me considerable thought," said the President. "Sometimes it seems as if he could, an' agin it seems as if he couldn't. De bizness of chilblains am to itch an' be oneasy. De bizness of de owner am to pacify de oneasiness. You can't talk to a chilblain, nor argy wid it, nor scare it away by threats. It takes mo' nerve to sot still for ten minits wid your feet ticklin' an' tinglin' an' itchin' dan it does to face a mad lion fur half an hour. It seems as if sunthin had got to be did, but what to do am de queshun. I believe dat genius should be invoked. I believe genius kin attach a nutmeg-grater to an iron rod an' fit de machine inside de boot, so dat when de oneasiness begins a movement of de rod will agitate de grater along de sole of de foot an' bring on a peaceful calm. I believe we have de genius in dis Club, an' fur de sake of bringin' him out I will hereby offer a reward of $25 from de treasury to de inventor of a successful chilblain-scratcher."

Something of the sort will no doubt be brought out soon, and the successful genius may look for a large sale and big profits.

"THANK YOU EVER SO MUCH."

The Secretary announced a further communication from Gardnerville, Tex., announcing that the name had been given to the new town in honor of the President of the Lime-Kiln Club. Brother Gardner was quite overcome for the moment, and might perhaps have broken down under his emotion had not Samuel Shin accidentally upset the water pail and filled the surrounding brogans with ice water.

CAN'T RECEIVE IT.

The Treasurer said that a majority of the honorary members were sending in punched quarters and halfes in payment of dues, and although he had plugged scores of pieces with lead and passed them off on the unsuspecting public, he hoped for some ruling in the case which would relieve him from the pressure. The President instructed him to hereafter make a discount of 1,000 per cent. on all mutilated bills or coins sent in, and most of the lamps being on the point of going out for the want of oil, the meeting was dismissed in due ancient form.

HAVE WE ANY ÆSTHETICS?

The Chairman of the Committee on Agriculture announced that he was ready to report on the query: "Have we any æsthetics among us?" The Committee had faithfully investigated for two long weeks, and had reached the conclusion that if there were any such persons in Detroit, they were hidden away in garrets. The Committee had run across sad-eyed girls, having a sorrowful pucker to their mouth and carrying sorrowful-hued parasols, but they were not æsthetics. They had merely been disappointed in not going to the seaside. The Committee had run across sad-eyed young men, carrying sad little canes and wearing spiritulle hats, but they smoked five-cent cigars and chewed raw peanuts, and æsthetics never do that. The Committee had labored diligently and well, and was forced to the conclusion that the only fools in Detroit were natural born ones.

THE CLOSE.

The Glee Club struck up, "Who Stole Dat Dog o' Mine," and a collection was taken up for the benefit of two theological students about to sail for Liberia. Brother Gardner announced that by accident somebody had dropped two cents in money into the hat, and the coin was voted into the Club incidental fund, and the meeting adjourned.

TO PATRIOTS.

"BE patriotic," began the old man as Pickles Smith swallowed a trunk-key which he had been holding in his mouth to cure dyspepsia—"be patriotic, but doan' emagine dat all de odder patriots am dead an' buried. I like a man who speaks well of his kentry, but it worries me when I see him carryin' dat kentry on his back. Be patriotic, but find out fust what patriotism means. Dis kentry fought fur her liberty. Put dat in your hat. Liberty in dis kentry eber since has bin as nigh a sham as a circus widout a menagerie, clown or performers. Put dat in your pipe. We fout England to unite de States. Den we turned aroun' an' fout each odder to dissolve 'em. We whoop an' hurrah fur our soldiers, but we gin de fat offices to our relashuns who didn't go to war. A general who lost a battle am all O. K. if he kin run a political party. A general who won one am forgotten in a y'ar if he doan' wote de right ticket. In one breath we flatter ourselves that we have de greatest statesmen on airth, an' in de next we convict 'em of todyism, nepotism, placehuntin' an' stealin'. We weep ober de orphans made by war, an' den turn about an' howl bekase dey am granted pitiful penshuns. We poke fun at our navy, an' yet refuse to wote money to strengthen it. We want de Injun licked out of his butes, an' yet we sell him de means to lick us.

"De man who sots out to be a patriot must go slow, or he will be taken for a lunatic or a rascal instead. It's a grand kentry, but de taxpayers have to foot de bill. It's a Republic of free speech, but you mus' agree wid de big guns or you will be sot down as a crank. We flatter ourselves dat we—we am thought some pumpkins by European powers, an' yet we select as our representatives abroad sich men as am played out at home. We talk about de pauper labor of Europe, an' yet we have two county houses to her one. We rap de Czar of Russia for his tyrany, an' yet we submit to laws an' practices, an' rappin's from policemen, an' arrests without warrants, and customs which would send de Russian into a war of rebellion. We dispise titles, an' yet toady to de rich. We warn kings dat deir days am short, an' den steal our own Presidents or shoot them into power.

"Be patriotic, my frens, but doan shoot off a hull battery of artillery to call yer dog when a whistle will do jist as well. Let us now enter upon de bizness which has culminated us togeder."

UNDER CONDITIONS.

The Secretary announced a communication from the Hon. Considerably Davis, of Jersey City, stating that he had invented a combined music-box and rat-trap, and wished permission to name the invention after the Lime-Kiln Club. In case it was granted, he would forward four of his machines by the first freight train.

Brother Gardner replied to the effect that permission could not be granted until he had witnessed the workings of the invention. The trap part might be all right, but what was the music? He did not propose to show his enmity by inflicting on this country anything worse than the average piano. He had one in his own humble home, and whenever he felt out of sorts with the world he sat down and began on "Home, Sweet Home." He could turn out every neighbor inside of three minutes, and in less than five he was sure to be shot at. Did this new invention possess power to soothe or irritate? Would it add to the number of lunatics, or would it soothe the feelings of a family just returned from a steamboat excursion? He could not grant the desired permission without further particulars.

ELDER TOOTS AT THE FRONT.

During the last two or three meetings Elder Toots had managed to keep awake most of the time by keeping a bit of ice on his head and permitting the melting stream to trickle aown the back of his neck, but on this occasion he had slept sweetly for twenty minutes, when he suddenly rose and offered the following resolution:

"*Resolved,* Dat dis Club do hereby express its sympathy fur de cause of liberty in Cuba."

During the deep silence which followed the reading of the above, Prof. High-Strung Smith was plainly heard chewing slippery elm, and a sudden sneeze from Gen. Overworked Johnson rattled along the ceiling and brought down hundreds of small pieces of plaster.

"Brudder Toots, what do you know 'bout Cuba?" asked the President.

"Nuffin, sah."

"What do you know 'bout de cause of liberty?"

"Nuffin."

"Who axed you to present dat resolushun?"

"Judge Gallipolee Thompson, sah."

"Brudder Toots, you go out an' soak de back of yer neck in cold tea! You has bin made a fool of! You are a purty middlin' aiverage ole nigger, but de mo' you sleep while present at our meeting de mo' benefit you will derive from de purceedins. As fur you, Brudder Thompson, you am hereby fined nine hundred dollars an' costs fur disruptin' de reg'lar purceedins. I may add at dis time dat de costs am about fo' hundred dollars."

The Judge fell to the floor in a dead faint, but was immediately drawn out of the Hall by the left leg, and business went right on.

HE'S A FRAUD.

A letter from a city official of Irwinton Ga., made inquiry if Pickles Smith had been sent down there to canvas for subscriptions to raise the funds to purchase 500 ice cream freezers for the negroes in Liberia. A person so calling himself was then in that city, and had collected seven or eight dollars. He was described as a low-built man, broad in the back, nose broken and skewed around to starboard, and four front teeth gone.

Brother Pickles Smith at once leaped to his feet and moved that the Club offer a reward of $5,000 for the arrest and conviction of the infamous imposter, and he was about to launch out into a speech thirty-four feet long when the President stopped him with:

"Doan' git excited, Brudder Smith. While de man am a fraud, an' while it am werry, werry wrong to blast de reputashun of a good man, dis Club won't offer ober $5 reward. Hundreds of white men have sold out for less. Sot down, Pickles—sot down an' ketch yer breath."

THE SICK.

The Committee on the sick reported that Brother General Jackson Cox had sent for them on the previous evening and they had arrived at his cabin in a one-horse wagon to find him out of his mind and evidently drawing near death's door. They recommended that he be allowed five dollars from the relief fund, and that two members be detailed to sit up with him.

"Brudder Cox didn't send for me," observed the President, as he placed the report on the window-sill, where it would blow into the street, "but I went over dar jist de same. I arrove dar 'bout half an hour after de Committee left, an' I found de Gineral lickin' de chill'en wid one hand an' eatin' cold corn beef wid de odder. His mind had got back an' so had his ole woman, an' de way she was rakin' him down made me weak in de knees. Doorin' de arternoon de Gineral had eaten two quarts of huckle-berries, a cherry pie, a loaf of bread, fo' biled aigs an' a due quantity of sassage, an' de strain on his constitution was a leetle too much. He won't git eny relief heah, an' de next time he shows up in dis Hall Ize gwine to talk to him in a way dat will make him lose six pounds of fat in five minits."

ASTRONOMY.

The Committee on Astronomy reported that it had used every possible effort to discover whether the moon was inhabited or not, but had been unable to satisfy twemselves that it was. Col. Jerusalem Todd, of the Committee, was pretty well satisfied that he had seen goats moving about up there, and Elder Higginbottom was dead sure that he could make out a troop of yellow dogs and a patch of blackberry bushes, but they had squinted in vain for a sight of human life.

WILL INVESTIGATE.

Giveadam Jones sent to the Secretary's desk a letter which he had received from Chicago, signed Ginger Jackson, preferring charges against a member of the Club residing there, named Cyclone Sampson. The charges were: Beating his fare on the street cars and mistaking a cooper shop for a saloon. Brother Gardner ordered the Committee on Elections to investigate and report, and if the charges are sustained Brother Jackson may prepare himself for a standing jump of thirty-two feet.

The solemn voice of the triangle now announced that the safety of the country was an assured fact, and as the water pail was turned bottom side up and the safe rolled back to place, the Glee Club burst into delicious song and the meeting fell asunder.

NO LUNATICS PRESENT.

"WHAT I war goin' to remark," began Brother Gardner, as the hour arrived and the triangle sounded, "am to ask who among you am insane? I should like to make out a list as soon as possible, an' I hope dat no lunatic will feel backward about handin' in his name.

"You look surprised," continued the old man, as he walked up and down in front of his desk, "but I am quite satisfied dat we have at least a dozen lunatics among us. De man who shot de President could read law an' plead it; he could cheat, lie, swindle, bilk hotels, buy an' sell, come an' go, push his claims fur office an' go on long journey, an' yet he am declared to be crazy. No one eber knowed it till he became an assassin. If he hadn't tried to commit murder he would still be looked upon as a dead-beat instead of a lunatic. Now I propose to take time by de 4-lock an' make a list of de lunatics in our Club fur de benefit of de purleece. Let each assassin stand up as his name is called by de Seckretary."

The Secretary went through the roll in his usual sing-song way, and not a member stood up.

"Werry well," said the President, "let de Seckretary make a note of dis. You hev all pleaded guilty to bein' perfeckly sane, an' you mus' take de consequences. If ary one of you walk out of a grocery wid a codfish under your coat, or am oberhauled by de purleece wid a bag of chickens on yer back, doan' try to shirk de consequences by pleadin' insanity."

NOT YET.

A letter from the Rev. Tobago Jones, of Mobile, asked if it was true that the Lime-Kiln Club had passed a resolution asking Congress to rob the treasury and divide up the money between them and go home and have done with it. The President said that such a resolution was now on his desk, and might be presented at the next meeting.

IT WILL.

The Secretary announced a further communication from Buggy Botton, Fla., stating the fact that the colored people in that vicinity had formed a "Saw-Dust Club," and desired to affiliate with the Lime-Kiln. Brother Gardner ordered the Secretary to open correspondence with red ink and corn-colored envelopes, and in case it was found that the "Saw-Dusters" were composed of sixteen members, and were provided with a three-hooped water-pail, a thermometer and a stove with regular hinges to the door, to say that the Lime-Kiln would affiliate up to the twenty-seventh degree.

"KINDER NEUTRAL."

"I has received a letter from de interior of de Stait," said the President, as he adjusted his spectacles, "axin' what part dis Lime-Kiln Club will take in de Emancipashun Proclimashun Celebrashun, to be held in August. I 'spect dat we shall take a kinder neutral posishun. If de cull'd folkses of Michigan, or any part dar'off, feel dat de anniversary of dat occashun calls fur a splurge, let 'em splurge. As fur me, I reckon dat de black man who chaws up chickens on Thanksgivin', hangs up his stockins on Christmas, gorges himself on New Year's, parades on Washington's birthday, feels bad on Decorashun Day an' busts de glory outer dis kentry on Fo'th of July, has 'bout all de bizness on han' he kin manage on an income ranging from $3 to $7 per week. We will lend 'em our flag an' water-pail, an' keep Paradise Hall open all day fur de weary, but dey needn't look fur anythin' furder."

ABSORBED.

Among the applications for membership was the Colored Philosophical Club of Atlanta, composed of twenty-seven of the most celebrated colored men of Georgia. The club was organized seven years ago, and at one time numbered over three hundred members. The letter forwarded by the Secretary stated that the club had decided to dissolve because the President had run away with a strange woman, its Treasurer had skipped with the funds and the Secretary was in jail on charge of having thirteen shovels hidden under his wood-shed.

ELECTION.

Pickles Smith, Chairman of the Committee on Applications, announced that he had no names of candidates to hand in, and an explanation being demanded, he said that he had a list of thirteen in his pocket to bring down, but lost it while assisting a white man to load a calf into a wagon.

Brudder Smith," replied the President, as he carefully wiped his spectacles, " de nex' time dat a spotted calf or a yaller dog, or anything else short of a cyclone or an airthquake, am permitted to interfere wid de reg'lar bizness of dis Club, dar will be a wacancy heah, an' you will no longer hev de privilege of spittin' tobacky on de fust jint of de stovepipe."

IT WAS PENSTOCK.

The Secretary then read a letter from January Jones, of Selma, Alabama, stating that he received a call some six weeks since from a person representing himself to be the Rev. Penstock. Said person borrowed $2 to help him on to the next town, and as the money had not been returned as promised, Mr. Jones had drawn a sight-draft on the Treasurer of the Club for the amount.

As the Secretary laid the communication down 117 pairs of eyes were turned upon Penstock. He rose up, choking with indignation, and as soon as he could unbutton his vest and push up his hair, he put in such an emphatic denial that one of the beartraps fell down upon Samuel Shin and rendered him unconscious for seven minutes. Penstock was not within fifty miles of Selma on his southern trip, and as for money, he reached home after an absence of almost four weeks with upwards of twenty-three cents to spare. He wanted a Committee of Investigation, and he wanted that committee to do its work in the most thorough manner. The President appointed Giveadam Jones, Colonel De Hue and Saratoga Thompson as such committee, with power to send for persons and papers and lemonade and cigars and a fifteen-cent lunch.

THE CLOSE.

The Glee Club having wrestled with a new song composed expressly for the fall season by some one signing herself "Mrs. L.," Elder Toots was drawn to one side, a new thirteen-cent pad-lock placed on the safe, and the meeting adjourned with such enthusiasm that several panes of glass were broken in the window looking down upon the alley.

TRAPPING A HYENA.

SOME three months ago, owing to various and repeated attempts to destroy Paradise Hall by fiends in human shape, Samuel Shin asked leave in open meeting to protect the Hall by an invention of his own. Leave was granted, and the result was seen as the Janitor opened the place Saturday afternoon to make ready for the usual weekly meeting at night. Mr. Shin's invention consisted of a pound of powder innocently stored away in an old nail keg, and the keg placed where a stranger would use it to look through the transom. A pressure of two pounds on the head of the keg would scratch a match and explode the powder. Some men would have grown weary of waiting, but Samuel knew that if he fished long enough he was certain to catch a whale.

Sometime during Thursday night a person whose name will never be known unlocked the street door with the crank of a coffee mill and slid up stairs with murder in his thoughts. Perhaps he expected to find Elder Toots asleep up there, and was prepared to dispatch him without mercy, or he may have simply intended to damage the Hall about $15,000 worth and then go away to secretly chuckle over his dastardly work. Be that as it may he reached the ante-room and paused for a moment to cast a glance of contempt at the stuffed opposum over the door leading into the lodge. There stood the innocent nail keg, and the transom was open.

The human hyena probably cackled with delight as he saw the easy way prepared for him, but it was his last cackle on earth. As he mounted the keg there was a dull explosion, which was heard by many people on the street and supposed to have been caused by the blowing up of a tug down towards Lake Erie.

When the Hall opened Saturday evening Mr. Shin had all the remains spread out on top of Waydown Bebee's plug hat. There was a button, seven hairs, the heel of a sock, a finger-nail, and a part of a document beginning with: "To the Hon. the Common Coun—." A hole in the roof through which twenty-seven stars looked placidly down on the Bear-Trap indicated the ulterior direction taken by the balance of the remains. The force of the explosion knocked the safe over and broke one hinge, and the pictures on the walls were more or less damaged, but Cadaver Smith came forward and offered to make good the damage out of his own pocket.

THE LESSON.

"Let dis be a warnin' to de wicked to pause," said Brother Gardner as the meeting opened. "Let it be a furder warnin to de good not to become wicked. Wickedeess doan' pay. If you turn gambler you may hide de joker up yer sleeve and win a few dollars, but de fust thing ye know some man will hide de fo' bowers in his hat an' skoop ye blind. If you turn robber you may stop some plumber on de highway an' make a haul of three hun'red dollars, but de nex' fing you know you bet on a hoss-race an' lose de pile. We have de proofs befo' us dat while de wicked am chucklin' an' grinnin' an' growin' fat, death am waitin' at deir elbow to lif' em higher nor a kite. De Committee on Privileges an' Repose will see to de repairs of de Hall, an' we will now ambulate to'rs de reg'lar order of bizness."

THE LAWYERS.

"Jist at dis moment," began Brother Gardner as the triangle called the meeting to order, " de press of de North, East, South an' West am cryin out at de increase of of crime an' de laxity of law. Judges an' juries am bein' plainly told dat dis turnin' loose of red-handed criminals must stop or de people will resort to lynch law, an' in many cases de long-sufferin' people hev dun taken de law inter deir own hands an' left de criminals dangling to de limbs of trees or lamp-posts. From de press an' workshop comes a cry for reform, an' men am axin' each odder whar de root of de evil lies. Heah am a letter from Ohio axin' me how I feel about it an' what I hev to recommend.

"Listen to me. Kin you name one single lawyer in dis kentry, outside of de salaried Prosecuting Attorneys, who has any fame as a defender of de law an' a convicter of criminals? Not one! On de odder hand you kin name hundreds who have grown rich an' famous by pullin' thieves, burglars an' murderers freu de meshes of de law. To be a lawyer is to be a law-breaker—not a law defender. To be a lawyer is to be a man, who, fur mo' or less money, will attempt to shield de man who steals his own fadder's corpse from de grave an' sells it to de surgeons. To be a lawyer is to be a man who will break up the happiest family fur a $20 greenback. Ef you hate your naybur go to de lawyer an' he will tell you how to play him some dirty trick. Ef a newspaper tells de truf 'bout you, go to a lawyer an' he will start a libel suit on 'speckulashun. Ef you want your wife sent to a mad-house, any lawyer will fix de case fur $50. Steal, rob, murder, an' lawyers will rush to your prison cell to get a fee for defendin' you. Our cities am full of gamblers. Why? 'Kase de lawyers encourage 'em. Embezzlement has become de rule. Why? Kase de lawyer settles de case fur a per cent. an' de embezzler comes out of it wid a character as pure as de snow. Who started de insanity dodge? De lawyers. Who encourage divorces? De lawyers. Who encourage crime in all its phases? De lawyers. You kin not hire de lowest, poorest black man to do fur money what lawyers am doin' every day. De public am deir prey. Misfortune am deir opportunity, an' man's weakness am deir glory an' profit. De public law has no majesty in deir eyes—de flreside grief rouses no sentiment in deir hearts. Whar dar am no lawyers dar am no litigashun an' but few crimes. Our judiciary, in too many cases, from Justice of de Peace cl'ar up, am entitled to no man's reverence an' may well fall under every man's suspicshuns. Too many lawyers am black egs, who deserve prison bars, an' many of our courts am nuffin better dan dens of robbers an' black-mailers. Dat's all fur dis time, an' we will now impel ourselves upon de reg'-lar order of bizness."

DON'T NEED ANY.

The Secretary announced a communication from Prof. Pecan Thomas, of Texas, offering to come to Detroit and deliver five lectures before the Club on the subject of "The Benefits of Philosophy," providing that the Club would pay his running expenses and guarantee him a purse of $100.

"We can't spar' de money, an' we doan' need de philosophy," said Brother Gardner in reply. "No doubt philosophy has its benefits: but a determined man, armed wid de Baptist religun an' a new white-wash brush, kin work all aroun' philosophy six days in de week, an' wake up wid a cl'ar head on Sunday mornin'. When taters am a dollar a bushel an' risin', two shillins in cash will go furder dan sixteen lectures on de purtiest philosophy eber stood up in a nine-pin alley to be knocked down by de cold han' of hunger.'

NOT ON THAT LAY.

The Secretary of the Scientific and Research Association of St Louis, composed of twenty-one barbers and a cook, forwarded a communication to the Club, asking in the name of the colored people of America, a contribution of $50 in cash towards another attempt to discover the North Pole.

Samuel Shin bobbed up to say that he favored the project, but one look settled him back, and on the matter being put to a vote, every one of the 129 mem-ders voted dead against it. If the colored people of America do any discovering during the next three or four years, they will not have to divide the honors with the Lime-Kiln Club.

THEY WILL AGREE.

The Chairman of the Committee on Internal Harmony reported that his committee had met a committee appointed by the State Legislature, and had come to a perfect understanding all around. The legislative body had agreed:

1. To take no steps to raise the poll-tax on colored men, without the assent of the Club.

2. To place no impediment in the way of introducing artistic whitewashing into school boards.

3. To name all new mountains, lakes and volcanoes discovered in this State after prominent colored persons to be named by the Club.

The Committee had agreed on the part of the Club:

1. Not to demand exemption from jury service on account of ignorance.

2. To restrain the number of dogs in a family to six.

3. Not to interfere with the next Senatorship.

Thus, by the exercise of a little diplomatic courtesy and common sense, these two powerful bodies will work together for the common good, and the result cannot be over-estimated.

WILL SEE ABOUT IT.

The Secretary further announced the receipt of a communication from the "Malone Corners Prevaricating Society," of Tennessee, asking to be taken into the Lime-Kiln Club in a body.

THE LIME-KILN CLUB. 277

Giveadam Jones moved to suspend the rules and vote the society in, but the Rev. Penstock objected. He said that a prevaricator was a liar, and he thought the Club had all the liars it could take care of. Judge Juneblossom jumped up and wanted to know if that was a personal fling at him. Col. Rainbow Smith followed suit, and in a minute forty members were on their feet waving their hands, shaking their fists and yelling at the top of their voices. During the paraliamentary excitement one of the bear-traps fell down, and struck old man Collins on the neck, and the bust of Andrew Jackson made a jump for Pickles Smith and laid him out, and somebody upset the sleeping Elder Toots and incited him to yell "murder!" at the top of his voice. Order could not be restored until the President picked up a four-pound weight and threatened to let it slide down the center aisle. It was then decided to refer the matter to a Special Committee, and the President added:

"Brudder Penstock, do not be too ready to charge humanity wid lyin' an' deceivin'. Brudder Juneblossom, do not be too quick to believe dat you am de only liar an' prevaricator in dis Club. All men lie an' all women prevaricate. We expect 'em to, an' in many cases we respect 'em for it."

RULES SUSPENDED.

At this moment the Janitor entered with a telegram from Comecloser Peters, of Baltimore, asking that his name be presented for membership. Mr. Peters is known throughout the State of Maryland as the only colored man in the South who can whistle six different tunes on his thumb-nail. He is an orator, a great financier, and makes "pig" rhyme with "everlasting" when writing poetry.

On motion of Royal Purple Saunders the rules were suspended and Mr. Peters was made a member.

REPORTS.

Owing to the great interest taken in the celebration of the Fourth by the members of the Club, the various committees were behind in their reports and had nothing to submit. The President stated his hopes that all committees would settle down to business at once, and after reproving Samuel Shin for asserting in a crowd that his forefathers died in the cause of liberty, and severely reprimanding Pickles Smith for asserting that Fourth of July was no better than Christmas, the meeting walked down stairs while the Glee Club sang: "'Twas the Midnight Howl of a Baby."

THE INFLUENCE OF MUSIC.

"I has received a letter from Boston," slowly remarked Brother Gardner as he squinted from Samuel Shin to Waydown Bebee. "I has received a letter from Boston axin' me fur my observashuns on de inflooence of music on mankind. I reply dat mankind widout music would be chawin' each odder up in half a day. Music am de stone wall dat surrounds marcy, peace, charity and humanity. Only last week I war writin' down my observashuns fur de last forty-seven y'ars, an' I will gib dem to de public as follows:

"De sound of a horse-fiddle brings up old recko-leckshuns an' starts de tears of regret. If played long 'nuff, an' de mind am in de right direckshun, it will cause de listener to shell out a subscripshun of $3,000 to'rds a new cull'd Baptist Church. Try it once an' be convinced.

"De sound of a harp hits a man below de belt. He begins to fink of all de mean fings he ever did, an' to wish he hadn't, an' at de eand of fifteen minits he am all ready to step ober an' pay his nayburs a dollar apiece fur de hens he shot in his garden las' spring.

"De sound of de fiddle grabs on to seben different heart strings to once, an' a man am knocked so flat dat he will esteem it a privilege to len' you $10.

"The jewsharp goes right to de soul. If your wife am all ready to 'lope off wid de hired man de notes of de jewsharp will take her bonnet off in sixteen seconds. If you keep a hired man you should also keep a jewsharp.

"Pianer music sometimes hits and sometimes misses. Ize known it to make an old bald-head go home an' pass two hull hours widout cuffin' de chill'-en, an' Ize known it to cause a young gal to slide down ober de roof of de kitchen an' 'lope off wid de owner of a side-show.

"De guitar always brings sadness an' a resolushun to begin on de 1st of January to quit runin' out nights an' playin' policy.

"De brass band might soothe a sorrowin' soul if de said sorrowin' soul didn't have all he could do to hold his hoss.

"De molodeon used to produce a desire on de part of de listener to be buried under a yew-yew tree, but

I h'ar dey have improved it so dat a pusson had as lief be buried under a basswood.

"De organ fills de soul wid awe an' strikes de heroic chord. If you am layin' fur a man doan' tackle him just arter he has been takin' in de note of an organ.

"De banjo—yum! If you want my dog—my hoss—my house an' lot, play me de banjo an' keep time wid yer fut. I spect de music of de anjelic harps am sweet an soft an' dreamy, but if dey want to keep us cull'd folks satisfied up dar a leetle mo' banjo an' a leetle less harp am de fust prescription. Let us now attack de bizness of de meetin'."

NIPPED IN THE BUD.

A hotel keeper in Leesburg, Va., notified the Club that on a late date a colored man, wearing two diamond pins, three watch chains and other evidences of the string game, called at his hotel to engage board for four weeks, and gave his name as Trustee Pullback, of the Lime Kiln Club. When his landlord asked him which eye Brother Gardner was blind of, the fellow took to his heels, and although pursued for three miles by two men and a dog, he eluded them in a blackberry patch.

A CLOSE SHAVE.

"Am brudder Blue Glass Henderson in de Hall to-night?" blandly inquired the President, as he stood up and looked around.

"Yes, sah."

"Will you please step dis way?"

The brother stepped. He didn't seem easy in his mind and he kept his eyes on the coffee-pot once owned by the poet Milton instead of facing the President.

"Brudder Henderson, you war in a butcher-shop on Beaubien street las' Wednesday forenoon?"

"Yes, sah."

"When you went out de butcher missed two slices of ham, an' you war follered an sarched."

"Yes, sah."

"In one of your coat-tail pockets dey found, not de two slices of ham, but a pound and a half of beef."

"Yes, sah."

"You couldn't tell whar you got dat beef to save your life, an' you let de butcher keep it."

"Yes, sah, but de charge was stealin' ham."

"Jist so, Brudder Henderson, jist so. Dey missed ham an' dey found beef. It am plain 'nuff dat you didn't take de goods charged but I want you to understan' dat when dey miss ham an' find beef on a member of dis Club dat member has had de werry closest sort of a shave from bein' bounced off'n our books an' outer de Hall. Take your seat, sah, an' let dis be de awfullest kind of a warnin' to you."

THE WEATHER.

The following streak of weather can be looked for this week.

SUNDAY—Pretty fair, considering that it has to spread out over the whole United States and Canada.

MONDAY—A little off, but good enough for wash-day.

TUESDAY—Opens to a large house and gives general satisfaction as far west as Omaha, and that's as far as good weather is expected to go.

WEDNESDAY—Signs of autumn; coal dealer says he wants the amount of the old bill first. Thunder showers in the Gulf States. Persimmons fair eating in Virginia, and Michigan watermelons come under the wire ahead.

THURSDAY—No fish.

FRIDAY—Next door to being a spooney day. Opaque atmosphere in the New England States, and all the women look lantern-jawed.

SATURDAY—Comes up to the scratch smiling, but no go. Wants to snow, but concludes to rain. Sort of dreariness settles down over the country, and cats usher in the evening with wild, glad yells.

A CHAMPION.

" Am Construction White in de Hall dis evenin'?" softly inquired the President as the hush came.

"Yes, sah," answered a voice from the back end of the room, and Brother White made his way to the platform with a look of puzzled wonder on his face.

"Construction White," continued the President, after drawing a long breath, " I understan' dat you have become a champion."

" I—I—I dunno, sah," stammered the Brother.

" I understan' dat you claim to be able to lift mo' wid your teef dan any odder man in America. One of de local papers say dat you kin lift 280 poun's wid your jaws, an' dat you kin sustain your own weight seben minits by cotchin' a strap in your mouf."

" I—I 'spect dat's so, sah."

"Brudder White, dis Club doan' go a cent on champions. Champion rowers am simply crooks. Champion wrestlers am only loafers wid clean shirts on. De champion runner am sooner or later an inmate of de workhouse. De champion walker walks away, from his bo'd bill. Show me a so-called champion an' I'll show you a bad citizen. Brudder White, you am a man wid an iron jaw."

"Yes, sah."

"Use dat jaw properly an' men will bless you. You have a wide field befo' you. You kin help to tear down houses wid dat jaw. You kin tow schooners up an' down de riber wid profit to yourself an' pleasure to commerce. You kin help de firemen—you kin aid de police—you need have no fear of bitin' off mo' dan you kin chaw. Do dis quietly an' modestly, an' widout any blowin' of ho'ns. Bite honestly when you strike a railroad spike, an' chaw on de squar' when you git hold of a piece of sheet-iron. Do dis, an' we shall be glad dat you are among us. Start out as a champion, an' off goes your name from our books. You kin now return to your seat an' analize yer thoughts, an' decide what course you will adopt."

THEY ARE FRAUDS.

The Secretary announced a letter under the blood red seal, from the council chamber of the Gee-haw-haw Club, of Jersey City, stating that six individuals who professed to hold membership in the Lime-Kiln Club had applied to the Gee-haw-haw Club for admission. The matter was laid on the table until the names could be forwarded for identification.

Brother Gardner at once denounced each and every one a fraud of the second water. No such persons ever belonged to the Lime-Kiln Club, and the only one of them who ever made application was rejected for walking home with a smoked ham which belonged to another man. Societies all over the country are warned against any person who claims to belong to the Lime-Kiln Club who cannot show a certificate in which the word correct is spelled with a big " K."

SIXTY COPIES WANTED.

Trustee Pullback stated that he had received a letter from Escanaba, Mich., to the effect that an Escanaba editor had in press a history of the colored troops in the war. It would be a book of 200 pages, illustrated with 150 cuts of the said editor leading the gallant sun-burned Africans into carnage, and would probably be sold for a dollar.

On motion of Samuel Shin it was resolved that the Kime-Kiln Club order sixty copies of the forthcoming work, and an amendment inviting the editor to lecture before the Club and describe his experiences in thirty-four battles was likewise adopted.

THE EASTERN QUESTION.

Elder Toots said he arose in the interests of harmony and peace, and to inquire if the American Government had meddled or proposed to meddle with the eastern question.

The President replied that this government was represented in Turkish waters by two naval vessels, and that Uncle Sam seemed to itch to be counted in.

THE LIME-KILN CLUB.

The Elder then offered a resolution to the effect that in the opinion of the Lime-Kiln Club the less this government meddled with foreign affairs the more it would please the great majority, and the same was adopted by a vote of 84 to 1—Sorghum Clydebottom voting in the negative to spite Pickles Smith for stepping on his heel.

REPORTS.

The Committee on Internal Harmony reported a peaceful state of affairs throughout the entire country.

The Committee on Agriculture had received reports from the peanut and melon crop which delighted their hearts.

The Committee on Judiciary reported a marked decrease of crime in most of the States, and recommended the passage of a law by the several States making the crime of murder a punishable offense.

The Committee on Astronomy had seen the comet and observed the spots on the sun, but were not prepared to say that either affair had any influence on the weather or the general welfare. It was their belief that if the heavens were allowed to run their own machine things would come out all right.

The Librarian reported that he had received three new books from Boston treating on the vegetable kingdom, and a further supply of almanacs of the date of 1857.

The Keeper of the Sacred Relics reported the receipt of a plaster cast of the head of Plato, which showed the old man to be very level-headed, a knife carried by DeSoto, and vest buckle supposed to have been lost by Napoleon in his retreat from Moscow.

All the other general business of the country was then placed in the refrigerator and the meeting went home.

PROF. ARTICHOKE HUGGINS.

"What I desire to say," began Brother Gardner, as the meeting opened, "am to de effeck dat Prof. Artichoke Huggins am in de ante-room an' ready to appear before us an' deliver his celebrated lecture on 'Am Life Wuth de Livin' Fur.' De Professor am a resident of Arkansas, in which state he has won seben silver medals fur makin' de longest jumps on record. He arrove here from Chicago last night on a mixed train, paid a boy two shillins to show him de way to my house, an' so fur as I kin judge from his talk an' de way he combs his hair, de man am a scholar an' a gem'len. Sir Isaac Walpole, you an' Giveadam Jones will put on yer white kids, blue neckties an' swaller-tailed coats an' escort Prof. Huggins inter de Hall."

The brothers mentioned retired to the dressing-room and donned their State apparel, and after the lapse of a few minutes they appeared in the Hall with the Professor between them. As he mounted the platform and was received by Brother Gardner he appeared to be a man about five feet ten inches high, prominent nose, retiring chin, eyes about the color of boiler-iron, and dressed in faultless taste. After slipping a troche into his mouth he bowed impressively and began:

"My friends, it pleases me exceedingly to behold sich a vast sea of intellectual faces befo' me. [Sensation.] I kin almost emagine myself looking down de aisle of de Senate Chamber of de United States. [More sensation.] De question: 'Am Life Wuth de Libin' Fur?' has often been axed, an' I believe that several parties besides me have put de same query from 'de rostrum. [Cheers by Samuel Shin, who had no idea what the word rostrum meant.] But I claim to be de only pusson in dis kentry who takes de negative side of dis momenchus inquiry. In de fust place we am bo'n. De fust year of our life am spent in cryin' wid pain an' sorrow. We see ghosts. We have bad dreams. We am seized by de colic. Our froats am tunnels down which dey pour soothin' syrup, paregoric, sweet milk an' what not, an' we wish we was dead. [Sobs by Pickles Smith, who lately lost his grandfather.] What comfort does any boy or gal take up to de aige of fifteen y'ars? Not a bit. De boys git licked an' de gals git spanked an' dey fall down stairs, have de chicken-pox, git boxed up wid de mumps, an' have to w'ar clothes which have been cut over an' dyed. [Sensation by Giveadam Jones as he recalled old recollections.]

"From de aige of fifteen to twenty," continued the orator, after pulling down his vest, "life am full of love an' jealousy an' bad fittin' coats, an' gwine to funerals, an' stayin home from circuses. Jist as a young man gits to thinkin' dat he am happy he diskivers dat his sleeve buttons am fifteen seconds behind de style, or dat his butes am de hundredth part of an inch too long, or dat his coat wrinkles in de back. [Groans from Trustee Pullback, who remembered when he was learning the barber's trade in Richmond.]

"From twenty to thirty we get married," continued the Professor as a sad smile crossed his face. "We love an' court an' hire libery rigs an' buy candy an' marry. What am de result? [Groans from all over the Hall.] We have to pay house rent, an' buy wood, an' go to meetin' an' git trusted fur groceries, an' puts up wid kicks an' cuffs an' howlin' babies an' a hull doahyard full of miseries. [Long-drawn sighs from eighty-four members.]

"Den we grow old, an' we take snuff an' smoke clay pipes an' spit on de ca'pet an' jaw de chill'en, and finally die. [Tears from Waydown Bebee.] Dat's life an' its eand. Whar's de comfort? What have we foun' wuth livin' fur? How much better if we had bin trees, or fence-posts, or picket fences! Life am a mad struggle. [Sighs.] We come up like a sunflower an' am cut down. [Faint groans.] To-day we may win de big turkey at de raffle—to-morrow we may have to pawn our overcoat to keep de stove gwine, [Significant winks and nods.]

"My friends, thankin' you fur your airnest an' inexplicable attenshun, an' trustin' dat my feeble remarks will be productive of overwhelmin' profit, I return you my heartfelt sympathies and resoom my seat."

For half a minute there was deep silence. Then Pickles Smith stood up and waved the empty water-pail around his head, and the enthusiasm broke forth and lasted so long that six policemen gathered on the corner and a barrel of beans was upset in the grocery below.

ANOTHER IMPOSTER.

After quietness had been restored and the announcement made that, owing to the lateness of the hour, no election would be held, the Secretary read the following:

PORTLAND, ME., January 8, 1832.

BROTHER GARDNER—A man claiming to be Elder Toots has been canvasing the colored population of this city soliciting subscriptions to aid the schools in Liberia. He is a man about fifty years of age, with a proclivity for getting drunk. He has secured several contributions. Will you state through the columns of the FREE PRESS if he is the original Elder?

And oblige,
SINCERITY JONES, 2d,
Secretary Atlantic Division Lime-Kiln Club.

The anger of Elder Toots broke out as soon as the Secretary had finished reading. He waved his arms, jumped up and down in his tracks, and but for the sudden discovery that he had lost a pound of pork bought before the meeting and placed in his coat-tail pocket to carry home for breakfast, he might have become a victim of apoplexy.

Brother Gardner said that the Portland man was a red, white and blue imposter of the deepest dye, and the Secretary was instructed to offer a reward of $25 to any vigilance commitsee who would catch and hang him.

CUSSIN' DE TIMES.

'DIS mawnin' ez I war walkin' out 'mong de sunflowers in de back yard," began Brother Gardner, as the Janitor finally got through sneezing, "Misser

Darius Green, de white man, came 'long, an' dere was a powerful sad look on his face ez he leaned ober de fence an' said:

"'Misser Gardner, dis sufferin' hez got ter come to a cease!'

"'Hez you got de shakes an' chills, I axed?'

"'Wuss dan dat, Misser Gardner. Ize workin' all de long week fur ten shillin' a day, an' whar de money goes I can't tell. De ole woman wants new clothes, de chillin' wants dis an' dat, de rent runs behin', an' I'ze gittin, desperit.'

"'Shoo! now, but let's make some figgers on de fence,' I tole him. 'Now den, you chew terbacker?'

"'Yes, I chew 'bout ten cents' worf a day.'

"'Dat's seventy cents a week!'

"'An' you drink lager?'

"'Well, of course I drink a glass now an' den— maybe fifteen glasses a week!'

"'Dat's seventy-five cents moah sah.'

"'What d'ye do on Sundays?'

"'Oh, go up to de beer garden.'

"'An' you spen' a dollar at least?"

"'I guess so—maybe two of 'em.'

"'Say twelve shillins, an' dat makes two dollars an ninety-five cents per week. I reckon you frow away at least free dollars ebery week sah!'

"Frow it away.'

"'Yes sah. Dat money would pay your rent an' buy your flour.'

"'But a feller must hev some comfort.'

"'De same, sah. De greatest comfort in de world am to see de rent paid up, de family dressed up, de table loaded down, an' de ole woman able to go to church.'

"'You frow away free dollars ebery week, sah, an' den you go roun' cussin' de times, de wedder, an' de man who hez saved his money.'

"Gem'len, dat white man called me an ole black fool, an' a dog-stealer; but dat didn't alter de case a bit. He is frowin' away one-third of his weekly wages, an' den blowin' 'roun' dat he's gittin' desperit an' ready to head a riot. Doan let me heah eny member o' dis club spinnin' dat yarn, kase if he does dar's gwine to be a committee of investigashun, an dat committee won't whitewash wurf a cent!"

IT PAYS TO BE GOOD.

There was great excitement in Paradise Hall as the members began to assemble. A Lithograph Company had for weeks been engaged in getting out a chromo entitled "Passing the Bean-box in Paradise Hall." The chromo shows the entire interior of the Hall, and the forms and faces of sixty or seventy members.

The first chromo printed was sent to the Janitor of the club, to be exhibited, and to say that the prominent members were pleased, gratified, knocked down and dragged out, would not cover the case.

Giveadam Jones, who looks the hero and statesman that he is, said of the chromo, "No respectable family should be without one."

Samuel Shin, who has his seat beneath the bear-trap, looked the picture over carefully fourteen times, and then observed, "Children will cry for it in every county in America."

Waydown Bebee's eyes glared with enthusiasm as he stood and contemplated the work of art, and turning to Rev. Penstock he softly whispered, "We don't look as beautiful as angels, but them benign expreshuns can't be beaten."

Various other members indulged in flattering remarks, and when Brother Gardner entered the Hall, there was hardly a dry eye in the house.

He stood in front of the picture in earnest contemplation for a few minutes, and then walked to his accustomed seat and opened the meeting by saying:

"It pays to be good. Don't be too good, but just good 'nuff.

"Christopher Columbus diskivered America, but has he eber bin put in a chromo? He was too good. Cap. Kidd, de pirate, neber eben had his photograph on sale. Why? Kase he was too bad. My advice to you is to hit de happy neutral groun' between Columbus and Kidd. One was too good to want to knock somebody's head off arter stubbing his toe on a stone; de odder was too bad to subscribe fur a religious publication.

As I tole you in a former lecktur, be purty good on de hull, an' a leetle bad on de averaige. If you fin' a lost wallet, don't give it up until you have counted de money in it, an' have de bes' of proof dat somebody lost it. If you lose your own wallet, doan, expect any better from de finder. Doan' be profane, an' yit doan' hesitate to giv' de English language full sweep when you cotch a boy girdlin' your apple trees.

Honor yer fader an yer mudder, but doan' lend de ole man any money onless you have good security. Cum down liberally to erect churches, but if you have any brick to sell, ask de contractor full price. Do yer dooty by orphan asylums, but doan' board any orphans fur less dan $3 a week. Love yer naybur as thyself, but see dat he returns yer shovel an' spade an' rake in good order, or make him pay de retail price.

THE WEATHER.

The report was accepted, and filed, and the Chairman of the Weather Bureau reported the following probabilities for the coming week:

SUNDAY.—Purty hot.

MONDAY—Purty hotter.

TUESDAY—No more signs of snow than yesterday.

WEDNESDAY—Lemonade with a stick in it.

THURSDAY—Cut on the bias and ornamented with forty-six buttons.

FRIDAY—Rather small-tailish, but good enough for common folks.

SATURDAY—Thunder showers in the morning to strengthen the taste of onions, and, perhaps, a tornado in the Missouri valley. Fish will bite well in the Lower Lake Region, and Sunday School picnics leaving Duluth should carry an average of a barrel of lemonade to every fat woman. The day closes cool and beautiful, with new potatoes down to forty cents per bushel.

ON THE SICK.

The Chairman of the Committee on the Sick reported as follows:

"Dis Committee war called 'pon to walk 'roun' to de humble cabin of Ephem'as Sundown, late of de

Stait of Noo York, who jined himself to dis yere Club in de early half of July. When we got dar an' 'spected to see de brudder wid his eyes rollin' in agerny, we foun' we was on de wrong plantashun. Misser Sundown said it was his sister-in-law who was sick wid de ager an' in want of quinine, an' he menshuned de fack dat he'd be much obleeged for about two dollars' worf of relief. Dis Committee sot down on de ideah to once, an' Misser Sundown was radder inclined to call de undersigned human hyenas of de latest fall fashun."

"It may do dat member a heap o' good to be walked up befo' de bear-trap," observed Brother Gardner, as he passed the report along. "Dis Club proposes to relieve its members in distress, but when it comes down to sister-in-law de motto mus' be: 'Let 'em shake.' Brudder Sundown hez got to be talked to."

ON EDUCATION.

The Committee on Education, having been at work for the past three weeks, were ready to submit the following:

"Dis Committee hez done a heap of walkin' roun' an' axin' queshuns. De cause of eddercashun can't be put in a bottle an' shook up an' poured out into a tumbler wid nutmeg an' sugar in de dottom of it, same as politics an' finance. We moved slowly, put down de figgers in plain English, an' we arrove at de followin' conclushuns:

"1. Gin de pupils forty different books to study. None of 'em hez ober thirty-five now, an' dey am wastin' heaps o' preshus time.

"2. Change de skule books about eight times a y'ar. Dey ain't changed but once in two months now, an' de chill'en get tired of 'em.

"3. Ebery department in ebery skule ought to have exactly fo' hundred rules. Dey have only three hundred an' eighty-five apiece now, an' dar's a possibul chance dat some scholar will git a noshun dat eddercashun am all vanity."

THE CLOSE.

The hour for adjournment having arrived, and there being no further business before the meeting, Brother Gardner said:

"Gem'len, de man who cheats you in a hoss-trade, or sells six quarts of peaches for a peck, may ride along on de top wave for a time, an' he may puff out an' grow fat an' be de biggest gun at a pole-raisin' or a coroner's inquest, but doan' you fool yerself! Justice hez got her eyes sot on dat chap, an' sooner or later he'll come down like a satchel from a baggage car."

BRUDDER HOWKER.

"Will Whalebone Howker please step dis way?" inquired Brother Gardner in his blandest voice as the meeting was declared open.

Mr. Howker had taken a seat on one of the back benches as if to escape observation. He moved forward at a slow pace, and finally halted in front of the President's desk.

"Brudder Howker," continued the President, "you am past de noonday of life, an' it grieves me to have to call you up heah an' tell you dat yer nayburs find fault wid de carryins on around yer cabin. Dey complain dat you fight wid your wife, keep late hours drink too much whisky, an' dat you nebber hev a good word fur any man. What hev you to say?"

The old man hung his head and was silent.

"You war a slave, an' dat am some excuse, but befo' mo' gray hairs come to yer head you hev much to l'arn. If ye didn't marry fur love ye hev no bizness libin' wid a wife. If ye did, den why do ye quarrel wid her? If ye can't agree—if ye can't be all to each odder—if libin togeder keeps yer temper up, de best thing ye can do am to walk right outer dat cabin. De Lawd neber 'tended dat man an' wife should call names an' pull ha'r an' indulge in midnight battles wid feet, fists an' broomsticks."

The old man raised his head to speak, but the words would not come.

"An' so you drink whiskey? Ole man, ye ar' layin' up a heap o' sorrow fur yer last y'ars! Better put power under yer cabin dan whisky down yer froat. It am a hole in yer pocket summer an' winter; it am an evil voice constantly urgin' ye to misdeeds; it am a gaunt wolf drinkin' yer blood; it am de voice of misery an' poverty—de clods on a coffin furnished by de Poo'-master! Let it alone! An' so ye slander folks? Whisky an' slander go togeder. Hev ye lived fifty long years widout knowin' dat de sunshine of life am in speakin' good words to an' of yer fellow men? All men hev deir faults an' weaknesses, but slander won't work a change. If we expect men to condone our faults we mus' excuse deirs. Go home an' speak well of yer naybur an' dey will speak well of you. Speak kindly to dem, an' kind words will come back. Dar am fifty million souls in dis kentry, Brudder Howker, but yit de pusson who am determined to be an enemy to de rest will soon come to feel dat he am all alone heah. Make a change, Brudder Howker—make it to-night. Dis Club hez got helpin' hands fur any man who wants to be a man."

COMMUNICATIONS.

The Secretary announced the reception of a letter from the Massachusetts Horticultural Society, asking the Club how long it took taffy seed to sprout and mature, and whether they produced a vine or a shrub.

"'Deed, I doan' 'zactly feel posted on dat queshun," replied the President as he scratched his head. "Kin any member present furnish de informashun?"

"Misser President, Ize surprised—yes I iz!" answered the Rev. Penstock as he arose. "I want to inquar', sah, if de honorable President of dis Club neber heard de 'spreshun of 'gibin us taffy?' and de talk 'bout 'taffy on a string?'"

The silence for the next half minute was so deep that every breath drawn by the sleeping Elder Toots sounded like the blowing of a whale.

"Brudder Penstock," observed the President in a low voice. "on mo' dan one occashun dis cha'r hez had to tell you to go slow. Dar am no doubt dat you know a heap, but dar am seberal matters left ober dat you havn't yit surrounded,"

"Am it possible dat de cha'r doan' know what taffy am!" exclaimed the Reverend.

"Order," called Samuel Shin.

"Disorder!" yelled Giveadam Jones.

"Sot down!" piped Whetstone Smith in his squeaky voice.

Waydown Bebee rapped on the Bear Trap with a monkey wrench, and order was finally restored.

"Brudder Penstock," replied the President, "dis cha'r knows what taffy am. He has bin acquainted wid de article for ober forty years. Dis chair kin refer you to ober ten different species of de goods, all warranted not to fade in de wash. If you kin give dis Club de desired informashun axed fur a few minits ago we'll take it; if not, you had better sot down an' git ready to sing alto wid de next song by de Glee Club.

"NO OBJECTIONS."

The Committee on the Judiciary, to whom was referred the subject of the Lesseps canal, with power to send for persons and papers, reported as follows:

"Dis Committee didn't stop fur any fried clams on de hull-shell, but went right to bizness. A butcher on Woodward avenoo said he fought de canal should be pushed right frew, as it would lower de price of lightnin'-rods. One of de city Alderman said he was opposed to it, as it would raise de price of rings. A grocer on Michigan avenue said he didn't want to give a decided opinyun, kase he 'spected to run fur offis next year. A dry-goods man said he was in favor of all kinds of canals, kase dey made good places to fish in. A hardware man said he couldn't favor de Lesseps plan, kase his uncle was drowned in a canal. A leadin clergyman likewise opposed it for fear dat it would tempt boys to drown cats on week days an' go fishing on Sundays. A great many people were spoken wid. Some were pro an' some were con, but de majority favored de ideah. Dis Committee also favors de ideah. It believes in encouraging all public enterprises, from de building of a steeple on a meetin' house to de unitin' of two great oshuns by a canal full of water."

Col. Wallflower then offered a resolution to the effect that the Club had no objection to the canal going through, and the same was unanimously adopted.

A DISAPPOINTEENT.

Col. Clawbone Fishback, a cultured and fluent orator residing in Chattanooga, had agreed to be present at this meeting and deliver his lecture on " Why Do Our Toes Turn In?" but a telegram from Cincinnati announced the fact that he had been obliged to lay off there for a few days, to assist in organizing a colored club to be known as "The Colored Parisians of America."

SUPPLY AND DEMAND.

The Committee on Supply and Demand announced that they had made a thorough investigation of the quantity of water in this country, including lakes, rivers, creeks and ponds, and that they were convinced that there was no real necessity for any person economizing on his share. The supply would permit each inhabitant the daily use of 150,000 gallons for the next seventy-five years, and at the end of that period some cheap substitute would probably be discovered.

THE JUDICIARY.

The Judiciary Committee announced that they were compelled to report adversely on the petition of fifty-six colored citizens of Indiana, asking the Club to use its influence for the protection of coons and possums of this country. While these two animals did not rank as dangerous wild beasts, they could not properly be classed as domestic or useful animals, and nature must have expected them to get up and dust and take care of themselves. Statistics prove that both species were on the increase, and this fact alone showed that there was no necessity for the law to stretch forth its protecting arm and say: "Touch not this coon."

INSTRUCTIONS.

The Committee on Agriculture were instructed to investigate and report on the inquiry: "Was there ever a race in this country which was subject to spavins?"

The Janitor was warned against further use of the Club's stove polish to shine his boots.

The Committee on Astronomy were requested to investigate and report on the inquiry: "What would be the effect of 365 continuous dark nights?"

THE END.

"Gem'len, in dissemblin' to our homes," said the President as time was up, "let us bear in mind de fack dat blackberries doan' ripen in winter. Expect of de world only what de world expects of you. Somebody wake up Elder Toots an put on his hat, an' den de meetin' will stand upsot for one week."